Grapes, seedless	1 pound	4 cups
Green peppers	1 pound	3 medium large peppers 3 cups, diced
Herbs, fresh	1 tablespoon	1 teaspoon, dried
Honey	1 pound	1⅓ cups
Lemons	1 lemon	3 to 4 tablespoons juice 1½ teaspoons grated rind
Lentils, dry	1 pound	2¼ cups dry 4½ cups, cooked
Lettuce	1 pound	6 cups, torn or shredded
Limes	1 lime	1⅓ tablespoons juice 1 teaspoon grated rind
Macaroni	1 pound	4 cups, uncooked 8 cups, cooked
Marshmallows	1 pound	64 large marshmallows 6 cups
	1 large marshmallow	10 miniature
Meat, uncooked boneless	1 pound	2 cups, chopped or ground
Meat, boneless cooked	1 pound	3 cups, chopped or ground
Milk, fresh	1 quart	4 cups
Milk, nonfat dry	1 pound	4 cups
Milk, evaporated	1 can (14½ oz.)	1⅔ cups
Molasses	1 pint	2 cups
Mushrooms	1 pound	5 cups, sliced raw 2 cups, cooked sliced
Noodles	1 pound	6 cups, uncooked 8 cups, cooked
Nuts, unshelled	1 pound	2 cups nutmeats
Nuts, shelled	1 pound	4 cups nutmeats
Oil	1 pint or 1 pound	2 cups

Onions	1 pound	3 medium 3 cups, chopped
Oranges	1 orange	½ cup juice 1 tablespoon grated peel
Peas in pod	1 pound	1 cup, shelled
Potatoes	1 pound	3 medium 2½ cups, cubed cooked 2 cups, mashed
Peaches or pears	1 pound	4 medium 2 cups, sliced
Prunes, pitted	1 pound	2 cups chopped 4 cups cooked
Raisins	1 pound	3 cups
Rhubarb	1 pound	3 cups, sliced raw 2 cups, cooked
Rice, uncooked	1 pound 1 cup	2½ cups, uncooked 3 cups, cooked
Rice, wild	1 cup (3 ounces)	4 cups, cooked
Rolled oats	1 pound	5 cups, uncooked 8 cups, cooked
Shortening	1 pound	2 cups
Spaghetti	1 pound	5 cups, uncooked 10 cups, cooked
Spinach, fresh	1 pound	10 oz. cleaned and stemmed
Split peas	1 pound	2¼ cups, uncooked
Strawberries	1 quart	3 cups, sliced 2 cups, crushed
Sugar, brown	1 pound	2¼ cups, packed
Sugar, confectioners'	1 pound	3½ cups
Sugar, granulated	1 pound	2¼ cups
Tomatoes,	1 pound	4 small
Tapioca, quick	1 pound	3 cups
Yeast, active dry	1 package	1 tablespoon

Mormon
Country Cooking

Mormon Country Cooking

Winnifred C. Jardine

Layout by Dick Scopes
Illustrations by Mary Scopes
Cover design by Jon Burton
Cover photography by Royce Bair, PhotoUnique

Bookcraft

Salt Lake City, Utah

LIBRARY OF CONGRESS
CATALOG CARD NUMBER: 83-73181

ISBN: 0-88494-516-2

Second printing, 1983

Lithographed in the United States of America
PUBLISHERS PRESS
Salt Lake City, Utah

This book is gratefully dedicated
to *Deseret News* readers
who contributed many of these recipes.

Foreword

Every homemaker appreciates a good cookbook, and *Mormon Country Cooking* is more than that. As the preface indicates, it is comprised of carefully selected, top-notch recipes geared to the Mormon audience, gathered over Winnifred Jardine's three-decade-plus career as food editor of the *Deseret News*, and carefully tested by this expert cook.

Similarly, every publisher appreciates a first-class addition to his listing. Bookcraft is pleased to be able to publish this excellent book, originally published by Deseret News Publishing Company, and to recommend it to our readers.

Paul Hap Green, Publisher
Bookcraft, Inc.
December 1, 1983

Preface

"I have four huge scrapbooks of your recipes—and a box full," wrote a Tooele, Utah homemaker to Winnifred Jardine recently. "I wish I had thought about putting them in folders years ago."

Mormon Country Cooking is the answer for that Tooele, Utah grandmother, and thousands of other *Deseret News* readers who find "food is fun" as presented by Winnifred.

For more than three decades, Mrs. Jardine has been food editor of the *Deseret News*, which was founded in 1850. This book represents the cream of thousands of her kitchen-tested recipes.

Winnifred Cannon Jardine's food-fixing background is as Mormon as the great turtle-shaped Tabernacle on Salt Lake City's Temple Square. She is a great granddaughter of Brigham Young, and a granddaughter of George Q. Cannon, who was an able editor of the *Deseret News* in the nineteenth centry. Two of his sons also served as editors and a grandson served as managing editor.

When she was a girl, Winnifred's parents' home in Ames, Iowa, was a gathering place for Mormons there. Her mother often served Thanksgiving dinner to more than fifty guests. In Ames her father headed Iowa State University's Dairy Husbandry Department. He was also the Mormon Bishop there.

Winnifred graduated from Iowa State University with a major in journalism and a minor in foods and nutrition. She later became home economics director of the American Meat Institute in Chicago. National awards for her food presentations have come from the American Dairy Association and the American Meat Institute.

Winnifred has been a member of the world-famed Salt Lake Mormon Tabernacle Choir. She has also traveled to various parts of the world as a member of the general boards of the Young Women's Mutual Improvement Association and the Young Women's Organization of The Church of Jesus Christ of Latter-day Saints (Mormon). She has authored homemaking lessons for the women's Relief Society organization of the Church.

With her numerous honors and achievements, Winn Jardine's greatest accomplishments have come in her home as a wife, mother and hostess. "My first priorities are my husband and our four children," she says. Her husband, Stuart B. Jardine, is an agent with a major insurance company.

Winnifred does most of her writing and food testing in her homey kitchen in the Jardine's beige-brick, one-story Early American type rambler, which is surrounded by a small garden, lawn and fruit trees.

She admits that when she has nothing to do these days, with most of her children grown, she moves to her kitchen and "whips up a recipe."

Who eats all the food? Her children, grandchildren, neighbors and scores of friends. Her home is a gathering place for Sunday dinners and soup suppers, with servings on soup plates that once belonged to her grandfather George Q. Cannon.

And many of Winnifred's dishes start right on the Bing cherry tree, peach trees, raspberry bushes, or tomato or zucchini plants in the Jardine home garden.

The *Deseret News* is proud of Winnifred Jardine. It is pleased to present her fifth book, *Mormon Country Cooking*.

Wendell J. Ashton
Publisher, *Deseret News*
September 12, 1980

Contents

Introduction

Originally, Mormon Country was Salt Lake Valley where pioneers settled 130 years ago. From there pioneer trails began moving into neighboring states as Brigham Young made assignments to colonize new areas.

Mormon Country was growing. With this growth came culinary traditions.

A former magazine food editor remarked on one visit that she could feel, in talking with cooks in this area, a definite influence of the Mormon Church on the meals served in this area.

The most obvious effect was from the Word of Wisdom, a statement by the early prophet Joseph Smith, who counseled his people to abstain from the use of alcohol, tea, coffee, tobacco and all foods that would impair human efficiency.

But there were positive aspects of the statement, too. He prescribed the use of "all wholesome herbs . . . every herb in the season thereof," and he declared that the flesh of the beasts and the fowls of the air are ordained for the use of man—but sparingly and in time of winter or cold or famine. All grain was ordered for the use of man to be the staff of life.

Further influence came with the establishment of the Mormon Church's welfare program in the early 1930's.

Counsel to Church members is to maintain a two-year supply of food, clothing and fuel. To make the program function on a practical level, stored food has to be rotated, with some foods being used on a regular basis and new supplies replacing them. Not only has this influenced the eating habits of Church members, but some non-members have adopted the food storage concept, too.

Families are advised to stay out of debt and build up savings. This calls for prudent living and members are complying by maintaining gardens and planting fruit trees.

In this spirit we have selected recipes that are built upon basic ingredients, requiring longer ingredient listings and more detailed instructions. But Mormons, although often busily involved in civic and/or educational activities, have learned to sandwich in fruit-canning, garden-growing, bread-making and bean-baking— "lengthening their strides," as the present-day prophet, President Spencer W. Kimball, calls it. Not all Mormons are equally skilled in time and energy management, but their efforts are felt in the cooking habits of Utah.

Foreign recipes influenced Mormon cooking long before general cooking trends took an international bent. Foreign recipes dating back to pioneer ancestors are still being used with pride in some homes. Added to these are recipes brought back from foreign lands by missionaries. It is not uncommon for a missionary returned from Italy, for instance, to make pasta regularly for his family, or for a returned missionary from South America to make his family black bean soup. Here are family traditions in the making.

Important, too, is the influence on Mormon cookery by non-Mormon friends living in the Salt Lake Valley. The Greek community, established nearly a century ago when men immigrated from Greece in search of meaningful work, is thriving in Utah and has provided many choice recipes (Walnut Honey Cake, Stuffed Cabbage, Stifado). The Japanese-American community has shared wonderful Oriental recipes.

Such were the influences we felt as we began recipe selections for this book. Because our assignment was to compile favorite *Deseret News* recipes from past years, we turned to our readers for help, and hundreds of letters poured in telling us what they have most enjoyed. But the number of recipes was too many. There was not room for all. Choosing from among them was like choosing from among my own children. As we closed the last chapter, we felt a little sadness over the many fine recipes that had to be omitted. Perhaps another day there will be another book.

Our thanks to our readers—a mighty force of women and men who through their interest have kept our column alive for over 30 years. We know some of our readers in person and some by mail and many by telephone voice. We appreciate them all.

A special thanks to Jay Livingood and Sally Archer, who served as editors, to Dick and Mary Scopes, the artists, and to Wendell J. Ashton who first conceived of the idea of *Mormon Country Cooking*. Thanks to our team of recipe testers: home economists Marion Jane Cahoon and Laura Cannon McCarrey and to Carol Gerth Bench and Shirley Taylor McKay. And thanks to my husband and children who checked proofs, read over manuscripts and were supportive in every way. It has been a grand adventure!

Winnifred C. Jardine
Food Editor, *Deseret News*
September, 1980

Appetizers and Beverages

To a Mormon the word beverage means fruit drinks, milk mixtures, ciders, punches, sodas, vegetable juices and plenty of clear, cold water. Such concoctions are Mormon proffers of refreshment and hospitality.

Friends are welcomed in summer with chilled glasses of Peach Melba Punch (made with fresh golden peaches and crimson raspberries) or Frosty Grape Juice Cocktail or Banana Slush, garnished with fresh mint from the backyard.

In winter the refreshment is more likely to be Hot Apricot Nectar, Hot Spiced Tomato Juice or fragrant Hot Wassail.

Beverages suitable for serving at receptions and open houses are Great White Punch, Mormon Punch (easy to make and easy on the pocketbook) and colorful Raspberry Float.

And French Chocolate, made with hot milk and soft mounds of chocolate whipped cream, provides elegant beverage service for "teas."

Underlying this singular approach to beverage choices is the Mormon "Word of Wisdom," which cautions that drinking "wine or strong drink" is "not good, neither meet in the sight of your Father" and that "hot drinks [specifically tea and coffee] are not for the body or the belly." The Word of Wisdom is described as a principle with a promise—that those who abide shall "run and not be weary, and walk and not faint."

Tomato Bouillon

2 QUARTS

4 cups or 2 cans (18 oz. each) tomato juice
3 cans (10¾ oz. each) condensed beef consomme or bouillon
1 tablespoon lemon juice
1 teaspoon Worcestershire sauce
1 teaspoon horseradish

Combine all ingredients in 3-quart saucepan; heat to boiling point. Serve immediately.

NOTE: May be heated on low setting in slow cooker for 2 to 3 hours.

Spiced Tomato Juice

6 SERVINGS

5 cups or 1 can (46 oz.) tomato juice
⅓ cup brown sugar, packed
6 whole cloves
2 full sticks cinnamon
4 slices lemon

Combine all ingredients in heavy saucepan. Bring to boil. Lower heat and simmer 5 minutes. Strain and serve.

Tomato Ice

12 SERVINGS

2 quarts tomato juice
1 medium onion, coarsely chopped
1 tablespoon marjoram, crushed
    Juice of 2 lemons (½ cup)
2 teaspoons sugar

Combine all ingredients in large saucepan. Bring to boil; simmer 5 minutes. Remove from heat, cover and cool. Strain. Pour into ice cube trays; freeze for at least 5 hours or overnight. Thirty minutes before serving time, remove from freezer; allow to stand at room temperature. With fork stir mixture into slush. Pile tomato crystals into individual serving cups or glasses. Garnish with sprigs of mint or parsley.

Hot Spiced Apricot Nectar

ALMOST 6 CUPS

    6 cups or 1 can (46 oz.) apricot nectar
    ½ lemon, sliced
    2 whole sticks cinnamon
    16 whole cloves
    8 allspice berries

Combine all ingredients in heavy saucepan, bring to boiling point, reduce heat and simmer 5 minutes. Remove from heat; allow to stand, covered, for 30 minutes. Strain; sweeten to taste, if desired. Serve hot.

Frosty Grape Juice Cocktail

5 SERVINGS (¾ CUP EACH)

    2 cans (6 oz. each) frozen lemonade concentrate
    2 cups water
    1 pint grape juice

Dilute lemonade concentrate with water; stir until blended. Freeze. When ready to serve, break lemon ice into small bits; mash into slush. Spoon into punch cups or cocktail glasses. Pour chilled grape juice over; serve.

Raspberry Float

4 QUARTS

3 packages (3 oz. each) raspberry flavor gelatin
4 cups boiling water
1½ cups sugar
4 cups cold water
½ cup lime juice
2¼ cups orange juice
1¼ cups lemon juice
1 quart ginger ale
2 packages (10 oz. each) frozen raspberries

Dissolve gelatin in boiling water; add sugar, cold water and juices. Cool, but do not chill. To serve, pour punch into punch bowl. Add ginger ale and frozen raspberries. Stir until raspberries break apart and are partially thawed. Serve immediately.

Rhubarb Ice Cocktail

12 6-OZ. SERVINGS

4 cups (1⅓ lb.) sliced fresh rhubarb
2 cups water
2 cups sugar
Ginger ale, chilled
Fresh mint, if desired

Wash and clean rhubarb; cut into 1-inch lengths. Combine with water and sugar in medium saucepan; cook until tender. Thoroughly strain juice from rhubarb, but do not press pulp through. Freeze juice. (Use drained rhubarb for pie or cobbler.) When ready to serve, break up rhubarb ice and mash into a slush. Spoon into punch cups or glasses; pour in chilled ginger ale. Garnish with mint leaves, if desired.

Appetizer Fruit Freeze

6 TO 8 SERVINGS

1 cup sugar
1 cup water
1 can (1 lb.) grapefruit sections, undrained
1 can (1 lb.) crushed pineapple, undrained
1 small bottle maraschino cherries, drained
  Ginger ale, chilled

Combine sugar and water; bring to boil, stirring to dissolve sugar. Cool. Add grapefruit, pineapple and maraschino cherries that have been cut into small pieces. Freeze to a slush. Spoon fruit into sherbet or cocktail dishes; pour chilled ginger ale over slush.

Ruby Grapefruit

8 SERVINGS

1 package (10 oz.) frozen red raspberries
2 to 4 tablespoons sugar (if desired)
4 large fresh grapefruit

Heat raspberries in small saucepan until completely thawed. If desired, add sugar to taste. Puree raspberries in electric blender or food mill; strain. Refrigerate in covered jar. To serve, spoon over fresh grapefruit sections. To peel fresh grapefruit, cut away rind of grapefruit with serrated knife, going round and round grapefruit as you might for an apple, cutting deep enough to remove white under-layer. Extract sections by cutting close to membrane on each side of fruit wedge and carefully slipping out whole section. Each grapefruit should yield 11 sections. Squeeze denuded membranes of any remaining juice into bowl with fruit.

Peach Melba Punch

1 GALLON

1 quart or 1 can (1 lb. 13 oz.) peaches, undrained
2 packages (10 oz. each) frozen raspberries, thawed
1 cup sugar or to taste
1 cup heavy cream
3 bottles (28 oz. each) club soda, chilled

In blender combine undrained peaches, thawed raspberries and sugar. Process at high speed until pureed. Press puree through strainer into large glass bowl to remove tiny seeds. Stir in heavy cream (not whipped). Cover bowl with plastic wrap and chill. At serving time pour punch mixture into large punch bowl. Slowly stir in club soda. Ladle into punch cups.

NOTE: To prepare one drink, mix ½ cup syrup with 1 cup chilled club soda.

Traditional Eggnog

2 QUARTS

2 eggs, well beaten
1 can (14 oz.) sweetened condensed milk
1 teaspoon vanilla
¼ teaspoon salt
1 quart whole milk
1 cup heavy cream, whipped
  Grated nutmeg

Combine eggs, sweetened condensed milk, vanilla and salt. Gradually beat in milk. Gently fold in whipped cream. Sprinkle nutmeg on top. Chill several hours.

Eggnog Punch

1½ GALLONS

6 eggs, well beaten
¼ cup sugar
¼ teaspoon ground cloves
¼ teaspoon ground ginger
½ cup lemon juice
2 quarts orange juice
2 quarts vanilla ice cream, softened
1 quart ginger ale
Nutmeg

In large punch bowl, combine beaten eggs, sugar, cloves, ginger and lemon juice. Add orange juice and ice cream; stir to blend. Slowly add chilled ginger ale down side of punch bowl. Sprinkle with nutmeg and serve.

Great White Punch

1½ GALLONS

1 can (6 oz.) frozen limeade concentrate
11 cups water
3 cups sugar
2 quarts lemon-lime carbonated beverage, chilled

Combine frozen limeade concentrate with water and sugar; stir until sugar dissolves. Freeze until solid. Two hours before serving, remove mixture from freezer and thaw in punch bowl. One hour before serving, add carbonated beverage; allow to soften, mashing occasionally with potato masher. Garnish with fresh lime slices.

Cocoa or Chocolate Milk Syrup

1 ¾ CUPS

½ cup cocoa
1½ cups sugar
1 cup water
⅛ teaspoon salt
½ teaspoon vanilla, if desired
Milk

In large saucepan combine cocoa, sugar, water and salt. Bring to boil, turn heat down and simmer for 5 minutes. Remove from heat. Add vanilla, if desired. Store in covered jar in refrigerator. Stir in 1 or 2 tablespoons syrup for each cup of milk. Drink cold or heat for cocoa.

French Chocolate

8 TO 10 SERVINGS

2½ squares (2½ oz.) unsweetened chocolate
½ cup water
¾ cup sugar
Dash salt
½ cup heavy cream, whipped
6 cups hot milk

Combine chocolate and water in saucepan; cook over low heat, stirring until chocolate melts and mixture is blended. Add sugar and salt; boil 4 minutes, stirring constantly. Cool. Fold in whipped cream and chill. To serve, spoon 1 rounded tablespoon chocolate mixture into each cup; pour in hot milk. Stir to blend. Garnish with dash cinnamon, if desired.

Quick Homemade Root Beer

1 GALLON

2 cups sugar
2 tablespoons root beer extract
1 gallon water
1½ lbs. dry ice or 1 quart bottled soda water

Combine sugar, root beer and water; stir until sugar is dissolved. Chill. Thirty minutes before serving, add dry ice. Or add carbonated soda water just before serving.

NOTE: Carbonation will last about 2 hours. The colder the root beer mixture, the longer the carbonation will last. Buy an extra pound of dry ice if it must be held several hours before using.

Mormon Champagne

Combine equal parts chilled apple cider and ginger ale. Serve as desired.

Homemade Buttermilk

1 QUART

3½ cups warm water
1⅓ cups instant nonfat dry milk
½ cup dairy buttermilk

Combine all ingredients. Place in clean, warm quart jar. Cover jar with waxed paper, then with clean, dry towel. Allow to stand at room temperature for 24 hours or until buttermilk begins to curd. Cover jar; store in refrigerator. Save last cup of buttermilk for making new batch.

Banana Slush

1 can (6 oz.) frozen orange juice concentrate
1 can (6 oz.) frozen lemonade concentrate
1 can (46 oz.) pineapple juice
5 large bananas, mashed
6 cups water
3 cups sugar
4 quarts lemon-lime carbonated beverage

Mix together the juices and fruit. In large saucepan cook water and sugar together until mixture forms a syrup. Combine with fruit mixture; stir to blend; freeze. To serve remove frozen mixture and allow to thaw to slush, beating to hasten the process, if desired. Combine with equal part of carbonated beverage.

Cranberry Nog

2 eggs
½ cup sugar
Pinch salt
¼ cup lemon juice (1 lemon)
1½ cups orange juice (3 oranges)
2 cups cranberry juice
Finely crushed ice

Beat eggs, sugar and salt together until thick. Stir in fruit juices. Pour immediately over crushed ice and serve.

Mormon Punch

2 GALLONS

5¾ cups sugar
  2 gallons water
  1 can (6 oz.) frozen orange juice concentrate
¾ cup lemon juice (3 lemons)
1½ tablespoons vanilla extract
1½ tablespoons almond extract
  1 oz. citric acid (available from pharmacist)

In 2 or 3 gallon container combine all ingredients but citric acid; stir until sugar is dissolved. Just before serving, stir in citric acid. May be served hot or cold.

Hot Wassail

2½ QUARTS

2¼ cups sugar
  4 cups water
  2 full-size sticks cinnamon
  8 allspice berries
10 cloves
  1 whole piece dried ginger root
  4 cups orange juice (10 oranges)
  2 cups lemon juice (8 lemons)
  2 quarts apple cider

Combine sugar and water; boil together for 5 minutes. Remove from heat. Add spices, cover and allow to stand in warm place for 60 minutes. Strain. Just before serving, add juices and cider; bring quickly to boiling. Remove from heat; serve at once.

White Gazpacho

1 packet (.19 oz.) instant chicken flavor broth or 1 chicken
  bouillon cube
1 cup boiling water
1 medium to large cucumber
⅓ clove garlic
½ pint (1 cup) dairy sour cream
1 teaspoon salt
1 teaspoon white vinegar
2 fresh tomatoes, diced
½ cup fresh parsley, chopped
1 cup slivered almonds, toasted and salted

Dissolve broth in hot water; set aside to cool. Peel and
halve cucumber; remove large seeds, and cut into 8 or 10
pieces. Combine cucumber with a little broth and garlic in
blender; process until smooth. Combine with remaining
broth; chill. When ready to serve, spoon sour cream into
large bowl and stir with wooden spoon until smooth.
Gradually add broth mixture, blending with wire whisk.
Add vinegar and salt. Chill. Serve in cups; garnish with
diced tomatoes, chopped fresh parsley and almonds. To
toast almonds, spread them in a thin layer in shallow
metal baking pan. Set pan on center rack of 350 degree
oven. Bake for 5 minutes or until almonds show first sign
of browning. Remove from oven. Toss with few drops of
cooking oil and light sprinkling of salt.

Grace's Cornmeal Crispies

375 degrees   4 CUPS

1 cup boiling water
2½ tablespoons butter
1 cup enriched cornmeal
½ teaspoon salt

Heat water to boiling. Add butter. Measure cornmeal and salt into dry bowl; make well in center. Add butter, stir until smooth. Spread batter onto well buttered cookie sheet in very thin layer with fingers or back of spoon. Bake for 20 minutes or until lightly browned and crisp. While still hot, sprinkle with onion or barbecue salt and shredded cheddar cheese, if desired. Or for a sweet treat, sprinkle with cinnamon and sugar. Break into corn chips.

Corned Beef Pinwheels

7 DOZEN

1 package (8 oz.) cream cheese, softened
Milk
1 tablespoon mayonnaise or salad dressing
2 teaspoons horseradish
⅛ teaspoon onion salt
Salt, pepper
2 packages (3 oz. each) sliced pressed corned beef
Crackers

Blend together cream cheese and milk until spreadable. Blend in mayonnaise, horseradish, onion salt, salt and pepper. Set aside but do not chill. Separate corned beef slices from one package (there should be 12 pieces); arrange on large piece of aluminum foil into flat rectangle, three pieces of corned beef across top, four pieces down, overlapping edges slightly. It will form one large sheet of corned beef. Carefully spread half of cream cheese mixture over surface; roll up corned beef jelly-roll style, starting from narrower edge. Wrap in foil and freeze. Repeat with second package of corned beef and remaining cream cheese mixture. An hour before serving, thaw corned beef rolls slightly. With very sharp knife (electric knife works well) cut into ¼-inch slices; place each pinwheel in center of cracker; serve.

Relish Wreath

1 bunch romaine or other leaf lettuce
2 cups cherry tomatoes
2 large green peppers
1 small head cauliflower
5 or 6 long ribs celery
3 or 4 medium carrots
1 pint Confetti Dip (see below)

Wash lettuce; drain well. Wash tomatoes. Cut top from one green pepper; scoop out seeds and veins to make cup for dip. Clean second green pepper; cut into julienne strips. Wash, separate and trim cauliflowerlets. Clean celery ribs and peel carrots; cut into slender 4-inch sticks. Refrigerate all raw vegetables in separate plastic bags. To serve, line 12- to 16-inch platter with lettuce leaves. Fill green pepper cup with Confetti Dip; set into middle of platter. Arrange alternate bunches of carrot sticks, cauliflowerlets, celery and green pepper sticks around edge of plate. Pile cherry tomatoes around green pepper cup, overlapping bundles of vegetables in wreath fashion.

CONFETTI DIP:

Combine 2 cups (16 oz.) dairy sour cream, ¼ cup Parmesan cheese and 2 individual packets spring vegetable dry soup mix. Chill in covered jar until ready to serve. Makes enough dip to refill green pepper cup once.

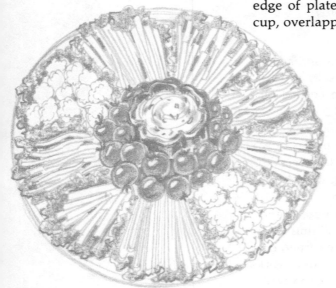

Mushroom Tarts

400 degrees   2 DOZEN

    2 dozen unbaked Dainty Tart shells (p. 240)
    1 cup (8 oz.) canned mushrooms, drained, or 1 cup (4 oz.)
      fresh mushrooms
    2 tablespoons butter
    1 tablespoon chopped chives or green onions, chopped
    1 tablespoon chopped parsley, chopped
    1 tablespoon lemon juice
    ½ cup light cream
  1½ teaspoons paprika

Make pastry shells as directed. Slice or chop mushrooms;
saute in butter. Add chives, parsley and lemon juice; simmer 5 minutes. Add cream and paprika. Mixture will be
thin. Put one teaspoonful of mixture into each tart shell.
Bake 20 to 25 minutes or until pastry is golden brown.
Cool 5 minutes; remove from pans.

Cheddar Cheese Straws

400 degrees   3 DOZEN

    1 cup (4 oz.) sharp Cheddar cheese, shredded
  1½ cups sifted flour
    ¾ teaspoon salt
      Dash pepper
      Dash cayenne pepper
    ½ cup (1 stick) butter

Grate cheese finely or rub through wire sieve. Sift flour
and seasonings together. Cream butter until light and
fluffy; add seasoned flour and cheese. Blend thoroughly.
Chill for 1 hour. Roll pastry ⅓-inch thick. Cut into 4-inch
squares. Cut each square into straws 4 inches long and ⅓-
inch wide. Lift carefully with spatula; place on ungreased
cookie sheet. Bake 8 to 10 minutes or until light golden in
color. Do not brown too much; they burn quickly and
easily.

Hot Mushroom Dip

400 degrees   35 SERVINGS

2 lbs. fresh mushrooms
½ cup (1 stick) butter
¼ cup flour
½ teaspoon salt
  Ground fresh pepper
  Lemon juice
1½ cups (6 oz.) Swiss cheese, shredded
⅔ cup fresh parsley, chopped
1½ cups sour cream
½ to ¾ cup chopped green onion
½ teaspoon paprika
  Few drops Tabasco sauce

Wash mushrooms; slice. In large skillet saute mushrooms in butter. Stir in flour, salt and pepper; blend thoroughly; cook 1 or 2 minutes. Remove from heat; stir in remaining ingredients. Spoon into 1½-quart casserole. Bake 10 minutes or until very hot. Serve with crackers, vegetable sticks or chips.

NOTE: Casserole may be assembled and refrigerated until time to bake. Remove from refrigerator 30 minutes before baking so casserole will warm up before going into hot oven.

Cheese Puffs

400 degrees   5 DOZEN

2 glasses (5 oz. each) Olde English sharp cheese
1 teaspoon Worcestershire sauce
  Dash cayenne pepper
½ cup (1 stick) butter, softened
1½ cups flour, stirred and measured

Cream together cheese, Worcestershire sauce, cayenne pepper and butter. Stir in flour; blend. Shape into balls the size of small walnuts; refrigerate for 2 hours. Bake on cookie sheet for 10 to 12 minutes.

Avocado Dip

1 PINT

1 medium avocado
1 small onion, finely grated
2 teaspoons sugar
1 tablespoon lemon juice
½ to 1 teaspoon Worcestershire sauce (or to taste)
  Dash Tabasco sauce
⅛ teaspoon garlic powder
1 cup mayonnaise

Grind avocado and onion with fine blade or chop in food processor with metal blade. Stir in sugar, lemon juice, seasonings and mayonnaise until smooth. Refrigerate in covered container. Serve as dip with vegetables.

NOTE: May be used as salad dressing with fruit or sea-food salad.

Stuffed Olive Cheese Balls

48 HALVES

1 package (8 oz.) cream cheese, room temperature
24 small stuffed olives
1 cup nuts, finely chopped

Cut cream cheese into 24 cubes. Press hole in side of each cube; insert olive. Mold cheese around it, completely covering and forming ball. Roll in chopped nuts and refrigerate. To serve, cut balls in half.

Mild Cheese Ball

1 LARGE OR 2 SMALL BALLS

1 jar (5 oz.) Roka cheese spread
2 jars (5 oz. each) Olde English cheese spread
1 package (8 oz.) cream cheese
2 tablespoons onion, grated
1 teaspoon Worcestershire sauce
1 cup pecans, chopped
⅓ cup parsley, chopped

Combine all cheeses and seasonings until well blended. Shape into one large or two smaller balls. Roll in pecans and parsley. Chill. Remove from refrigerator at least 1 hour before serving with crackers.

"Plains Special" Cheese Ring

1 8-INCH RING

4 cups (1 lb.) sharp Cheddar cheese, shredded
1 cup nuts, finely chopped
1 cup mayonnaise
1 small onion, finely grated
Grated black pepper
Watercress
Dash cayenne pepper
Strawberry preserves, optional

Combine cheese, nuts, mayonnaise and onion. Season to taste. Place in lightly greased ring mold (5 or 6 cup capacity). Cover with plastic wrap; refrigerate until firm, several hours or overnight. Unmold on serving platter. Garnish with watercress. If desired, fill center with strawberry preserves. Serve with crackers.

Chicken Nuggets

400 degrees   30 NUGGETS

    4 chicken breast halves
    ½ cup unseasoned fine dry bread crumbs
    ¼ cup Parmesan cheese, grated
    ½ teaspoon salt
    1 teaspoon crushed thyme leaves
    1 teaspoon crushed basil leaves
    ¼ cup (½ stick) butter or margarine, melted

Bone chicken breasts; remove skin. Cut breast meat into strips, then into 2½ x 2-inch pieces. Combine bread crumbs, cheese and seasonings. Dip chicken pieces in melted butter, then in crumb mixture. Place in single layer on foil-lined baking sheet. Bake 15 minutes or until light golden brown.

NOTE: Simmer chicken bones and skin in water to cover with 1 stem of celery leaves, 1 small carrot, 3 onion slices and 6 peppercorns for 2 hours. Strain; use for chicken stock.

Frozen Shrimp Cocktail

                                               40 SERVINGS

    3 quarts tomato juice
    2 bottles (12 oz. each) cocktail sauce
1¾ cups (14 oz.) catsup
    2 tablespoons fresh horseradish
    1 head celery, cleaned and finely diced (about 8 cups)
    3 cans broken shrimp, drained and rinsed

Combine all ingredients; freeze. Remove from freezer 1 or 2 hours before time to serve. Spoon frozen cocktail into dishes; serve immediately.

Jellied Chicken Spread

SPREADS ABOUT 80 CRACKERS

    4 cups cooked chicken (2 broiler-fryers)
    1 bottle (4 oz.) stuffed olives (about 20)
    6 hard cooked eggs
 1½ cups mayonnaise
    3 tablespoons Worcestershire sauce
    2 tablespoons horseradish
    2 dashes Tabasco sauce
    2 teaspoons onion, grated
    1 tablespoon lemon juice
    2 envelopes (1 T. each) unflavored gelatin
 ¼ cup cold water
    1 can (10¾ oz.) chicken broth

Finely chop the chicken, olives (saving 2 for garnish) and eggs. Add mayonnaise and seasonings; mix thoroughly. Soften gelatin in cold water; combine with chicken broth; stir and heat until gelatin is completely dissolved. In bottom of 5-cup mold, pour thin layer of gelatin mixture (about ⅛ inch); arrange in it a flower design of the reserved sliced olives and parsley stems. Refrigerate to set. In meantime, combine gelatin and chicken mixtures. When gelatin design has set, pour chicken mixture into mold; chill for several hours. Unmold onto serving platter. Garnish with parsley and cherry tomatoes.

Crab Cocktail Surprise

10 SERVINGS

    1 can (46 oz.) tomato juice
    2 cans (1 lb. each) grapefruit, drained and broken into
        pieces
    1 can (6½ oz.) crab, broken apart
    1 cup (8 oz.) catsup
    1 teaspoon Worcestershire sauce
        Pinch salt
 ¾ cup lemon juice (3 lemons)

Combine all ingredients; chill thoroughly. Serve in cocktail dishes or cups.

Buffet Meatballs

1 cup dry bread crumbs (2 cups soft crumbs)
1 lb. lean ground beef
1 envelope (.07 oz.) bleu cheese salad dressing mix
½ cup milk

Combine ingredients; mix thoroughly. Shape into 36 small balls, using 1 tablespoon meat mixture for each meat ball. Arrange meat balls in cold skillet. Place over medium heat; cook until meat balls are browned, loosening with spatula and shaking skillet to rotate them. When all are browned, turn heat to low, cover skillet; cook for 5 minutes. Drain. Transfer to chafing dish to keep hot. Serve with toothpicks. Meatballs may be cooked, chilled and reheated in microwave oven for 2 minutes or in skillet over medium heat until just heated through.

Deviled Ham Snack Spread

15 TO 20 SLICES

1 loaf French bread
1 package (8 oz.) cream cheese, softened
¼ cup (½ stick) butter, softened
1 can (4½ oz.) deviled ham
1 teaspoon seasoned salt
¼ teaspoon crushed dill weed
1 can (2 oz.) mushrooms, chopped finely

Cut bread lengthwise into two flat halves. Blend together thoroughly cream cheese, butter, deviled ham, seasoned salt and dill weed. Stir in mushrooms. Spread mixture on both halves of bread. Place on baking sheet; broil until golden brown, about 5 minutes. Cut into slices and serve hot.

Quick and Yeast Breads

Mormons seem to be involved in baking—especially in baking breads. And among their favorite recipes are some to be found in this chapter—Best Bread Sticks, Apple Banana Bread, feather-light Butterflake Rolls and quick-baked Favorite French Bread. All accommodate themselves to busy schedules.

The penchant for breadmaking and baking may have come to Mormons from their pioneer ancestry. But more likely it has been encouraged by the hundreds of pounds of wheat stored in the cool basements of Mormon homes.

Wheat is the heart of a Church-endorsed program of preparedness that calls for every family to maintain a two-year supply of food. Such provision is intended to sustain families not only during natural disasters, but also during personal crises—unemployment, disability, financial reverses.

Mormons who comply find the practice not only a source of security but also a convenience and an economic advantage. Quantity buying generally means lower prices and buying ahead seems to slow down the bite of inflation.

Mormon kitchens are often equipped with hand or electric wheat grinders. And with a turn of the handle or switch, grains of wheat are instantly ground into mounds of soft, fine graham flour. Grinding one's own wheat is a gratifying experience. And a cook with culinary bent can hardly resist such an invitation to bake bread.

Baking Powder Biscuits

450 degrees   16 MEDIUM BISCUITS

　2 cups sifted flour
　4 teaspoons baking powder
　½ teaspoon salt
　½ teaspoon cream of tartar
　2 teaspoons sugar
　½ cup shortening
　⅔ cup milk

In large mixing bowl sift together flour, baking powder, salt, cream of tartar and sugar. Cut in shortening until mixture forms coarse crumbs. Add milk all at once; stir until dough follows fork around bowl. Turn out onto lightly floured surface. Pat or roll dough ½ inch thick; cut with biscuit cutter. Bake on ungreased cookie sheet for 10 to 12 minutes.

Cinnamon Stack Biscuits

425 degrees   12 BISCUITS

　2 cups flour, stirred and measured
　3 teaspoons baking powder
　½ teaspoon cream of tartar
　½ teaspoon salt
　3 tablespoons sugar
　½ cup shortening
　⅔ cup milk
　¼ cup (½ stick) butter or margarine, melted
　¼ cup sugar
　1 tablespoon cinnamon

In large mixing bowl stir together dry ingredients. Cut in shortening until mixture forms coarse crumbs. Add milk; stir until mixture forms ball. Turn onto lightly floured board; knead gently 4 or 5 times. Roll dough into rectangle 16 x 10 inches. Brush with melted butter; sprinkle with mixture of ¼ cup sugar and cinnamon. Cut lengthwise into five 2-inch strips. Stack the five strips; cut into 12 pieces. Place cut-side down in 12 greased muffin tins. Bake 12 to 15 minutes.

Cottage Cheese Stollen

350 degrees   1 STOLLEN, 14 INCHES

½ cup (1 stick) butter
2 tablespoons shortening
1½ cups sugar
3 eggs
2 teaspoons vanilla
1 teaspoon almond extract
   Grated rind, 1 large lemon
2 cups white raisins
5 cups flour, stirred and measured
5 teaspoons baking powder
1 teaspoon salt
2 cups (16 oz.) cottage cheese
   Melted butter
   Confectioners' sugar

In large bowl cream together butter, shortening, sugar, eggs, vanilla, almond extract and lemon rind. Stir in raisins. Sift together flour, baking powder and salt; add alternately to dough with cottage cheese, mixing until well blended. Turn dough onto lightly floured board. Roll into circle, 14 inches in diameter. Fold in half; place on buttered cookie sheet. Bake for 60 minutes. While still warm brush with melted butter; dust with confectioners' sugar.

Raisin Surprises

400 degrees   1 DOZEN

1¾ cups flour, stirred and measured
 1 tablespoon sugar
 3 teaspoons baking powder
½ teaspoon salt
⅓ cup shortening
¾ cup milk
   Raisin Filling (see below)
   Melted butter or margarine
   Granulated sugar

Sift flour, sugar, baking powder and salt in mixing bowl. Cut in shortening until small pieces are formed. Add milk; mix to moderately stiff dough. Roll out on lightly floured board to an oblong about 12 x 9 inches (dough will be about ¼-inch thick). Cut into 12 3-inch squares. Drop spoonful of raisin filling in center of each square. Bring four corners of each square together; twist lightly at the top. Place in greased muffin cups (medium size). Brush each "surprise" with melted butter or margarine; sprinkle with sugar. Bake 15 to 20 minutes.

RAISIN FILLING:

 1 cup light or dark raisins
¼ cup brown sugar, packed
 1 teaspoon cinnamon
 2 tablespoons butter or margarine

Mix raisins, brown sugar, cinnamon and melted butter together until blended.

Popovers

Cold oven   12 POPOVERS

 3 eggs
 1 cup milk

1 cup flour, stirred and measured
½ teaspoon salt

Prepare 12 muffin tins by greasing generously. In mixing bowl combine eggs, milk, flour and salt. Beat vigorously until just blended; do not worry about lumps. Fill cold muffin pans three-fourths full. Place in cold oven, set oven controls at 450 degrees and turn oven heat on. Bake for 30 minutes without opening oven door. Serve immediately.

Pineapple Muffins

350 degrees   16 TO 18 MUFFINS

½ cup almonds, sliced
1 can (1 lb. 4 oz.) crushed pineapple
2 cups sifted flour
1 teaspoon soda
1 teaspoon salt
1 package (3 oz.) cream cheese
1 cup sugar
2 teaspoons vanilla
1 large egg, beaten
½ cup dairy sour cream
    Glaze (below)

Heavily grease muffin pans; sprinkle with almonds. Drain pineapple, reserving syrup. Resift flour with soda and salt. Beat cheese, sugar and vanilla together until smooth. Blend in egg. Add flour mixture alternately with sour cream. Fold in drained pineapple. Spoon into prepared muffin pans. Bake for 35 minutes, until muffins are brown and test done. Cool 10 minutes. Turn out onto wire rack and spread Glaze over warm muffins.

GLAZE: Combine 1 tablespoon soft butter or margarine, 1 cup sifted confectioners' sugar and 1 tablespoon syrup drained from pineapple; blend smooth.

Whole Wheat Pancakes or Waffles

1¼ cups sifted whole wheat flour
3 teaspoons baking powder
3 tablespoons sugar, brown or granulated
¾ teaspoon salt
3 eggs, well beaten
1¼ cups milk
3 tablespoons cooking oil

Stir together dry ingredients. Combine eggs, milk and oil; stir into flour mixture. Bake on ungreased griddle until golden brown, then turn. Or bake in waffle iron.

NOTE: For lighter pancakes or waffles, eggs may be separated and stiffly beaten egg whites folded into batter just before baking.

German Pancake

400 degrees   4 SERVINGS

3 eggs
½ cup flour, stirred and measured
½ cup rich milk
¼ teaspoon salt
2 tablespoons butter or margarine

Set 9-inch clear glass pie dish into hot oven on lowest oven shelf until very hot. Meanwhile, mix eggs, flour, milk and salt in small mixer bowl, blender or food processor. Beat until smooth, about 3 minutes. Remove pie dish from oven; add butter and rotate pie dish until butter is melted. Add batter immediately. Bake on lowest oven shelf for 20 minutes or until golden. Serve with hot syrup, jam or applesauce.

NOTE: For serving a large group, triple recipe and bake in 9 x 13-inch baking pan.

Sonja's Ableskivers

2 DOZEN

    3 eggs, separated
  ⅓ cup sugar
    2 cups buttermilk
    2 tablespoons butter, melted
1¾ cups flour, stirred and measured
  ½ teaspoon salt
    1 teaspoon baking powder
       Applesauce or jelly, if desired

Beat egg whites until stiff; set aside. In another bowl beat together egg yolks and sugar; add buttermilk and melted butter; stir in sifted dry ingredients; blend well. Fold in egg whites. Bake in ableskiver iron, spooning a bit of applesauce or jelly into center of each ableskiver before turning.

Whole Wheat Muffins

425 degrees

12 LARGE MUFFINS

    1 cup sifted flour
    1 cup sifted whole wheat flour
  ½ teaspoon salt
    4 teaspoons baking powder
  ½ cup brown sugar, packed
    1 cup milk
    2 eggs, slightly beaten
  ⅓ cup oil
  ½ cup nuts, coarsely chopped

Grease 12 large (2½ inch) muffin cups. In large mixing bowl stir together until blended flours, salt, baking powder and brown sugar. Add combined milk and eggs; then oil and nuts; stir just until moistened. Spoon batter into prepared pans. Bake 15 minutes.

NOTE: Raisins or chopped dates may be used in place of or in addition to nuts.

Sour Cream Waffles

6 WAFFLES

1 cup sifted cake flour
1 teaspoon baking powder
1 teaspoon soda
⅛ teaspoon salt
1 teaspoon sugar
3 egg yolks
2 cups thick sour cream
3 egg whites

Sift together flour, baking powder, soda, salt and sugar. In separate bowl beat egg yolks until light; add sour cream. Combine with dry ingredients. Beat egg whites until stiff but not dry; fold into batter. Bake in hot waffle iron. Delicious with fresh fruit or ice cream.

NOTE: To substitute all-purpose flour for cake flour, sift and measure 1 cup all-purpose flour. Remove 2 tablespoons flour; add 2 tablespoons cornstarch. Sift flour-cornstarch mixture three times.

Cheese Spoon Bread

375 degrees   6 TO 8 SERVINGS

1 cup milk
1 cup yellow cornmeal
1 cup cold milk
1 teaspoon salt
¼ cup (½ stick) butter or margarine
1½ cups (6 oz.) sharp Cheddar cheese, shredded
4 eggs, separated

Heat 1 cup milk in heavy saucepan. Combine cornmeal, cold milk and salt. Pour into hot milk, stirring constantly. Cook about 5 minutes, stirring frequently, until thickened.

Remove from heat; stir in butter and cheese. Beat egg yolks until thick and lemon-colored. Stir small amount of hot cornmeal mixture into egg yolks; then add egg mixture to remaining cornmeal, stirring constantly. Carefully fold in stiffly beaten egg whites. Pour mixture into well buttered 2-quart casserole. Bake for 35 to 40 minutes. Serve immediately with butter or margarine, if desired. Good with honey or maple syrup.

NOTE: If desired, cheese may be omitted from recipe for plain spoon bread. Or 1 cup of grated cooked vegetable, such as zucchini, might be added.

Drop Doughnuts

375 degrees (hot oil)   2 DOZEN

    2 eggs
⅓ cup sugar
    2 tablespoons melted shortening
⅓ cup milk
    2 cups flour, stirred and measured
1½ teaspoons baking powder
½ teaspoon salt
    1 teaspoon cinnamon
¼ teaspoon nutmeg

Beat eggs until very light. Add sugar, melted shortening and milk. Add dry ingredients which have been sifted together. Mix well. Drop by teaspoonfuls into deep hot fat. Fry on all sides until golden brown. Drain on unglazed brown paper; sprinkle with confectioners' sugar.

Apricot Nut Bread

350 degrees 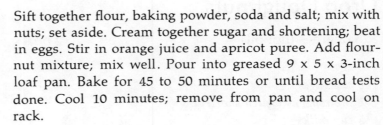 1 LOAF

2 cups flour, stirred and measured
¾ teaspoon baking powder
½ teaspoon soda
½ teaspoon salt
½ cup nuts, chopped
⅔ cup sugar
⅓ cup shortening
2 eggs
3 tablespoons orange juice
1 cup pureed apricots

Sift together flour, baking powder, soda and salt; mix with nuts; set aside. Cream together sugar and shortening; beat in eggs. Stir in orange juice and apricot puree. Add flour-nut mixture; mix well. Pour into greased 9 x 5 x 3-inch loaf pan. Bake for 45 to 50 minutes or until bread tests done. Cool 10 minutes; remove from pan and cool on rack.

Banana Nut Bread

300 degrees 2 LOAVES

4 eggs
5 large ripe bananas
1 cup shortening
2 cups sugar
4 cups sifted flour
2 teaspoons soda
1 teaspoon salt
1 cup walnuts, coarsely broken

In large bowl beat eggs until thick; add bananas and beat until smooth and liquid. In second bowl, cream together shortening and sugar until fluffy. Beat in egg-banana mixture. Sift flour with soda and salt; add to creamed mixture. Stir in walnuts. Bake in two well greased 8½ x 4½ x 2½-inch loaf pans for 75 minutes or until bread tests done. Cool 10 minutes; turn out onto racks to cool.

Glazed Lemon Nut Bread

350 degrees   1 LOAF

¼ *cup (½ stick) butter*
¾ *cup sugar*
 2 *eggs*
 2 *teaspoons grated lemon peel*
 2 *cups flour, stirred and measured*
2½ *teaspoons baking powder*
¾ *teaspoon salt*
¾ *cup milk*
½ *cup walnuts, chopped*
 2 *teaspoons lemon juice*
 2 *tablespoons sugar*

Cream together butter and sugar until light and fluffy. Add eggs and lemon peel; beat well. Sift together flour, baking powder and salt; add to creamed mixture alternately with milk, beating after each addition. Stir in nuts. Pour into well greased 9 x 5-inch pan. Bake for 55 minutes or until done. Cool in pan for 10 minutes; then spoon mixture of lemon juice and 2 tablespoons sugar over top. Remove from pan; cool.

Apple Banana Bread

350 degrees   1 LOAF

    1 small banana
       Applesauce
    ½ cup shortening
    ¾ cup sugar
    2 eggs
    3 tablespoons buttermilk or sour milk
    2 cups flour, stirred and measured
    1 teaspoon soda
    1 teaspoon salt

Mash bananas; add enough applesauce to measure 1 cup;
set aside. Cream together shortening and sugar. Add eggs;
beat well. Add sour milk and banana-applesauce mixture.
Sift together dry ingredients; add to creamed mixture;
blend well. Pour into greased 8½ x 4½ x 2½-inch loaf pan.
Bake for 45 minutes or until done.

Zucchini Bread

350 degrees   1 LOAF

    ¾ cup shortening
    1 cup sugar
    3 eggs
    ⅓ cup molasses
    2 teaspoons vanilla
    ¼ cup milk
    2 cups zucchini, grated
    2 cups flour, stirred and measured
    ½ cup whole wheat flour, stirred and measured
    1 teaspoon salt
    1 teaspoon soda
    ½ teaspoon baking powder
    2 teaspoons cinnamon
    ¾ cup nuts, broken

Grease and flour 9 x 5 x 3-inch loaf pan. Cream together shortening and sugar. Add eggs, one at a time, beating well after each addition. Add molasses and vanilla, mixing well. Add milk and zucchini; mix well on low speed. Sift together all dry ingredients. Add all at once to creamed mixture; stir gently until well blended. Stir in nuts. Pour batter into prepared pan. Bake 70 minutes.

NOTE: Grated yellow crookneck squash may be used in place of zucchini squash.

Coconut Pumpkin Bread

350 degrees   2 LOAVES

1⅓ cups oil
4 eggs
2 cups cooked or canned pumpkin
2 cups flour, stirred and measured
2 cups sugar
1 teaspoon salt
1 teaspoon soda
1 teaspoon cinnamon
1 teaspoon nutmeg
2 packages (3 oz. each) coconut pudding and pie filling mix
1 cup nuts, coarsely chopped

Beat together oil, eggs and pumpkin. Add sifted dry ingredients along with pie filling mix; blend. Stir in nuts. Bake in two well greased 9½ x 4 x 2-inch loaf pans for 60 minutes or until done.

NOTE: If loaves brown too quickly, lay brown paper over top till loaves are done.

Old Fashioned Date Nut Bread

350 degrees   2 LOAVES

         2 teaspoons soda
         2 cups boiling water
         2 cups (8 oz.) pitted dates, chopped
         2 tablespoons butter
         1 cup sugar
         2 eggs
         2 cups nuts, coarsely chopped
         4 cups flour, stirred and measured
    1½ teaspoons baking powder
      ¼ teaspoon salt

Add soda to boiling water; pour over chopped dates and
set aside. Cream together butter and sugar; beat in eggs.
Add date mixture and nuts. Stir in sifted dry ingredients.
Pour batter into two well greased 8½ x 4½ x 2½-inch loaf
pans. Bake for 60 minutes or until done.

Herb Batter Buns

400 degrees   12 TO 16 BUNS

        1 package active dry yeast
      ⅓ cup warm water (115 degrees)
        2 tablespoons sugar
      ¾ teaspoon salt
      ½ teaspoon powdered sage
      ¼ teaspoon nutmeg
        1 teaspoon caraway seeds
      ¾ cup warm water
    2½ cups sifted flour
        1 egg
        2 tablespoons soft shortening

Soften yeast in ⅓ cup warm water. In large mixing bowl combine sugar, seasonings, seeds and ¾ cup warm water. Stir yeast into cooled herb mixture. Add half of flour; beat until smooth. Add egg, shortening and remaining flour; beat again until smooth. Scrape batter down from sides of bowl. Cover; let rise in warm place until doubled, about 30 minutes. Stir down; spoon into 12 to 16 large greased muffin cups (2¾ inches), filling about half full. Let rise in warm place until dough reaches top of muffin cups—20 to 30 minutes. Bake 15 to 20 minutes. Serve warm.

Sweet Rye Rolls

350 degrees   2 DOZEN

   1 package (1 T.) active dry yeast
   ¼ cup warm water (115 degrees)
   1 cup milk
   1 cup water
   ¼ cup shortening
   ½ cup (scant) sugar
   1 teaspoon salt
   ¼ cup dark molasses
   1 cup rye flour
   5 cups all-purpose flour

Soften yeast in ¼ cup warm water. Heat together milk and 1 cup water. In large mixing bowl combine with shortening, sugar, salt and molasses; cool to lukewarm. Stir in dissolved yeast. Add rye flour; blend well. Add enough all-purpose flour to make soft dough. Turn out onto lightly floured board; knead 8 to 10 minutes or until smooth. Place in greased bowl, turning to coat; cover. Allow to rise in warm place until double in bulk—1 to 1½ hours. Turn out onto lightly floured board. Pinch off pieces the size of a large egg; place onto greased baking sheets. Brush with oil. Allow to rise until double in bulk— about 1 hour. Bake for 20 minutes or until done. May be shaped into two round loaves; bake 50 to 55 minutes.

12-Hour Butterhorns

375 degrees   32 BUTTERHORNS

1 package (1 T.) active dry yeast
¼ cup warm water (115 degrees)
½ cup butter or margarine, melted
¾ cup milk, scalded
½ cup sugar
¾ teaspoon salt
3 eggs, well beaten
4 to 5 cups flour
½ cup (1 stick) butter, melted

Soften yeast in warm water. Combine melted butter and scalded milk. Stir in sugar, salt and eggs. Cool. Stir in softened yeast and enough flour to make a soft dough. Cover; allow to rise in cool place for 5 or 6 hours. Turn out onto lightly floured board; knead just to coat dough with flour. Dough is very soft and should remain so. Divide dough. Roll each half into 14-inch circle. Spread each circle with ¼ cup melted butter. Cut pie-fashion into 16 pieces. Roll each piece loosely from large end to small. Place on greased cookie sheet. Allow to rise in cool place 5 to 6 hours. Bake 12 to 15 minutes or until lightly browned.

STATLER HOUSE ROLLS: Divide dough in half. Roll each half into rectangle 8 x 14 inches. Spread with ¼ cup melted butter, sprinkle with 2 tablespoons granulated sugar and ¼ cup chopped raisins. Roll loosely, starting from long side, and pinch edges together. Slice into 12 pieces; place, cut side down, in buttered muffin pans. Cover lightly; allow to rise 5 to 6 hours in cool room. Bake for 12 to 15 minutes. While hot, brush with powdered sugar icing (1 cup powdered sugar, 1 tablespoon warm water and ½ teaspoon rum extract). Remove from pans. Makes 24 rolls.

STICKY ORANGE ROLLS: Divide dough in half. Roll each half into rectangle 8 x 14 inches. Spread each with half of orange filling. (Cream together ½ cup or 1 stick butter with ½ cup sugar and grated rind of 1 orange.) Continue as for Statler House Rolls, flavoring frosting with ½ teaspoon almond extract.

BUTTERSCOTCH ROLLS: Divide dough in half. Roll each half into rectangle 8 x 14 inches; spread each half with ¼ cup soft or melted butter; then spread with ½ cup (packed) brown sugar. Continue as for Statler House Rolls, but do not frost.

CHRISTMAS TEA RINGS: Divide dough in half. Roll each half into rectangle 8 x 14 inches. Spread each half with ¼ cup melted butter; then sprinkle with 2 tablespoons granulated sugar, candied fruit and nuts. Roll as for Statler House Rolls. Shape each roll into circle on buttered baking sheet, pinching ends together. With scissors cut two-thirds into circle at one-inch intervals; then twist each 1-inch piece one-half turn to left to make tea ring. Allow to rise 5 to 6 hours; bake as for rolls. Frost with rum-flavored icing; (see Statler House Rolls) decorate, if desired, with candied cherries and nuts.

FREEZE-AHEAD ROLLS: Any of the rolls may be frozen ahead of time by shaping as desired, then immediately placing rolls onto baking sheet and quick freezing. Remove frozen rolls from baking sheet; place in heavy plastic freezer bag. Twist bag closed; keep for up to 2 weeks. Six hours before time to bake, remove from freezer and arrange on greased baking sheet or in greased muffin tins, according to recipe. Allow to thaw and rise for 5 to 6 hours; bake as directed.

Fast-Rising Rolls

400 degrees   3 DOZEN

    2 packages (2 T.) active dry yeast
    ½ cup warm water (115 degrees)
    ¼ cup sugar
    6 cups flour, scooped
    ½ cup nonfat dry milk (instant or regular)
    1 tablespoon salt
    2 cups warm water
    2 eggs, beaten
    ½ cup oil

Soften yeast in ½ cup warm water to which sugar has been
added. In large bowl stir together flour, dry milk and salt.
Making well in center, add 2 cups water, yeast mixture,
eggs and salad oil in that order. Stir until well mixed, adding more flour, if needed, to make soft dough. Cover;
allow to rise in warm place until double—about 1 hour.
Turn out onto light floured board. Knead a few times to
make dough easy to handle. Pinch off smooth round
pieces about egg size; arrange 2 inches apart, on greased
baking sheet. Cover lightly with clean towel; allow to rise
20 minutes. Bake 10 minutes or until golden brown.
Dough may be used for cinnamon or other kinds of rolls.

Whole Wheat Rolls

400 degrees   2 DOZEN ROLLS

    2 packages (2 T.) active dry yeast
    ½ cup warm water (115 degrees)
    ⅓ cup cooking oil
    ⅓ cup brown sugar, packed
    2 eggs, well beaten

1 cup warm water
2 teaspoons salt
½ cup nonfat dry milk (instant or regular)
4½ to 5 cups whole wheat flour

Soften yeast in ½ cup warm water. In large mixing bowl combine oil, brown sugar, eggs, 1 cup water and salt. Add yeast mixture; stir thoroughly. Add dry milk and enough flour to make soft dough. Turn out onto well floured board; knead until smooth and satiny. Place in greased bowl, turning to coat surface. Allow to rise until slightly less than double—1½ to 2 hours. Shape into 24 round balls or other desired shapes. Place on greased baking sheet. Allow to rise in warm place until slightly less than double—about 1 hour. Bake 15 to 20 minutes.

Old Fashioned Wheat Bread

375 degrees   2 LOAVES

1 package (1 T.) active dry yeast
⅓ cup warm water (115 degrees)
1 tablespoon shortening
1 tablespoon honey
1 tablespoon molasses
2 teaspoons salt
3 cups milk, scalded
6 cups whole wheat flour, stirred and measured

Soften yeast in warm water. Melt shortening; combine with honey, molasses, salt and scalded milk. Cool to lukewarm; combine with yeast mixture. Add flour enough to make soft dough. Knead thoroughly, using extra flour as needed. Shape into two loaves. Place in greased 8½ x 4½ x 2½-inch loaf pans. Allow to rise until not quite double in bulk—1½ to 2 hours. Bake for 45 minutes or until done.

Butterflake Rolls

425 degrees   4 DOZEN ROLLS

> 2 packages (1 T. each) active dry yeast
> ½ cup warm water (115 degrees)
> 2 eggs
> ⅓ cup sugar
> 1 tablespoon salt
> 1¼ cups evaporated milk
> ¾ cup hot water
> 5 to 7 cups flour, stirred and measured
> ½ cup (1 stick) soft butter or margarine
> ⅓ cup soft shortening

Soften yeast in ½ cup warm water. In large mixing bowl beat eggs lightly. Add sugar, salt, evaporated milk and hot water; beat thoroughly. Stir in yeast mixture gradually, add up to 4½ cups flour gradually to make soft dough; mix well. Turn onto pastry cloth that's been lightly covered with flour. Knead until smooth and elastic, adding barely enough flour to make it workable but no more than necessary. With rolling pin, roll dough into rectangle ½-inch thick. Spread with one-third of the soft butter. Fold half of dough over other half; roll to original shape and size. Spread with half the shortening; fold and roll. Spread with half of remaining butter, fold and roll out again. Spread with remaining shortening; fold and roll. Spread with remaining butter; make fold and roll to rectangle ½-inch thick. Cut out with biscuit cutter, place in well greased muffin tins. Allow to rise until double, 2 to 4 hours. Bake 8 to 12 minutes or until golden brown. Serve hot.

NOTE: After rolls have been cut out, they may be laid close together on baking sheet and quick frozen, then kept frozen 1 or 2 weeks in freezer bags that have been tightly closed. About 4 hours before serving, remove from freezer, set into greased muffin tins and allow to rise and bake as directed.

Favorite French Bread

400 degrees   2 LOAVES

2¼ cups warm water (115 degrees)
  2 tablespoons sugar
  2 packages (1 T. each) active dry yeast
  1 tablespoon salt
  2 tablespoons soft shortening or oil
  6 cups flour, stirred and measured

In large mixing bowl combine warm water and sugar. Sprinkle yeast over top; allow to soften. Add salt, shortening and 3 cups flour; beat well. Add remaining flour, stirring well with heavy spoon. Leave spoon in batter and allow dough to rest 10 minutes; stir down with spoon; allow dough to rest 10 minutes; stir down again. Repeat this process until dough has been stirred down five times. Turn dough out onto floured board; knead two or three times to coat dough with flour so it can be handled. Divide into two parts. Roll each part of dough into rectangle 9 x 12-inches. Roll dough up, starting from long side; pinch edge of loaf to seal. Arrange seam side down on large baking sheet that's been sprinkled with cornmeal, allowing room for both loaves. Repeat with second part of dough. Cover lightly; allow to rise for 30 minutes. With very sharp knife, cut three gashes at an angle in top of each loaf; brush entire surface with egg wash (1 egg beaten slightly with 1 tablespoon water). If desired, sprinkle with sesame or poppy seeds. Bake for 30 minutes or until brown. Cool on racks.

NOTE: For crustier loaf, a pan of hot water may be set on bottom of oven while bread is baking.

Armenian Pocket Bread

475 degrees   12 SERVINGS

   2 cups warm water (115 degrees)
1⅓ packages (1 tablespoon plus 1 teaspoon) active dry yeast
   1 tablespoon salt
   4 cups white or whole wheat flour, stirred and measured

In large bowl soften yeast in warm water. Stir in salt and
enough flour to make soft dough. Cover; let rise 1 hour
(dough will be sticky). Turn out onto floured board.
Knead lightly for a few minutes. Leaving dough on board,
cover with towel; let rise 30 minutes. Divide dough into
six balls. Roll each ball into 8-inch circle, using as few
strokes as possible and rolling only on one side. Place on
cookie sheet. Center rack in oven. Bake for 8 minutes or
until circles puff up like pillows and are lightly brown. Do
not over-bake or bread will be too crisp. Cut or break
bread in half and fill pockets with Taboola (p. 188) or
Barbecued Pork (p. 107). Pocket bread may be packed in
reezer bags, tightly sealed and frozen.

Cool Rise White Bread

400 degrees   2 LOAVES

   2 packages (1 T. each) active dry yeast
   ½ cup warm water (115 degrees)
1¾ cups warm milk
   2 tablespoons sugar
   1 tablespoon salt
   3 tablespoons soft margarine
5½ to 6½ cups all-purpose flour, stirred and measured

Grease two 8½ x 4½ x 2½-inch loaf pans. In warm mixing bowl soften yeast in warm water. Add warm milk,
sugar, salt and margarine. Srir in 2 cups flour; beat until

smooth, about 1 minute. Add 1 cup more flour; beat vigorously with wooden spoon until smooth, about 150 strokes. Gradually stir in enough of remaining flour to make soft dough which leaves sides of bowl. Turn onto lightly floured board. Knead until smooth and elastic, 5 to 10 minutes. Cover with plastic wrap, then with towel. Let rest 20 minutes. Divide dough into 2 equal portions. Shape into loaves; place in prepared pans. Brush surfaces with oil. Cover pans loosely with waxed paper brushed with oil; then top with plastic wrap. Place pans in refrigerator. Refrigerate 2 to 24 hours. When ready to bake, remove from refrigerator; uncover dough. Let stand at room temperature 10 minutes. If air bubbles have formed on top of bread, prick with toothpick. Bake 30 to 35 minutes or until done. Remove from pans; brush with melted butter. Recipe may be doubled.

WHOLE WHEAT COOL RISE BREAD: Use 3 to 4 cups all-purpose flour, 2½ cups whole wheat flour. Beat 1 cup all-purpose flour into yeast mixture. Add whole wheat flour; beat vigorously with wooden spoon. Stir in enough of remaining all-purpose flour to make soft dough. Continue as above.

Twin Mountain Muffins

375 degrees   1 DOZEN

¼ cup (½ stick) butter
¼ cup sugar
1 egg, beaten
½ teaspoon salt
3 teaspoons baking powder
1 cup milk
2 cups flour, stirred and measured

Cream butter and sugar. Add egg; blend. Add sifted dry ingredients alternately with milk. Bake in buttered muffin pans 25 minutes.

Herb Bread

350 degrees   2 ROUND LOAVES

1 package (1 T.) active dry yeast
¼ cup warm water (115 degrees)
¾ cup scalded milk
2 tablespoons shortening
2 tablespoons sugar
½ teaspoon salt
3 cups flour or more
2 teaspoons celery seed
1 teaspoon ground sage
1 egg, slightly beaten

Soften yeast in warm water. Combine hot milk and shortening. Add sugar and salt. Cool to lukewarm. Stir in 1 cup flour and herbs; beat thoroughly. Blend in yeast mixture and egg. Add additional flour to make soft dough. Knead until smooth and satiny. Place in lightly greased bowl, turning to coat with shortening. Cover lightly; let rise to double in bulk. Shape in two round loaves; place in greased 9-inch pie dishes. Allow to rise until nearly double in bulk—no higher. Bake for 20 to 30 minutes. Cut in pie-shaped wedges to serve.

Best Bread Sticks

400 degrees   1 DOZEN

1 package (1 T.) active dry yeast
1 tablespoon honey
1½ cups warm water (115 degrees)
1 tablespoon malted milk powder
1 teaspoon salt
4 to 4½ cups flour, stirred and measured

In large mixing bowl soften yeast and honey in warm water. Add malted milk powder and salt; blend. Add flour gradually, blending in with wooden spoon until dough pulls away from sides of bowl to form a ball. Divide dough into 12 pieces. Roll each piece between hands or stretch and roll on floured pastry board or cloth to make sticks about 10 to 12 inches long. Place lengthwise on large greased baking sheets, allowing six sticks to each sheet. Brush with beaten egg; sprinkle with desired seasonings—coarse salt, poppy or sesame seeds, Parmesan cheese, etc. Allow to rise 10 to 15 minutes, if desired, but not necessary. Bake for 15 minutes or until browned.

NOTE: If desired, this dough may be shaped into 24 smaller bread sticks. Bake 10 minutes.

Refrigerator Bran Bread Sticks

400 degrees   8 LONG BREAD STICKS

⅔ cup shortening
½ cup sugar
1½ teaspoons salt
1 cup boiling water
1 cup shreds of wheat bran cereal
2 packages (1 T. each) active dry yeast
1 cup warm water (115 degrees)
2 eggs, beaten
5 to 5½ cups flour, stirred and measured

In large bowl combine shortening, sugar, salt and boiling water. Add bran; cool to lukewarm. Soften yeast in warm water. Stir into cooled bran mixture along with beaten eggs. Stir in enough flour to make soft dough; mix thoroughly. Cover with plastic wrap; store in refrigerator overnight. Remove dough from refrigerator. Turn out onto lightly floured surface; shape into 8 long bread sticks. Set into greased breadstick pans (about 14½ inches long) or arrange on greased baking sheets about 2 inches apart. Allow to rise 10 to 15 minutes. Bake for 20 to 25 minutes or until golden brown. Serve hot.

NOTE: Dough may be shaped into cloverleaf or other rolls and placed in greased muffin tins. Makes 2 dozen.

Eggs and Cheese

Eggs must have been in Mormon country for as long as the Mormons themselves, for chickens were brought across the plains with pioneers in early 1847. And having eggs for cooking in those early days would have made it lots more interesting. The addition of eggs seems to signify "making it better."

Egg bread seems more special than regular bread. A six-egg cake brings a greater claim to fame than a plain old two-egg cake. A three-egg omelet is more deluxe than a one-egg affair. Even having an egg in your malt commands respect. It costs more!

Eggs and cheese together make a nutritious, delicious combination that is grand for a people who have been counseled to use meat "sparingly." Note the Quiche Lorraine, Top Hat Cheese Souffle Breakfast Casserole and Cheese with Spinach Strata.

Keep in mind these three things about eggs. 1-Store them in the refrigerator. 2-Cook them over low heat. 3-Never overcook them.

Remember these three things about cheese. 1-Store cheese in the refrigerator, but do remove it one hour before serving. 2-Cook cheese over low heat—just high enough to melt and blend it with other ingredients. 3-Avoid long cooking periods; cook only long enough to melt.

With such similar handling conditions, no wonder eggs and cheese are such compatible cooking partners!

Deviled Egg Casserole

325 degrees   12 SERVINGS

12 hard-cooked eggs, deviled (see below)
¼ cup (½ stick) butter or margarine
¼ cup flour
2 cups milk
1 can (10½ oz.) cream of mushroom soup
1 tablespoon lemon juice
2 cups (⅔ lb.) diced cooked ham
¼ lb. fresh mushrooms, sliced and browned lightly in butter
   Chopped parsley

In 7½ x 11½-inch casserole arrange deviled egg halves, filled side up. In medium saucepan melt butter, stir in flour; add milk. Cook and stir until thick and smooth. Add soup and blend. Stir in lemon juice, ham and mushrooms. Pour over deviled eggs. Sprinkle with chopped parsley. Bake for 20 minutes or until bubbly hot.

NOTE: In place of ham 1 can (12 oz.) corned beef, cubed, or 1 can (12 oz.) luncheon meat, cubed, may be used.

NOTE: 1 can (4 oz.) sliced mushrooms, drained, may be used in place of fresh mushrooms. Liquid drained from canned mushrooms may be frozen and used in soup, white sauce or as substitute for dry red or white wine in cooking.

Deviled Eggs

1 DOZEN

6 eggs
3 tablespoons mayonnaise
¼ teaspoon onion salt
1 teaspoon Dijon mustard
½ teaspoon vinegar
   Dash white pepper
   Dash Tabasco sauce

Dash monosodium glutemate
Dash paprika
Salt and pepper

Arrange eggs in medium saucepan. Add cold water to cover 1 inch above eggs. Bring to boil. Cover; remove from heat. Allow to stand for 20 minutes. Plunge eggs into cold water immediately; crack and remove shells. Cut cooled eggs in half lengthwise. Carefully remove yolks into small mixing bowl. Mash yolks with remaining ingredients; season to taste. Pile mixture back into egg halves. Sprinkle with paprika.

Swiss Cheese Fondue

6 SERVINGS

2 cups white grape juice or chicken bouillon, divided
1 clove garlic, mashed
4 cups (1 lb.) aged Swiss cheese, shredded
3 tablespoons cornstarch
¾ teaspoon salt
½ teaspoon Worcestershire sauce
¼ teaspoon white pepper
¼ teaspoon nutmeg
1 loaf French bread

In top of double boiler but over direct heat, heat 1¾ cups white grape juice or chicken bouillon with garlic until very hot. Remove garlic. Place pan over boiling water. Add Swiss cheese, stirring constantly until cheese is melted. (At this point cheese may not be thoroughly combined with liquid.) Combine cornstarch, salt, Worcestershire sauce, white pepper and nutmeg with ¼ cup cold white grape juice or chicken bouillon. Stir into cheese mixture. (When cornstarch is added, cheese will combine with liquid for smooth blend.) Continue heating and stirring until smooth and hot. Serve from chafing dish with cubes of French bread.

Cheese And Spinach Strata

350 degrees   8 TO 10 SERVINGS

2½ cups (10 oz.) sharp Cheddar cheese, shredded
  2 packages (10 oz. each) frozen chopped spinach, thawed
    and squeezed dry, or 1 package (10 oz.) fresh spinach
    leaves, cleaned and chopped
⅔ cup onion, chopped
 18 thin firm-type white bread slices (about one 1-lb. loaf)
½ cup (1 stick) butter or margarine, softened
  4 eggs
  4 cups milk
  1 tablespoon prepared mustard
1½ teaspoons salt
 ¼ teaspoon pepper

Toss together 2 cups cheese, spinach and onion; set aside.
Spread bread slices lightly on both sides with butter; place
6 bread slices in bottom of greased 9 x 13-inch baking
dish. Top bread slices evenly with ½ cheese mixture, 6
bread slices and remaining ½ cheese mixture. Cut remaining 6 bread slices diagonally into quarters; top casserole
with overlapping bread triangles and remaining shredded
cheese. Beat together eggs, milk, mustard and seasonings;
pour carefully over casserole. Cover; refrigerate at least 1
hour or overnight. Bake 60 to 65 minutes or until knife
inserted in center comes out clean. Let stand 15 minutes.
Cut into squares.

Summer Macaroni And Cheese

6 SERVINGS

¼ cup (½ stick) butter or margarine
1¾ cups (7 oz.) elbow macaroni
  1 large onion, chopped
  1 medium green pepper, chopped
½ teaspoon salt
½ teaspoon garlic salt

⅛ teaspoon pepper
½ teaspoon oregano
⅛ teaspoon dry mustard
2 cups water
1 tablespoon flour
1 can (13 oz.) evaporated milk
2 tablespoons pimiento, chopped
2 cups (8 oz.) sharp Cheddar cheese, shredded

In large skillet melt butter over low heat. Add macaroni, onion, green pepper and seasonings. Cook, stirring occasionally, over medium heat for 7 minutes, or until onion becomes transparent. Add water; bring to boil. Cover; simmer for 20 minutes or until macaroni is tender. Sprinkle flour over mixture; blend well. Stir in evaporated milk, pimiento and shredded cheese. Simmer 5 minutes longer, stirring occasionally, until cheese has melted. Serve hot.

Savory Eggs

6 SERVINGS

9 eggs, hard cooked
1 tablespoon onion, minced
2 teaspoons prepared mustard
1 tablespoon lemon juice
¼ cup stuffed olives, chopped
Few drops Tabasco sauce
Mayonnaise
Salt, pepper to taste
3 English muffins, split and toasted
1 recipe Cheese Sauce (p. 212)

Cut eggs in half lengthwise; remove egg yolks, place in small bowl; set egg whites aside. Mash yolks; add onion, mustard, lemon juice, stuffed olives, pepper sauce, mayonnaise to moisten, and salt and pepper to taste. Fill egg whites with mixture. Place 3 egg halves on toasted muffin half. Top with hot cheese sauce. Garnish with parsley.

Quiche Lorraine

375 degrees   6 SERVINGS

    1 unbaked 9-inch pastry shell
    8 strips bacon
    1 teaspoon bacon fat
    1 small onion, chopped
1½ cups Swiss cheese, shredded
    2 egg yolks
    2 eggs
  ½ cup heavy cream
  ½ teaspoon salt
  ¼ teaspoon nutmeg
    Dash cayenne pepper

Prepare pastry shell. Fry bacon strips until crisp. Crumble; set aside. In reserved bacon fat cook onion till tender. Sprinkle Swiss cheese, bacon bits and onion over bottom of pastry shell. Beat together egg yolks, whole eggs, cream, salt, nutmeg and cayenne pepper; pour into pastry crust. Bake 40 minutes. Best served hot, but may be served cold.

Breakfast Casserole

300 degrees   8 TO 10 SERVINGS

    8 slices bread, cubed
    2 cups (½ lb.) Cheddar cheese, shredded
  20 (1½ to 2 lbs.) pork sausage links
    4 eggs
2¼ cups milk
  ¾ teaspoon dry mustard
    1 can (10½ oz.) cream of mushroom soup
  ½ cup milk

Arrange bread cubes in bottom of greased 9 x 13-inch baking pan. Sprinkle with shredded cheese. Brown pork sausage links; drain and cut into fourths; arrange on top of cheese. Beat eggs with milk and dry mustard. Pour over sausage, cheese and bread. Refrigerate overnight. Dilute cream of mushroom soup with milk; pour over casserole. Bake 1½ hours.

NOTE: Good for Christmas morning breakfast.

Macaroni And Cheese

350 degrees   6 SERVINGS

1½ cups (6 oz.) elbow macaroni
3 tablespoons butter or margarine
¼ cup onion, minced
3 tablespoons flour
1½ cups milk
½ teaspoon salt
Dash pepper
3 cups (12 oz.) sharp Cheddar cheese, shredded
¼ teaspoon paprika
Tomato slices, if desired

Cook macaroni in boiling, salted water until tender, according to package directions. Drain. In another saucepan, melt butter. Add onion; cook until soft. Blend in flour and milk. Cook and stir until thick. Add salt, pepper and cheese. Heat and stir until cheese is melted. Mix sauce with macaroni. Pour into greased 1½-quart casserole. Sprinkle with paprika; then top, if desired, with an arrangement of tomato slices that have been sprinkled with salt. Bake 30 minutes or until bubbly and browned.

Top Hat Cheese Souffle

300 degrees   4 TO 6 SERVINGS

  ¼ *cup (½ stick) butter or margarine*
  ¼ *cup flour*
  ¾ *teaspoon salt*
     Dash cayenne pepper
1½ *cups milk*
  2 *cups (½ lb.) sharp Cheddar cheese, shredded*
  6 *eggs, separated*

Melt butter or margarine in medium saucepan. Add flour and salt; blend. Add milk. Cook and stir until thick and smooth. Add cheese; stir until melted. Remove from heat. Add beaten egg yolks; mix well. Cool slightly. Pour slowly into stiffly beaten egg whites, cutting and folding mixture thoroughly together. Pour into ungreased 2-quart casserole. With teaspoon draw a line around the casserole 1 inch in from edge to form a crease. Bake 75 minutes. Serve at once. (When baked, souffle will have a "top hat" that pops up.)

Scandinavian Scrambled Eggs

4 SERVINGS

  6 *eggs*
  ¾ *cup cottage cheese*
  2 *tablespoons milk*
  1 *tablespoon chives, chopped*
  ½ *teaspoon salt*
  ⅛ *teaspoon ground pepper*
  2 *tablespoons butter*

In mixing bowl beat eggs. Add cottage cheese, milk, chives, salt and pepper; beat lightly until blended. Melt butter in skillet over low heat. Add eggs to butter; cook slowly, turning portions of cooked egg with spatula as they begin to thicken. Do not stir; do not overcook. As soon as eggs are cooked, remove from heat and serve.

Cottage Cheese Pancakes

10 PANCAKES

  2 eggs
½ cup cottage cheese
¾ cup thin sour cream
¾ cup flour, stirred and measured
  2 tablespoons (or more) wheat germ
½ teaspoon baking soda
½ teaspoon salt

In blender combine eggs, cottage cheese and sour cream. Add remaining ingredients. Bake on lightly greased griddle.

NOTE: For sour cream, you may measure 2 teaspoons vinegar into glass measuring cup; add enough evaporated milk to measure ¾ cup; allow to stand 5 minutes.

Cheese And Egg Puffs

6 SERVINGS

  6 eggs
¾ cup sifted flour
1½ teaspoons baking powder
½ teaspoon salt
½ teaspoon onion salt
1½ cups (6 oz.) sharp Cheddar cheese, shredded
      Butter or margarine
      Spanish Sauce (p. 101)

Beat eggs at high speed until thick, about 10 minutes. Sift together flour, baking powder, salt and onion salt; gradually add to eggs, beating only until blended. Fold in cheese. Immediately drop batter on lightly buttered griddle, using about ¼ cup for each puff. When brown, turn and finish cooking. Serve 3 puffs for each serving, topped with ½ cup Spanish Sauce.

Caraway Cheese Omelet

350 degrees   4 TO 5 SERVINGS

    4 eggs, separated
    ½ teaspoon salt
       Dash ground black pepper
    ¼ cup milk
    1 tablespoon butter
    ½ cup sharp Cheddar cheese, shredded
    2 slices bacon, cooked crisp and crumbled
    ½ teaspoon caraway seed
       Fresh parsley

Beat egg yolks until thick and light. Add salt, pepper and milk. Fold into stiffly beaten egg whites. Turn into buttered hot 9-inch omelet or frying pan with oven-proof handle. Cook over low heat until omelet puffs up and is golden brown on the bottom, about 3 to 5 minutes. Peek underneath by lifting edge of omelet with spatula. Sprinkle cheese, crumbled bacon and caraway seed on omelet. Bake immediately for 10 to 15 minutes or until top springs back when pressed with finger. Remove from oven. Make 1-inch cuts at opposite sides and crease with back of knife. Fold in crease by slipping spatula or pancake turner under half the omelet. Slide onto platter; garnish with parsley. Serve immediately.

Strata A L'Augusta

350 degrees   4 TO 6 SERVINGS

    2 cups (8 oz.) sharp Cheddar cheese, shredded
    ½ cup mayonnaise
    3 tablespoons fresh parsley, chopped, or 1 tablespoon dried
       parsley
    ¾ cup chopped ripe olives (optional)
    6 slices enriched, day-old white bread, crusts removed

```
 3  eggs
¾  teapsoon salt
 1  teaspoon dry mustard
½  teaspoon dill weed
½  teaspoon ground pepper
 2  cups milk
12  ripe olives, whole (optional)
```

Make a paste of shredded cheese, mayonnaise and parsley. Stir in olives. Spread mixture on 3 slices of trimmed bread. Cover with remaining slices in sandwich fashion. Cut each sandwich twice diagonally to make four triangles and arrange, points up, in buttered 8 x 8-inch baking dish. Beat eggs with salt, mustard, dill weed and pepper; stir in milk. Pour eggs and milk over triangles so they are all moist. Arrange whole ripe olives between triangles for garnish. Refrigerate several hours or overnight. Bake 35 minutes or until set.

Baked Shrimp Cheese Strata

350 degrees   6 SERVINGS

```
 6  slices enriched day-old white bread
 2  cups (8 oz.) sharp Cheddar cheese, shredded
 2  cans (4½ oz. each) shrimp, broken or halved
 3  eggs
1½  cups milk
½  teaspoon dry mustard
½  teaspoon salt
```

Remove crusts from bread. Cut two slices in half diagonally. Place 4 full slices bread in bottom of well buttered 8 x 8-inch baking dish. Top with shredded cheese, then drained shrimp. Arrange remaining bread triangles overlapping across center of casserole. Beat eggs. Add milk, mustard and salt; blend well. Pour over shrimp and cheese casserole. Refrigerate several hours or overnight. Bake 40 minutes or until done.

Swiss Scrambled Eggs

400 degrees   4 TO 6 SERVINGS

     3 tablespoons butter or margarine
     8 eggs
     ½ cup milk
     ⅛ teaspoon ground pepper
     ¼ teaspoon seasoned salt
     2 cups Swiss cheese, thinly sliced
     1 tablespoon fine bread crumbs

Melt 2 tablespoons of the butter in skillet. Beat eggs with
milk, salt and pepper; pour into skillet, stirring constantly
with fork. Continue to stir until eggs are set but still soft
and not dry. Pour into buttered 9 x 1½-inch round baking
dish. Sprinkle lightly with seasoned salt. Top with slices
of Swiss cheese; then dot with small portions of remaining
butter. Sprinkle with bread crumbs. Bake 10 minutes until
top is lightly browned.

Cheese Strata

350 degrees   6 SERVINGS

    12 slices day-old enriched white bread, crusts removed
     2 cups (8 oz.) sharp Cheddar cheese, shredded
     4 eggs
    2½ cups milk
     1 teaspoon dry mustard
     1 tablespoon onion, chopped
    1½ teaspoons salt
     ¼ teaspoon white pepper

Arrange 6 slices of trimmed bread in bottom of well
buttered, 12 x 7 x 2-inch baking dish. Cover with cheese,
then with remaining slices of trimmed bread. Beat eggs;
then add milk, mustard, onion, salt and pepper; pour mix-

ture over bread and cheese. Cover with plastic wrap; refrigerate several hours or overnight. Bake for 60 minutes or until done. Serve immediately.

Farmer's Noodle Casserole

350 degrees   6 SERVINGS

   1 *package (6 or 6½ oz.) wide noodles*
   ⅓ *cup (⅔ stick) butter or margarine*
   3 *tablespoons flour*
   1 *teaspoon salt*
   ¼ *teaspoon ground pepper*
   2 *cups milk*
   ½ *cup Parmesan cheese*
   ¼ *cup green onion, sliced*
   1 *cup dairy sour cream*
   1 *cup large curd cottage cheese, undrained*
   ¼ *cup cornflake crumbs*

Cook noodles as directed on package; drain. Melt 3 tablespoons of the butter in saucepan. Combine flour, salt and pepper; stir into butter. Add milk, stirring constantly. Cook and stir until sauce is smooth and thickened. Blend in ¼ cup of the Parmesan cheese, green onion, sour cream, cottage cheese and cooked noodles. Pour into 2-quart casserole. Melt remaining butter; add cornflake crumbs and remaining ¼ cup Parmesan cheese; blend. Spoon crumbs around edge of casserole. Bake 30 to 40 minutes or until thoroughly heated. Serve with dollop of sour cream and sprinkling of chopped, fresh parsely, if desired.

Grains, Pastas and Legumes

A Mormon larder is planned around foods that will store for two years, foods such as wheat, barley, rice, oats and corn along with dried beans, split peas, lentils and enriched pastas.

These foods hold the promise of hearty good eating, but the promise can be fulfilled only when they're cooked according to a good recipe.

Split Pea Soup with Sausage Balls is an all-time favorite among *Deseret News* readers. It was discovered in a *News*-sponsored pioneer recipe contest over 30 years ago. It has never lost its place of grace.

Kindred to it in deep hearty flavor is Gypsy Chowder, which combines dried lentils with ham, tomato sauce, carrots, onions and marjoram. It is served with sour cream.

Speaking of lentils, you'll want to try the chilled Lentil Salad served on crisp lettuce leaves or piled into fresh tomato cups. And there is the Barbecued Lima Beans which even non-lima lovers will relish.

As for the pastas, toss drained hot spaghetti, cooked "al dente," into homemade herb-filled Pesto Sauce, a treat found in another chapter. Fit company for any meal, Spaghetti with Pesto Sauce is destined to become a food storage favorite.

Ready-To-Eat Cereal

225 degrees   6 QUARTS

8 cups regular rolled oats
6 cups rolled wheat
2 cups untoasted wheat germ
2 to 3 cups shredded coconut (unsweetened preferred)
2 teaspoons salt
1¼ cups brown sugar
½ cup honey
1 cup cooking oil
1 cup warm water
1 tablespoon vanilla
1 pound sunflower seeds or broken nuts, if desired
1 pound seedless raisins

In large bowl combine rolled oats, wheat, wheat germ, coconut, salt, and sugar; mix well. Combine honey, cooking oil, water and vanilla; pour over cereal; mix until all flakes have been coated and separated. Stir in nuts, if desired. Spread onto cookie sheet (will cover 4 large sheets); bake for 90 minutes, stirring occasionally, until mixture is toasted. Bake two baking sheets of cereal at a time, if desired, alternating cookie sheets from time to time. Remove from oven; stir in raisins. Store in air tight containers so raisins won't dry out. Need not be refrigerated.

Bulgur

1 ½ CUPS

1 cup whole wheat
1 cup water
½ teaspoon salt

Use a large pot (such as cold packer) with tight-fitting lid; place rack in the bottom. Add water almost to level of rack. In smaller pot place wheat, water and salt and set onto rack in larger pot. Cover large pot. Bring water in kettle to boil over high heat; then reduce heat and steam until wheat absorbs water in smaller pot. Spread bulgur on baking sheet in single layer. Dry completely in oven at 200 degrees for 1 hour. Crack in mill or blender. Store in covered jar in cool dry place indefinitely. To use as cereal, heat in steam for 10 to 20 minutes or boil in an equal amount water for 5 minutes. Serve hot and sweeten to taste.

Wild Rice Casserole

350 degrees   7 SERVINGS

¼ cup (1½ oz.) wild rice
1 tablespoon butter
1 small onion, finely diced
½ cup celery, chopped
2½ cups beef or chicken broth
1 teaspoon dried parsley flakes or 1 tablespoon fresh
  parsley, chopped
½ teaspoon salt
½ teaspoon Kitchen Bouquet
¼ teaspoon ground sage
¼ teaspoon crushed sweet basil leaves
1 can (4 oz.) sliced mushrooms, drained
¾ cup uncooked long grain white rice
1 cup (8 oz.) dairy sour cream, if desired

Wash and drain wild rice. Melt butter in medium skillet. Add onion, celery and wild rice; cook until onion is tender. Pour into 1½-quart casserole. Heat broth, pour over; add parsley, salt, seasonings and drained mushrooms. Cover. Bake 45 minutes. Stir in white rice; bake 45 minutes longer or until all liquid is absorbed and rice is tender. Serve at once. Stir in dairy sour cream, if desired. Either way is delicious.

Oven Baked Rice

400 degrees   4 SERVINGS

2½ tablespoons butter
  2 tablespoons onion, minced
  ½ teaspoon garlic, minced
  1 cup uncooked long grain white rice
1½ cups chicken broth
  3 sprigs parsley
  1 sprig fresh or ¼ teaspsoon dried thyme
  ½ bay leaf

Melt half the butter in heavy oven-proof saucepan; cook onion and garlic, stirring, until onion is translucent. Add rice; stir briefly over low heat until grains are coated with butter. Pour in stock, stirring until rice grains are separated. Add parsley, thyme and bay leaf. Cover with close-fitting lid. Bake 17 to 22 minutes. Remove cover; discard parsley, thyme and bay leaf. With fork, stir in remaining butter. Serve immediately.

Rice Pilaff

350 degrees   6 SERVINGS

1½ cups long grain white rice
  1 large onion, chopped
  ½ cup (1 stick) butter or margarine
  2 tablespoons parsley, chopped
1½ cans (10¾ oz. size) condensed beef consomme
  1 cup water
  ½ to 1 cup shelled pine nuts (optional)

Cook rice and chopped onion in butter in skillet until rice is golden. Combine with parsley, consomme and water; pour into 2-quart greased casserole. Cover; bake for 30 minutes or until rice feels tender between fingers and all water is absorbed. Uncover at once. To serve, fluff up rice with fork. Spoon onto large tray or into serving bowl; sprinkle with pine nuts.

Barley Pilaff

6 SERVINGS

  6 tablespoons (¾ stick) butter
  1 large onion, minced
  1 cup regular pearl barley
  1 cup (¼ lb.) sliced fresh mushrooms
  3 cups chicken bouillon
½ teaspoon salt
½ teaspoon ground pepper
  1 cup raw carrots, cut into thin short sticks (optional)

In skillet melt butter over medium heat. Add onion, barley and mushrooms; saute until lightly browned. Add chicken bouillon, salt, pepper and carrots. Cover skillet. Bring to boil. Reduce heat to simmer; cook until barley and carrots are tender and bouillon has been absorbed, about 45 minutes.

NOTE: 2 cups diced raw or cooked chicken may be added to brown and cook along with barley.

Seasoned Rice

325 degrees   8 SERVINGS

  1 cup brown rice
½ cup (1 stick) butter
  1 can (10½ oz.) beef consomme
⅔ cup water
  1 can (4 oz.) button mushrooms, drained

Wash rice; drain thorougly. Brown rice in melted butter in heavy skillet, stirring constantly. In 1½-quart casserole, combine rice and butter with consomme, water and mushrooms. Cover casserole; bake for 90 minutes or until rice is tender.

Refried Beans

2 CUPS

1 cup dried pinto beans
Water for soaking
2½ cups water
1 clove garlic, minced
⅓ cup onion, chopped
1 tablespoon bacon drippings or shortening
1 teaspoon salt
¼ cup bacon drippings or shortening
½ cup shredded Monterey Jack or Cheddar cheese

Sort and soak beans by one of these two methods: (1) soak in water to cover 8 to 10 hours, or (2) cover beans with water, bring to boil and cook 2 minutes; remove beans from heat; cover and let stand for 1 hour. Drain. In medium saucepan combine drained soaked beans with 2½ cups water, garlic, onion, 1 tablespoon bacon drippings or oil and salt. Bring to boil; reduce heat. Cover; simmer until beans are tender, 1½ to 2 hours. Beans should easily mash against side of pot with wooden spoon. Drain beans in colander, reserving liquid. In large skillet, melt 2 tablespoons bacon drippings or shortening. When hot, add 1 cup cooked beans, mashing with fork, wooden spoon or potato masher. Stir in remaining 2 tablespoons bacon drippings or shortening and add remaining beans, mashing them also. Leave some beans whole or half-mashed, if desired. Continue cooking and stirring until all shortening is absorbed. If thinner consistency is desired, stir in reserved cooking liquid, a small amount at a time. Add cheese. Cook and stir until cheese melts. Serve with dob of dairy sour cream, if desired.

NOTE: Red beans, red kidney beans or pink beans may be used in place of pinto beans.

Country Baked Beans

300 degrees   6 TO 8 SERVINGS

1 lb. (2¼ cups) small white or navy beans
Water for soaking
6 cups water
1 large onion, diced
1 can (1 lb.) pineapple chunks, drained
1 cup (8 oz.) catsup
½ lb. lean bacon, cut into pieces
¾ cup brown sugar, packed
¼ teaspoon garlic salt
1½ tablespoons prepared mustard
1 tablespoon horseradish
1½ tablespoons Worcestershire sauce

Sort and rinse beans. Soak in tepid water to cover for 6 to 8 hours. Drain; discard soaking water. Combine soaked beans and 6 cups water. Bring to boil; reduce heat. Cover and simmer 1½ hours or until barely tender, checking frequently. Drain beans, saving cooking water. In 2½-quart bean pot or casserole combine drained beans with remaining ingredients. Cover; bake 4 to 6 hours or until beans are tender, stirring and checking frequently. Stir in more cooking liquid as needed to keep beans just covered while cooking.

NOTE: 1 can (28 oz.) pork and beans may be used in place of cooked beans. Bake 3 to 4 hours. Makes 5 to 6 servings.

Red Beans And Rice

10 SERVINGS

1 lb. (2½ cups) dry red kidney beans
1 cup onion, chopped
¼ cup green onion tops, thinly sliced
¼ cup green pepper, chopped
1 clove garlic, minced
1 tablespoon fresh parsley, finely minced
1 to 2 lbs. ham hocks or ham bone with meat
¼ teaspoon ground black pepper
Dash Tabasco
1 bay leaf
½ teaspoon (or more) thyme
½ teaspoon basil
1 quart cold water (approximately)
½ lb. pepperoni sausage, thinly sliced (optional)

Soak beans overnight in cold water to cover; drain. Put beans and remaining ingredients into heavy pot or kettle, adding enough water to cover—approximately 1 quart. Bring to boil; then reduce heat; simmer on low heat for 5 or 6 hours or until beans are tender and thick natural gravy has formed. Add additional water if mixture appears too dry. Scrape down sides and across bottom of kettle frequently to prevent scorching. Season to taste. Serve over hot steamed rice.

Thrifty Lima Pot

8 SERVINGS

1½ cups (12 oz.) large dry lima beans
3 cups cold water
1 can (1 lb.) tomatoes, cut up
¼ cup onion, chopped
½ teaspoon salt
1 can (12 oz.) luncheon meat, cubed
1 beef bouillon cube
⅛ teaspoon pepper
1 cup milk, regular or skim

3 tablespoons flour
1 teaspoon Kitchen Bouquet, if desired

Rinse beans; place in large saucepan; add water. Bring to boil, cover and simmer 2 minutes. Remove from heat and let stand 1 hour. Do not drain. Add tomatoes, onion and salt; cover and simmer for 75 minutes. Add luncheon meat, bouillon cube and pepper. Bring to boil; reduce heat; simmer 15 minutes, stirring occasionally. Combine milk and flour; add to stew mixture. Cook, stirring constantly, till thickened; stir in Kitchen Bouquet.

Barbecued Lima Beans

300 degrees   8 TO 10 SERVINGS

2 cups large dried lima beans
8 cups water
¼ lb. bacon, cut into ½-inch pieces
1 small onion, chopped
2 cloves garlic, minced
¼ cup (½ stick) butter or margarine
1 teaspoon prepared mustard
2 teaspoons Worcestershire sauce
1½ teaspoons chili powder
1 can (8 oz.) tomato sauce
2 tablespoons brown sugar
¼ lb. bacon slices
2 tablespoons vinegar

Sort and rinse beans; do not soak. In 4-quart saucepan, combine rinsed beans, water and ¼ lb. diced bacon. Bring to boil; reduce heat. Cover and simmer until beans are almost tender, 1 to 1½ hours, checking several times. Add hot water as needed to keep beans just covered while cooking. Drain, reserving ½ cup liquid. Brown onion and garlic in butter. Add remaining ingredients except drained limas and sliced bacon. Cook 5 minutes; add to lima beans. Place in greased 2-quart casserole; top with sliced bacon. Cover; bake for 2 hours, adding reserved bean liquid if necessary.

Pioneer Stew

8 SERVINGS

1¼ cups (8 oz.) dried pinto or kidney beans
3 cups cold water
2 bay leaves
1 teaspoon salt
½ to 1 lb. ground beef
½ cup onion, chopped
½ cup green pepper, finely diced
1 can (1 lb.) whole kernel corn, drained
1 can (l lb.) tomatoes, undrained
1½ teaspoons chili powder
1 teaspoon salt
1 tablespoon flour
½ cup (2 oz.) sharp Cheddar cheese, shredded

In large saucepan place washed and drained beans, cold water, bay leaves and 1 teaspoon salt. Bring to boil; cover and simmer 2 minutes. Remove from heat; let stand for 1 hour. Return to heat; simmer 1¼ hours. In skillet cook ground beef, chopped onion and green pepper until meat is browned and vegetables are tender; drain off fat. Add meat mixture, corn, tomatoes, chili powder and salt to taste to beans; simmer 20 minutes. Combine flour with 2 tablespoons water. Stir into stew; cook and stir until bubbly. Stir in cheese. Serve.

Macaroni Salad

6 SERVINGS

4 cups cooked (2 cups uncooked) small elbow macaroni
¼ cup French dressing
1½ cups celery, diced
½ cup green onions and tops, sliced thinly
¼ cup pimiento, chopped
⅓ cup sweet gherkin pickles, chopped

1 cup (4 oz.) Cheddar cheese, diced
½ to ⅔ cup Modified Mayonnaise (p. 201)
   Salt and pepper
   Crisp greens

Cook macaroni according to package directions, stirring to keep pieces separated. Drain; rinse with warm water; drain again thoroughly. Stir in French dressing; chill. Add celery, green onions, pimiento, pickles, cheese and Modified Mayonnaise; stir to blend. Season to taste. Spoon into salad bowl lined with crisp salad greens; sprinkle with paprika. Refrigerate, covered, until time to serve.

NOTE: Hard-cooked egg and/or chilled cooked peas may be added, as desired.

Macaroni Souffle

350 degrees   8 SERVINGS

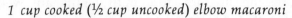

  1 cup cooked (½ cup uncooked) elbow macaroni
  1 cup milk, scalded
  2 cups fresh bread crumbs
½ cup (1 stick) butter or margarine, melted
  1 cup (4 oz.) sharp Cheddar cheese, shredded
  1 can (2 oz.) pimiento, drained and chopped
  2 teaspoon dried parsley flakes or 2 tablespoons fresh
    parsley, chopped
  1 teaspoon salt
  1 green pepper, finely diced
  5 egg yolks, beaten
  5 egg whites, stiffly beaten
    Mushroom Sauce (p. 211)

In large bowl combine all ingredients but egg whites and Mushroom Sauce. Fold egg whites into macaroni mixture; pour into 2-quart casserole. Set casserole in pan of hot water. Bake 35 minutes or until done. Serve immediately with hot Mushroom Sauce.

Lentil Salad

6 SERVINGS

1 cup dried lentils
1 quart water
1 teapsoon salt
½ cup salad oil
¼ cup vinegar
1 teaspoon salt
½ teaspoon dry mustard
½ teaspoon paprika
¼ teaspoon pepper
¼ cup sweet relish
½ cup green onion, sliced
¼ cup shallots, finely chopped

Rinse lentils in cold water. In large saucepan cover lentils with 1 quart water and 1 teaspoon salt. Bring to boil; simmer 20 to 30 minutes or until tender. Drain. Combine remaining ingredients in large bowl. Add hot, drained lentils to dressing mixture; toss until lentils are well coated. Refrigerate for at least 2 hours.

NOTE: For Lentil and Tomato Salad, wash and trim six medium tomatoes and section partly through. Open up as for petaled flowers and serve lentil salad inside.

Split Pea Soup With Sausage Balls

12 SERVINGS

1 lb. (2¼ cups) green split peas
3 quarts water
2 teaspoons salt
½ teaspoon pepper

¼ teaspoon marjoram
1 lb. bulk pork sausage
1 cup celery, diced
1 cup potatoes, diced
1 cup onion, diced
  Salt to taste

Wash split peas; cull. In large saucepan combine water and seasonings; bring to boil. Add peas gradually so water does not stop boiling. Shape sausage into 1-inch balls (about 28 of them); roll in flour. Drop into soup. Cover; simmer until peas are tender—2½ to 3 hours. Thirty minutes before serving time, add vegetables; cook until tender.

Gypsy Chowder

6 SERVINGS

1 cup dried lentils
5 cups water
1 can (15 oz.) tomato sauce
1 cup carrots, finely diced
½ cup onion, chopped
½ lb. ham scraps or seasoning ham
1½ teaspoons salt
½ teaspoon marjoram
  Dairy sour cream (optional)
  Ground nutmeg (optional)

Combine all ingredients except sour cream and nutmeg in 3-quart kettle. Bring to boil; reduce heat and simmer, covered, about 2 hours or until lentils are very tender. Top each serving with dollop of sour cream and sprinkling of nutmeg, if desired.

Meat, Fish and Poultry

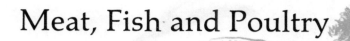

    Although counseled to eat meat and poultry "sparingly," Mormons still build many of their main meals around them. But they do not seem to eat large quantities. A look at the recipes in this chapter will show that most of them extend meat with other foodstuffs. Mormons also eat a great deal of fish.

  Buying meats in quantity and preserving are other phases of the Mormon's food storage program and provide a homemaker with a nice variety for her menus. Some families raise their own meat animals.

  For many families, hunting in the fall provides a definite part of their food supply. Venison and game birds are counted on for winter eating. These families have developed methods of preparing succulent game meat and prefer it above other meats.

  Skier's Stew and Barbecued Pork are reader favorites, also Chili-Ghetti and Quick Meatballs with all their variations. Sesame Baked Chicken Breasts and Chicken With Golden Rice are two poultry favorites. The abundance of recipes using tuna and salmon reflects the feelings of readers who find canned fish more compatible with their budgets than fresh or frozen.

American Pizza

CRUST:

> 1 package (1 T.) active dry yeast
> 1 cup warm water (115 degrees)
> 2 teaspoons sugar
> 3½ cups flour, stirred and measured
> 1 tablespoon cooking oil
> 1½ teaspoons salt

FILLING:

> 1 lb. lean ground beef
> ½ lb. bulk pork sausage
> 2 cans (6 oz. each) tomato paste
> 1¼ cups canned tomatoes, drained or ½ can (8 oz. size)
>   tomato sauce
> ½ teaspoon sweet basil, crushed
> ½ teaspoon oregano, crushed
> ¼ teasooon salt
>   Dash pepper
> ½ cup onion, minced
> 3½ cups (14 oz.) mozarella or Monterey Jack cheese, shredded
> 2 cans (3 oz. each) sliced mushrooms, drained
> ⅔ cup (3 oz.) Parmesan cheese

TO MAKE DOUGH: Soften yeast in 1 cup warm water. Add sugar; beat in 1½ cups flour. Mix in oil and salt. Stir in remaining flour; knead until smooth and elastic, about 10 minutes. Dough will be very firm. Place in greased mixing bowl; turn to bring greased side up. Cover; let rise in warm place until more than double (1 hour, 45 minutes). Dough will have decided yeasty odor. Punch down and place in refrigerator until cold. Cut dough into two parts. Roll and/or pat each into a 10-inch circle. Place on greased cookie sheets or pizza dishes or pans. Clip at 1-inch intervals around edge and press so edge stands up slightly. Gash bottom every two inches to prevent bubbles. Brush with oil.

TO MAKE FILLING: Brown ground beef and sausage in heavy saucepan, using a bit of olive oil, if needed; set aside. In large bowl combine tomato paste, tomatoes, basil, oregano, salt, pepper and minced onion. Shred cheese; set aside.

TO ASSEMBLE PIZZA: Spread each dough circle with one-fourth of tomato mixture. Cover with meat and mushrooms, then sprinkle with mozarella cheese. Top with remaining tomato sauce; sprinkle with Parmesan cheese. Bake at 425 degrees for 20 minutes. Garnish with broiled mushroom caps, if desired. Serve hot.

NOTE: One loaf of frozen bread, thawed just enough to roll out, and divided into two portions, will make the crust for two 10-inch pizzas.

NOTE: Leftover pizza may be refrigerated or frozen to be reheated later.

Sloppy Joes

16 SERVINGS

  2 lbs. ground beef
  2 medium onions, chopped
½ can (10½ oz. size) tomato soup
½ cup (4 oz.) catsup
  2 tablespoons brown sugar, packed
1½ teaspoons chili powder
1½ teaspoons Worcestershire sauce
  1 teaspoon salt
1½ teaspoons dry mustard
½ teaspoon curry powder
16 hamburger buns

Cook ground beef slowly in heavy saucepan, stirring to break up meat. Add onions; continue to cook until soft and transparent. Drain. Add remaining ingredients; simmer 20 to 30 minutes. Serve ¼ cup mixture in each hamburger bun.

Hot Italian Spaghetti

8 SERVINGS

½ lb. hot Italian sausage
1 lb. lean ground beef
1 large onion, coarsely chopped
1 large green pepper, chopped
1 can (4 oz.) sliced mushrooms, drained
1 can (16 oz.) tomato sauce
1 can (12 oz.) tomato paste
1 can (29 oz.) or 1 quart whole tomatoes
1½ teaspoons garlic powder
¼ to ½ teaspoon dried hot chilies, crushed
1½ teaspoon leaf oregano
4 bay leaves
1 large green pepper, thinly sliced
4 medium zucchini, washed and sliced thinly
   Salt and pepper
1 lb. cooked long spaghetti

Remove sausage from casing; brown with ground beef in large heavy saucepan along with chopped onion, chopped green pepper and drained mushrooms. Add tomato sauce, tomato paste, tomatoes and seasonings; simmer for 2 to 2½ hours. Add sliced green pepper and zucchini; simmer, covered, for 30 minutes longer. Season to taste with salt and pepper. Mix immediately with spaghetti and serve.

SPAGHETTI AL DENTE: Bring 2 gallons water (1 quart per serving of spaghetti) to rolling boil; add 2½ tablespoons salt (1 teaspoon per quart of water). Add spaghetti in portions (to minimize cooling of water); stir gently to avoid sticking. Bring water back to boiling as quickly as possible, stir pasta again, then cook for 8 to 12 minutes, until spaghetti, when tested, is biteable but not soft, crunchy or rubbery. Drain spaghetti in large colander, allowing it to drain thoroughly for 1 or 2 minutes.

Barbecued Hamburgers

1½ lbs. lean ground beef   **12 PATTIES**
   1 egg
  ¾ cup dry bread crumbs or quick cooking oats
  ¾ cup evaporated milk
1½ teaspoons salt
  ⅛ teaspoon ground black pepper
  3 tablespoons onion, finely chopped
  3 tablespoons vinegar
  2 tablespoons sugar
  1 cup catsup
  ½ cup water
  3 tablespoons onion, grated
  ¼ teaspoon dry mustard

Combine beef, egg, crumbs, milk, salt, pepper and 3 tablespoons onion. Shape into 12 patties, using ¼ cup mixture per patty. Brown in hot skillet, using a little oil, if necessary. Combine remaining ingredients in large heavy saucepan. Simmer 5 minutes. Put drained patties carefully into barbecue sauce, making sure sauce has been spooned over all of them. Simmer 1 hour. Serve each patty in a bun with 1 teaspoon sauce over top.

Saturday Meat Loaf

350 degrees   **6 SERVINGS**

  ⅔ cup dry bread crumbs
  1 cup milk
1½ lbs. lean ground beef
  2 eggs, slightly beaten
  ¼ cup onion, chopped
  1 teaspoon salt
  ⅛ teaspoon ground pepper
  ½ teaspoon ground sage
    Catsup Sauce (p. 212)

Combine all ingredients except sauce. Shape in loaf pan (7½ x 3½ x 2½ inches). Spread with Catsup Sauce. Bake 1¼ hours.

Ground Beef Fricassee

4 SERVINGS

1 lb. lean ground beef
½ cup onion, chopped
1 cup celery, diced
3 tablespoons green pepper, chopped
2 tablespoons flour
1½ cups hot water
1 beef bouillon cube
1 teaspoon salt
⅛ teaspoon pepper
½ teaspoon onion salt
½ teaspoon garlic salt

Cook ground beef in a skillet until lightly brown, using fat if necessary. Add onion, celery and green pepper; cook until onion is soft and transparent. Blend in flour, then add hot water in which bouillon cube has been dissolved. Cook and stir until slightly thickened. Add remaining ingredients. Cover skillet; simmer over low heat for 30 minutes or until flavors are blended. Adjust seasoning. Serve on fluffy rice, fried noodles, mashed potatoes or baked potatoes.

NOTE: 1 cup chopped cooked meat may be used in place of ground beef.

NOTE: If desired, 1½ cups coarsely grated carrot may be added to mixture along with seasonings.

Quick Meatballs

40 MEATBALLS

1 lb. lean ground beef
1 cup dry bread crumbs
½ cup milk
½ teaspoon salt
½ teaspoon Worcestershire sauce

Combine all ingredients. Shape mixture by level tablespoons into 1-inch meatballs. Arrange in single layer in large unheated skillet. Set over medium heat and brown, loosening and turning with spatula as necessary.

NOTE: For Quick Make-Ahead Meatballs, prepare in large mixing bowl 4 times the recipe to make 160 meatballs. Arrange in single layer in large dripper pan. Bake at 400 degrees for 12 to 15 minutes, loosening and turning with spatula once or twice, until nicely browned. To freeze, arrange meat balls on large cookie sheet; freeze for 30 to 60 minutes. Place in 1-lb. portions in 1½-pint freezer containers or in heavy plastic bags; seal tightly. Store in freezer no longer than two months. To thaw, set into refrigerator for 24 hours. Use in any of the following recipes: Meatballs With Spaghetti (p. 102), Oriental Meatballs (p. 101), Meatballs With Rice (p. 100), Meatballs And Gravy On Colcannon (below), Sweet and Sour Meatballs (p. 100).

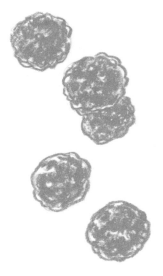

Meatballs And Gravy On Colcannon

6 SERVINGS

2½ cups boiling water
  6 beef bouillon cubes
  3 tablespoons cornstarch
½ cup cold water
  1 1-lb. recipe Quick Meatballs (p. 98)
  3 cups (1½ lbs.) hot potatoes, mashed
  3 cups (½ medium) hot cooked cabbage, shredded
½ cup sliced green onions

In medium saucepan, dissolve bouillon cubes in boiling water. Blend together cornstarch and cold water; stir into hot bouillon. Cook and stir until thick and clear. Add meatballs; heat through. Serve over mounds of colcannon, made by combining hot mashed potatoes, hot drained cabbage and green onions that have been seasoned to taste.

Sweet And Sour Meatballs

6 SERVINGS

1 can (15½ oz.) pineapple chunks
½ cup brown sugar, packed
3 tablespoons cornstarch
1 cup water
⅓ cup vinegar
1 tablespoon soy sauce
½ teaspoon dry mustard
¼ teaspoon ground cloves
1 beef bouillon cube
1 1-lb. recipe Quick Meatballs (p. 98)
1 green pepper, cut into strips
1 can (5 oz.) water chestnuts, drained and thinly sliced
3 cups hot fluffy rice

Drain pineapple chunks, saving syrup. Combine pineapple syrup, brown sugar, cornstarch, water, vinegar, soy sauce, mustard, cloves and bouillon cube. Cook and stir until thick. Add meatballs, pineapple chunks, green pepper and water chestnuts. Cover; simmer until all ingredients are hot, stirring occasionally. Serve over hot rice with additional soy sauce, if desired.

Meatballs With Rice

6 SERVINGS

1 1-lb. recipe Quick Meatballs (p. 98)
½ cup water
1 can (10½ oz.) cream of mushroom soup
1 can (10½ oz.) cream of tomato soup
3 cups hot fluffy rice

Make Quick Meatballs as directed. Combine soups and water in large saucepan; bring to boil. Add meat balls; simmer 5 minutes or until meat balls are thoroughly heated. Serve over hot fluffy rice.

Oriental Meatballs

3 tablespoons oil
1 medium onion, sliced
2 cups diagonally sliced celery
½ cup carrots, thinly sliced
1 can (10¾ oz.) beef bouillon
½ cup snow peas or ½ green pepper, cut in strips
1 teaspoon sugar
1 1-lb. recipe Quick Meatballs (p. 98)
1 can (1 lb.) bean sprouts, drained, or 1 lb. fresh bean
   sprouts
2 tablespoons cornstarch
3 tablespoons soy sauce
1 tablespoon cold water
1 can (5 oz.) Chinese noodles

Heat oil in hot skillet or wok. Stir in onion, celery and car-rots; cook, stirring, for 2 or 3 minutes or until barely soft. Stir in bouillon, snow peas or green pepper, sugar, and meat balls. Cover; simmer 10 minutes or until meatballs are hot, stirring occasionally. Add bean sprouts. Cook 1 minute longer. Blend together cornstarch, soy sauce and cold water. Add to meatball mixture; cook until thick. Serve immediately over Chinese noodles.

Spanish Sauce

3½ CUPS SAUCE

6 tablespoons (¾ stick) butter or margarine
1 cup green pepper, chopped
¾ cup onion, chopped
2 teaspoons flour
1 can (15 oz.) tomato sauce
2 cans (4 oz. each) sliced mushrooms, drained
2 teapoons sugar

In saucepan melt butter; saute pepper and onion until tender. Blend in flour. Stir in tomato sauce, mushrooms and sugar. Cook over low heat, stirring constantly until mixture thickens. Cook 2 additional minutes.

Meatballs With Spaghetti

6 SERVINGS

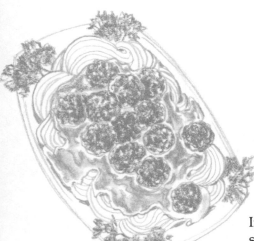

1 medium onion, chopped
1 clove garlic, minced
2 tablespoons oil
1 can (1 lb.) tomatoes
1 can (12 oz.) tomato paste
2 cups water
½ teaspoon sugar
1 teaspoon salt
¼ teaspoon ground black pepper
½ teaspoon dried sweet basil or 1 bay leaf
1 1-lb. recipe Quick Meatballs (p. 98)
1 package (8 oz.) spaghetti
Freshly grated Parmesan cheese

In heavy saucepan cook onion and garlic in hot oil until soft. Add tomatoes, tomato paste, water and seasonings. Cook slowly for 1 hour. Add meat balls; cook over low heat for 15 minutes. In meantime, cook spaghetti in boiling, salted water as directed on package until tender; drain. Serve with meat balls and sauce.

Chili-Ghetti

350 degrees   10 TO 12 SERVINGS

2 tablespoons butter
¾ cup onion, chopped
1 lb. lean ground beef
1 can (1 lb. 13 oz.) tomatoes
1 can (32 oz.) mild flavored chili
1 package (8 oz.) spaghetti
3 cups (12 oz.) Cheddar cheese, shredded
1 cup (8 oz.) dairy sour cream
½ lb. fresh mushrooms (optional)
¼ cup (2 oz.) Parmesan cheese, grated

In large skillet melt butter; cook onion and ground beef until tender and brown. Drain. Add tomatoes and chili; simmer 45 minutes. In the meantime, cook spaghetti according to package directions; drain. Remove skillet from heat; stir in cheddar cheese until melted. Fold in sour cream. Combine chili mixture and spaghetti. If using mushrooms, wash, pat dry, slice and cook in 1 to 2 tablespoons oil over high heat in medium skillet until lightly sauteed; add to chili-ghetti. Pour mixture into 4-quart casserole. Top with Parmesan cheese. Bake, covered, for 45 minutes; remove cover last 15 minutes.

Chili

12 SERVINGS

    3 cups (1 lb.) dry small red beans
    6 cups water
    2 or 3 bay leaves
    2 lbs. lean ground beef
    ½ lb. bulk pork sausage
    3 large onions, chopped
    3 garlic buds, minced
    1 can (29 oz.) or 1 quart tomatoes
    1 tablespoon chili powder
    2 small dried red chili peppers
    ¾ teaspoon curry powder
    1 tablespoon powdered cumin seed (or cominos)
    1 tablespoon salt
    ¼ teaspoon Tabasco

Wash and sort chili beans. Put into large kettle with water and bay leaves; cook until tender. In skillet, brown meat, onions and garlic. Add to drained beans along with remaining ingredients. Simmer together for 1 hour. Serve hot. Or chill and reheat.

NOTE: For less rich chili, use 1 lb. ground beef.

MEAT/FISH/POULTRY 103

Lasagne

350 degrees   12 TO 14 SERVINGS

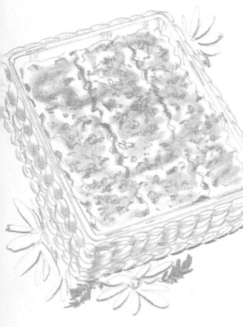

  1 package (10 oz.) frozen spinach, chopped or leaf
  2 lbs. lean ground beef
  ¼ lb. bulk pork sausage
1½ teaspoons salt
  ¼ teaspoon pepper
  ½ teaspoon oregano
1½ tablespoons Worcestershire sauce
  1 package (10 oz.) lasagne noodles
  1 lb. (4 cups) mozarella or Monterey Jack cheese, shredded
  2 cans (10½ oz. each) cream of mushroom soup
1½ cups milk
  1 can (8 oz.) tomato sauce
  ½ cup Parmesan cheese, grated

Cook frozen spinach as directed on package; chop, if necessary; set aside. Brown ground beef and pork sausage in skillet; drain. Add salt, pepper, oregano and Worcestershire sauce; stir in chopped spinach. Cook lasagne noodles as directed on package; drain and rinse thoroughly. In greased 9 x 13-inch pan arrange (in order given) half of noodles, half of meat mixture, half of shredded cheese; repeat, using remaining ingredients. Heat soup and milk in medium saucepan until well blended. Pour over top of casserole, letting it seep down into noodles. Spread tomato sauce over top. Sprinkle generously with Parmesan cheese. Bake for 30 minutes or until bubbling hot.

Stuffed Cabbage Leaves

12 LARGE STUFFED CABBAGE LEAVES

1 large head cabbage
1 lb. lean ground beef
½ cup uncooked rice

1 medium onion, chopped
1 teaspoon fennel seeds, crushed
1 teaspoon dried dill weed
2 tablespoons fresh parsley, chopped, or 2 teaspoons dried
2 tablespoons fresh mint, chopped, or 1 teaspoon dried
1 teaspoon salt
½ teaspoon pepper
¼ cup lemon juice (1 lemon)
1 can (1 lb.) or 2 fresh whole tomatoes, chopped
2 beef bouillon cubes
1 cup water

Wash cabbage. Cut off stem end; separate off 12 large leaves. Pour boiling water over leaves; drain. Combine remaining ingredients except bouillon cubes and water. Place 2 tablespoons mixture into center of each leaf. Roll up, folding in ends to make a tight package. Arrange, open edge down, in heavy casserole, stacking as needed. Dissolve bouillon cubes in water; pour over cabbage along with juices from meat; cover and simmer for 1 hour. If necessary, lay plate down on top of stuffed cabbage leaves while cooking to help them hold their shape.

Pork Pineapple Bake

375 degrees   4 SERVINGS

1 can (12 oz.) pork luncheon meat
2 teaspoons Dijon mustard
1 can (9 oz. or 4 slices) sliced pineapple
2 tablespoons brown sugar, packed

Cut pork luncheon meat slightly more than half through loaf into 8 sections. Place in ungreased baking dish. Spoon ½ teaspoon mustard between every other cut. Cut pineapple slices in half. Insert half-slice in each cut; top loaf with remaining half-slice. Insert whole cloves in pineapple, if desired. Sprinkle brown sugar over pork. Bake for 20 minutes.

Quick Rouladin

5 SERVINGS

1 tablespoon dry chopped onion or 3 tablespoons fresh
  onion, chopped
1 teaspoon parsley flakes or 1 tablespoon fresh parsley,
  chopped
½ teaspoon salt
5 slices bacon, diced
½ cup soft bread crumbs
1 tablespoon Worcestershire sauce
1 cup (¼ lb.) mushrooms, cleaned and chopped
5 cubed beef steaks
  Flour
½ cup grapefruit juice
1 cup beef bouillon
1 can (10½ oz.) golden mushroom soup
1 cup (¼ lb.) fresh mushroom, sliced
½ cup dairy sour cream
¼ cup stuffed green olives, sliced

Combine onion, parsley, salt, bacon, crumbs, Worcestershire sauce and 1 cup chopped fresh mushrooms. Place
equal portions of stuffing on each cube steak. Roll up
steaks; fasten securely with wooden toothpicks or tie with
string. Dredge rolls in flour. Brown well on all sides in hot
oil in skillet. Place rolls into pressure cooker containing
grapefruit juice and bouillon. Pour golden mushroom
soup over top. Assemble pressure cooker. Cook, according to manufacturer's directions, for 20 minutes. Turn
heat indicator off; unplug cord; let pressure drop of its
own accord. Add sliced mushrooms; allow to stand,
covered, but without heat, for 3 minutes, until mushrooms
are heated. Arrange rouladin on serving platter. Top with
sour cream; garnish with stuffed olives.

NOTE: Rouladin may be baked, covered, at 325 degrees
for 1 hour or until tender.

Skier's Stew

275 degrees   8 TO 10 SERVINGS

2½ lbs. beef cubes, cut in 1½-inch pieces
  8 medium potatoes, quartered
  8 large carrots, cut in 4 chunks each
  2 bay leaves
  1 package (1½ oz.) dried onion soup (or see p. 220)
  1 can (10½ oz.) cream of mushroom soup
  1 can (10½ oz.) cream of celery soup
  1 can (8 oz.) tomato sauce

In large Dutch oven with tight-fitting lid make a layer of half the beef, then half the vegetables; repeat. Top with bay leaves, soups and tomato sauce. Bake for 6 to 8 hours, baking at 250 degrees for the longer period of time.

Barbecued Pork

FILLING FOR 16 OR MORE BUNS

  3 to 3½ lb. pork roast
  1 bottle (18 oz.) hickory flavored barbecue sauce with onion
    bits
½ cup catsup
½ teaspoon prepared mustard
  1 tablespoon cider vinegar
½ teaspoon curry powder
2½ tablespoons butter
  1 tablespoon onion, minced
½ teaspoon oregano
  1 teaspoon salt

Cook pork roast in slow cooker or heavy saucepan over low heat for several hours or until meat is very tender. Shred pork. Combine remaining ingredients; pour over drained meat. Cover and simmer for at least 3 hours or until thick. Serve in buttered, toasted sesame seed buns.

Oriental Beef With Cauliflower

6 SERVINGS

1 package (7 oz.) frozen or ½ lb. fresh pea pods
1 lb. beef tenderloin, partially frozen
3 tablespoons oil, divided
⅓ cup onion, chopped
1 clove garlic, minced
4 cups raw cauliflower, thinly sliced
1 cup condensed beef broth
1½ tablespoons cornstarch
2 tablespoons soy sauce
½ cup water

Pour boiling water over frozen or fresh peas, breaking apart with fork, if necessary; drain immediately. Slice partially frozen beef tenderloin paper thin. Heat 1 tablespoon oil in large skillet. Add half the beef; cook briskly, turning over and over until browned. Remove to dish. Heat skillet again, add 1 tablespoon oil; and add remaining beef; brown in same way; remove to dish. Add 1 tablespoon oil to skillet. Cook onion and garlic only a few seconds. Add cauliflower and broth; cook 3 minutes until cauliflower is crisp tender, stirring carefully. Blend together cornstarch, soy sauce and water until smooth; stir into vegetable mixture. Add browned beef and pea pods. Cook and stir until thick and clear. Serve with fluffy rice.

NOTE: 1 green pepper, cut in strips, may be used in place of fresh pea pods. Add at same time as cauliflower.

Quick Sauerbraten

325 degrees

6 TO 8 SERVINGS

2 cups red wine vinegar
2 cups water
1 teaspoon salt
¼ teaspoon ground black pepper
½ cup onion, chopped

2 tablespoons fresh celery leaves, chopped
2 teaspoons whole mixed pickling spice
1 5-lb. chuck roast of beef
½ cup sugar
18 (more or less) old-fashioned gingersnaps, crushed

Combine vinegar, water, salt, pepper, onion, celery leaves
and pickling spice to make marinade. In large bowl or
crock place meat; pour over marinade, making sure meat
is covered with liquid. Cover; let stand in refrigerator for 2
hours. Add sugar. In heavy kettle or Dutch oven bake
meat in marinade, covered, for 3 hours or until tender. Or
simmer, covered, on top of range for 3 hours. Remove
meat to platter; keep hot. Strain liquid to remove spices.
Return liquid to cooking pan; stir in gingersnap crumbs to
thicken gravy; simmer until thick. Serve wtih Potato Pancakes (p. 170).

Stifado (Greek Stew)

4 TO 6 SERVINGS

2 lbs. beef stew meat
  Salt and pepper
½ cup butter
1 can (6 oz.) tomato paste
⅓ cup water
2 tablespoons red wine vinegar
1 tablespoon brown sugar
1 clove garlic, minced
1 bay leaf
1 small cinnamon stick
½ teaspoon whole cloves
¼ teaspoon ground cumin (or cominos)
2 cans (16 oz. each) boiled onions, drained partially

Season meat with salt and pepper. Melt butter in large
heavy pot. Brown meat slightly. Add remaining ingredients except onions. Cover and simmer for 2½ hours.
Add onions; simmer another 30 minutes.

Stuffed Pork Chops

325 degrees   6 SERVINGS

   6 rib pork chops, cut 1 inch thick
   2 cups dry bread cubes
1½ tablespoons onion, chopped
   ½ cup apple, chopped
   ½ teaspoon salt
   ⅛ teaspoon pepper
   ¼ teaspoon ground or rubbed sage
   ⅛ teaspoon poultry seasoning
   2 tablespoons butter, melted, and stock to moisten
   ½ cup hot water

Have pocket cut in each pork chop for stuffing. Combine bread cubes, onion, apple and seasonings. Moisten with butter and liquid; toss gently. Stuff dressing loosely into pork chops. Brown chops on both sides in hot fat; season lightly with salt and pepper. Transfer pork chops to casserole. Add ½ cup water, cover tightly and bake for 45 minutes or until tender, adding more water, if needed. Or water may be added to pork chops in skillet; cover tightly and simmer over low heat until tender—about 45 minutes to 1 hour.

Glazed Ham With Pineapple

325 degrees   12 SERVINGS

5½ to 6-lb. boneless ham, fully cooked
   3 cans (9 oz. each) pineapple or 12 large slices
      Ham Glaze (below)
      Fresh parsley
      Spiced crab apples

Have butcher cut ham into ⅓-inch slices; reassemble in its original form by tying slices together with cord. Place ham on rack in roasting pan; bake, uncovered, for 1½ hours.

Remove ham from oven. Increase oven heat to 400 degrees. Cut string around ham, insert drained pineapple slices between ham slices, and re-tie with string, if necessary. Brush generously with Ham Glaze. Return to oven; bake 15 minutes longer, basting 2 or 3 times. To serve, lift ham and pineapple to serving platter, cut and remove string, and garnish with fresh parsley and spiced crab apples. If desired, add a little pineapple juice to remaining glaze. Reheat; serve with ham.

HAM GLAZE: Combine 1 cup maple-flavored syrup, ¾ cup (packed) brown sugar and 2 tablespoons prepared mustard in small saucepan; heat until blended.

Brown Beef Stew

6 TO 8 SERVINGS

    2 lbs. beef chuck, cut in 1½-inch cubes
    2 tablespoons fat
    4 cups boiling water
    1 teaspoon lemon juice
    1 teaspoon Worcestershire sauce
    1 medium onion, sliced
    2 bay leaves
    1 tablespoon salt
    ½ teaspoon ground pepper
    ½ teaspoon paprika
       Dash allspice or cloves
    1 teaspoon sugar
    6 carrots, quartered
    1 lb. (18 to 24) small white onions

Thoroughly brown meat on all sides in hot fat. Add water, lemon juice, Worcestershire sauce, sliced onion, bay leaves and seasonings. Simmer 2 hours stirring occasionally to keep from sticking. Add carrots and onions. Continue cooking 20 to 30 minutes or until vegetables are done. Remove meat and vegetables; thicken liquid for gravy. Combine and serve.

Chow Mein

1 lb. pork, cut into strips, 1½ x ½ inches
1 tablespoon oil
¾ cup water
2 cups onions, slivered stem to stem
3 cups celery, cut on slant
1 can (8 oz.) bamboo shoots
½ lb. fresh mushrooms, sliced
4 tablespoons oil for frying vegetables
½ lb. fresh bean sprouts
½ tablespoon fresh ginger root, grated
1 teaspoon sugar
3 tablespoons soy sauce
3 tablespoons cornstarch
  Extra chicken or turkey stock as needed

In heavy saucepan fry pork pieces in 1 tablespoon hot oil until very brown. Remove meat; add water; heat and stir until drippings are absorbed to make stock. In wok or skillet, saute each vegetable separately except bean sprouts in 1 tablespoon oil until barely tender but still crisp; remove and set aside in separate piles, saving all vegetable juices. (This can be done ahead of time and re-frigerated, if desired.) To serve, reheat meat in beef stock and vegetable juices; add vegetables one by one and heat. Add bean sprouts and ginger, then stir in mixture of sugar, soy sauce, cornstarch and chicken stock as needed. Heat slowly until thick. Serve over crisp noodles.

NOTE: Do not use cast iron skillet.

NOTE: Recipe may be multiplied as many times as desired.

Sweet And Sour Pork

2 pork chops
 Cornstarch
½ cup cooking oil
¼ cup catsup
 6 tablespoons vinegar
 6 tablespoons sugar
 2 tablespoons soy sauce
 1 cup water
 3 cups prepared vegetables*
1½ tablespoons cornstarch
 2 tablespoons cold water

> *Any combination of diced carrots, green pepper, celery, onions, water chessnuts, mushrooms, bamboo shoots, bean sprouts, etc., each kept in separate units before cooking.

Cut meat into small pieces from bone. Roll in cornstarch; allow to stand until juices of pork dissolve cornstarch coating. Heat oil in heavy skillet over medium high heat. Add pork pieces; stir with chop sticks until meat is evenly browned. Remove pan from heat; with slotted spoon remove meat from pan; drain on paper toweling. In meantime, combine in large saucepan catsup, vinegar, sugar, soy sauce and 1 cup water; bring to boil. To sauce add hard vegetables (carrots, celery, water chestnuts, bamboo shoots); simmer for 10 minutes. Then add soft vegetables (onions, bean sprouts, green peppers, mushrooms); simmer 2 minutes more. Blend together cornstarch and 2 tablespoons water. Add to sauce, cooking and stirring, until thick and translucent. Stir in meat, heat and serve immediately with unsalted steamed rice.

Corned Beef Hash

4 medium (1½ lbs.) potatoes
1 large onion, chopped
¼ cup (½ stick) butter or margarine
½ small (2 cups) cabbage, shredded
½ cup water
1 teaspoon salt
1 can (12 oz.) corned beef, cubed

Scrub or pare potatoes, as desired. Cook until tender; cube. Chop onion. In large heavy skillet melt butter, add onion; cook until transparent, about 3 minutes. Add potatoes; cook and stir about 5 minutes. Add cabbage, water and salt. Cook, uncovered, over medium high heat until liquid is absorbed and hash is browned, about 10 minutes. Add corned beef; turn mixture with spatula. Cook about 3 minutes longer or until meat is heated through.

Frankfurt And Vegetable Stew

4 TO 6 SERVINGS

6 slices bacon (about ⅓ lb.) cut into 1-inch lengths
1 cup onion, sliced
1 clove garlic, minced
4 small to medium (4 cups) zucchini, sliced
2 cups raw cauliflower, sliced
1 can (1 lb.) tomatoes, undrained
½ teaspoon basil leaves, crushed
1 teaspoon salt
½ teaspoon sugar
1 can (10½ oz.) condensed tomato soup
1 lb. frankfurts, cut into thirds
1 medium green pepper, cut into 1-inch squares

Fry bacon crisp. Drain bacon pieces on absorbent paper; save 2 tablespoons drippings. Saute onion and garlic in drippings until onion is limp. Add zucchini, cauliflower, tomatoes, basil, salt and sugar. Cover; cook until vegetables are almost tender, about 15 minutes. Blend in soup. Add franks and green pepper; heat well. Sprinkle bacon over top.

Lamb Shish Kabobs

Broil   6 SERVINGS

   2 to 3 lbs. lamb shoulder or leg, cut into 1½-inch cubes
   1 teaspoon ground ginger
   1 teaspoon dry mustard
   1 teaspoon monosodium glutamate
   2 teaspoons sugar or molasses
   ½ cup soy sauce
   ¼ cup salad oil
   3 cloves garlic, mashed and minced
   ½ cup pineapple juice

Combine all ingredients but lamb in glass or pottery bowl. Let stand 24 hours at room temperature. Add lamb cubes, spoon marinade over all pieces and allow to stand in refrigerator for 6 to 8 hours. Arrange meat cubes on 6 skewers, allowing space between every two pieces. Broil over hot coals or 3 inches from source of heat for 15 minutes, turning frequently. If desired, thread whole canned mushrooms and small onions onto skewer alternately with pieces of lamb. Add small whole tomatoes for last 5 minutes of cooking, if desired. Serve immediately with Rice Pilaff (p. 82).

Veal Birds With Cream

350 degrees   4 SERVINGS

1½ lbs. veal, pounded
2 tablespoons onion, finely chopped
¼ cup celery, finely chopped
1 tablespoon butter
1 cup dry bread crumbs
  Pinch sweet herbs (basil, thyme, sage, marjoram, etc.)
1 teaspoon salt
  Ground pepper
1 teaspoon lemon juice
1 egg, beaten
1 teaspoon water
8 teaspoons butter, melted
1 cup light cream

Pound veal or have it run several times through cuber by meat dealer. Cut into eight 2½ x 4-inch pieces. Chop any trimmings of meat; saute with onion and celery in 1 tablespoon butter. Combine with crumbs, seasonings, lemon juice, egg and water. Place spoonful of dressing into center of each piece of meat; moisten each with 1 teaspoon melted butter. Roll each piece and tie with clean white string. Dredge veal birds in flour; then brown in additional butter in hot skillet. Arrange meat in baking dish, add cream and cover. Bake for 30 minutes or until tender. Or pour cream over veal birds in skillet, cover and reduce heat to cook below simmering for 30 minutes or until tender. If desired, thicken cream drippings before serving.

Venison Jerky

1 venison tenderloin
  Salt
  Pepper

After venison meat has aged, cut tenderloin into very thin strips across the grain. Sprinkle strips generously with salt and pepper; allow to stand in cool place for 24 hours to fully absorb seasonings. Hang meat strips over thin wire in cool, dry place; allow to remain for at least a week. When fully dry, gather beef jerky. Store in clean cloth bag in cool, dry place.

Venison Pot Roast

10 TO 12 SERVINGS

    6 to 8-lb. venison pot roast
 ¼ cup (½ stick) butter or margarine
 ¼ lb. salt pork or bacon, cut into strips
    3 medium onions, chopped fine
    2 bay leaves
    1 clove garlic, crushed
    3 large carrots, quartered lengthwise
2½ cups vegetable stock or water
 ¼ teaspoon allspice
 ¼ cup honey
    2 tablespoons vinegar
    2 cups dairy sour cream
    2 tablespoons flour
      Salt and freshly ground pepper

Rub roast thoroughly with salt and pepper. In large heavy kettle with lid, melt butter. Add pot roast; sear and turn until browned on all sides. Place salt pork or bacon strips over top. Add onions, bay leaves, garlic, carrots, hot vegetable stock or water, allspice, honey and vinegar. Stir liquids thoroughly; bring mixture to boil. Reduce heat; simmer 2 to 2½ hours. Remove pot roast to warming oven. Strain stock; return to kettle. Stir in blended mixture of sour cream and flour. Taste for seasoning. Return pot roast to gravy. Heat but do not boil. Serve sliced meat and gravy over hot noodles, if desired.

German Fish Skillet

1 lb. fresh or frozen fish fillets (haddock, perch, cod, etc.)
¼ lb. (about 5 slices) bacon, diced
½ cup flour
½ teaspoon paprika
½ teaspoon salt
⅛ teaspoon pepper
1½ lbs. red boiling potatoes (4 medium), cooked and sliced
¾ cup onion, chopped
1 tablespoon vegetable oil
1½ tablespoons flour
¾ cup water
¾ cup vinegar
¼ cup sugar
¼ teaspoon salt
⅛ teaspoon pepper
2 tablespoons parsley, chopped

Thaw fish if frozen. In large skillet fry bacon until brown and crisp; remove from skillet and set aside. Combine flour, paprika, salt and pepper; dip fillets in flour mixture to coat. Fry fish in bacon drippings, adding additional vegetable oil, if needed. Keep fried fish warm while preparing potatoes. In second skillet saute onion in 1 tablespoon oil. Blend in flour; gradually add water and vinegar. Stir in sugar, salt and pepper. Heat mixture to boiling, stirring constantly. Boil for 1 minute. Stir in potatoes and parsley. Top with fried fish and heat to serving temperature. To serve, place potato mixture in warmed serving dish with fillets arranged on top. Sprinkle with bacon pieces.

Quick Shrimp Divine

½ cup green onion, chopped
1 tablespoon butter
1 can (10 ¾ oz.) cream of shrimp soup
1 cup (½ pint) dairy sour cream
1 can (7 oz.) small deveined shrimp, drained and rinsed
4 pastry tart shells

In skillet cook onion in butter until tender. Stir in soup, sour cream and shrimp. Barely heat through. Serve immediately in pastry shells, in puff paste shells or over hot steamed rice.

Halibut Au Gratin

350 degrees   4 TO 6 SERVINGS

1 lb. fresh or frozen halibut
4 slices onion
2 bay leaves
¼ cup (½ stick) butter or margarine
¼ cup flour
2 cups milk
2 cups (½ lb.) Cheddar cheese, shredded
½ teaspoon salt
   Grated pepper
½ cup buttered bread crumbs
1 tablespoon parsley, chopped
   Paprika

Arrange halibut on rack in skillet with a little water; lay onion slices and bay leaves over halibut. Cover; steam for 30 minutes, adding water as needed. In meantime, melt butter, stir in flour and add milk. Stir and cook until sauce thickens and is smooth. Add cheese; stir until melted. Season to taste. Separate halibut into serving size pieces; place in buttered 1½-quart casserole. Pour over cheese sauce; sprinkle with buttered crumbs, then with parsley and paprika. Bake 30 minutes or until bubbling hot.

Baked Stuffed Fish

350 degrees   6 TO 8 SERVINGS

    1 tablespoon flour
    2 onions, sliced and separated into rings
    3 to 4 lb. fish, dressed for stuffing
      Salt and pepper
    1 package (5 oz.) seasoned stuffing mix
  ¼ cup butter or margarine, melted
    1 tablespoon lemon juice.

Shake flour in family size (14 x 20 inches) brown-in-bag; place in 2-inch deep roasting pan, large enough to allow fish to lie flat. Place onion rings in bottom of bag. Rinse fish and wipe dry. Cut fish inside along each side of backbone and remove bone but leave skin uncut. Sprinkle inside and out with salt and pepper. Prepare stuffing mix by package directions. Stuff fish with mixture. Close stuffed area with toothpicks. Place prepared fish on onion rings in bag. Spoon on melted butter or margarine and lemon juice. Close bag with twist tie; make six half-inch slits in top of bag. Bake for 40 minutes or until fish flakes easily when tested with a fork through bag.

NOTE: Fish may be garnished by cutting slits across top of baked fish at 2-inch intervals or where serving cuts will be made and inserting lemon wedges. Or top fish with lightly cooked bacon strips.

Pan Fried Trout

                                           1 TROUT PER SERVING

    1 trout (about 10 oz.) per serving
  ½ cup flour
    1 teaspoon salt
  ½ teaspoon monosodium glutamate
  ¼ teaspoon paprika
  ⅛ teaspoon ground pepper
  ½ cup (1 stick) butter

Clean and scale trout; roll in mixture of flour and seasonings. Melt butter in heavy skillet. Add trout; fry until golden brown, 15 to 20 minutes, turning frequently. Serve on heated platter with Dill Sauce (p. 211) or Cucumber Sauce (p. 125).

Trout In Bacon Wrap

1 SERVING

1 small trout (about 10 oz.)
1 teaspoon salt
½ teaspoon monosodium glutamate
¼ teaspon paprika
⅛ teaspoon ground pepper
2 or 3 bacon slices
   Lemon Butter Sauce (below)

For each serving, season one small trout that's been cleaned and scaled, with a mixture of above seasonings. Wrap fish completely in bacon slices. Fasten with small skewers or wooden picks. Place in basket-style steak broiler. Grill 3 inches from coals, turning once, until bacon is very crisp, about 7 minutes. Serve with Lemon Butter Sauce.

Lemon Butter Sauce

1 CUP

1 cup butter
2 tablespoons lemon juice
¼ teaspoon salt
¼ teaspoon paprika
⅛ teaspoon freshly ground pepper
¼ cup fresh parsley, chopped

Heat all ingredients but parsley in small saucepan. Add parsley. Serve over cooked fish, or omit parsley and use as basting sauce for cooked fish.

Rich Crab Casserole

325 degrees   8 SERVINGS

    1 can (7½ oz.) crab, drained and flaked
    1 cup mayonnaise
    1 cup soft bread crumbs
    1 cup light cream
    6 hard-cooked eggs, diced
    ½ teaspoon salt
    1 tablespoon parsley, chopped
    1 tablespoon onion, finely chopped
      White pepper
    ¾ cup buttered bread crumbs

Combine all ingredients except buttered bread crumbs. Place in 2-quart casserole. Sprinkle with buttered bread crumbs. Bake 30 minutes or until bubbly hot.

NOTE: Casserole can be covered and refrigerated over night before baking, if desired.

Skillet Tuna Casserole

                                                               6 SERVINGS

    ¾ cup onion, chopped
    ⅓ cup green pepper, chopped
    2 tablespoons butter
    1 cup uncooked rice
    1 can (10½ oz.) condensed tomato soup
    2 cups water
    ½ teaspoon salt
    ¼ teaspoon dried marjoram
    1 can (12½ oz.) or 2 cans (6½ oz. each) tuna
    4 slices (4 oz.) Cheddar cheese
    ⅓ cup ripe olives, quartered

In large skillet cook onion and green pepper in butter until soft. Add rice; stir. Add tomato soup, water, salt and marjoram. Bring to boil; cover and turn heat to low. Cook 30 minutes or until rice is tender. Remove cover. Fold in drained and flaked tuna fish. Top with cheese slices, cut into thin strips, and then olive wedges. Cover; heat gently until cheese melts.

Sweet And Sour Tuna

6 SERVINGS

1 can (12½ oz.) or 2 cans (6½ oz. each) tuna, drained
2 tablespoons butter
1 green pepper, cut in strips
1 cup celery, diagonally sliced
1½ tablespoons cornstarch
¼ teaspoon ginger
1 can (1 lb. 4 oz.) pineapple chunks
2 tablespoons vinegar
2 teaspoons soy sauce
1 chicken bouillon cube
3 to 4 cups hot cooked rice

Drain tuna fish; if packed in oil, oil may be used in place of butter. Heat butter or tuna oil in skillet. Add green pepper and celery; cook over high heat about 2 minutes, stirring constantly. Measure cornstarch and ginger into 2-cup measure. Add syrup drained from pineapple, vinegar and soy sauce; stir to blend. Add enough water to make 1½ cups. Add liquid to skillet along with tuna, pineapple and bouillon cube. Cook, stirring constantly until bouillon cube is dissolved and mixture is thick and hot. Serve over hot fluffy rice.

Simple Simon Pie

350 degrees   8 SERVINGS

⅔ cup uncooked long grain rice
1⅓ cups boiling water
½ teaspoon salt
2 tablespoons fresh parsley, chopped
1 can (1 lb.) pink salmon
⅓ cup (⅔ stick) butter or margarine
⅓ cup flour
2½ cups salmon liquid plus milk
½ teaspoon salt
¼ teaspoon ground pepper
½ teaspoon celery seed
⅛ teaspoon nutmeg
2 tablespoons lemon juice
1 cup (4 oz.) sharp Cheddar cheese, shredded
Biscuit Dough (below)

In 1½-quart saucepan gradually pour rice into boiling salted water. Turn heat to low, cover saucepan and cook 25 minutes (makes 2 cups cooked rice). Combine cooked rice and parsley; place in greased 2-quart casserole. Drain and flake salmon, saving liquid to combine with milk for white sauce; set aside. In medium saucepan melt butter; stir in flour. Add milk-salmon juice mixture; cook and stir until thick and smooth. Add seasonings, lemon juice and cheese. Stir in salmon. Pour over rice. Cover with Biscuit Dough. Bake 30 minutes.

BISCUIT DOUGH:

1 cup flour, stirred and measured
¼ teaspoon salt
¼ teaspoon baking powder
⅓ cup shortening
3 tablespoons cold water
1 tablespoon lemon juice

In medium bowl stir together flour, salt and baking powder. Cut in shortening. Stir in cold water and lemon juice. Turn out onto lightly floured board; knead once or twice. Roll into crust; cut gashes for escape of steam; fit into casserole. (If desired, 1½ cups biscuit mix and ½ cup milk may be used for crust.)

Salmon With Cucumber Sauce

6 SERVINGS

6 salmons steaks or fillets
Melted butter
Fresh lemon juice
3 cucumbers
1½ teaspoons salt
⅛ teaspoon pepper
3 tablespoons chives or green onion, chopped
1 cup dairy sour cream
2 tablespoons fresh lemon juice

Brush both sides of salmon steaks or fillets generously with melted butter or salad oil; broil over hot coals or in broiler (about 6 inches from source of heat) for 15 minutes on each side, or until done, brushing occasionally with mixture of melted butter and lemon juice. Serve hot with cold Cucumber Sauce.

CUCUMBER SAUCE:

Pare and thinly slice cucumbers. Combine with remaning ingredients; chill until ready to serve.

Crunchy Salmon Omelets

SALMON FILLING:

    1 can (7¾ oz.) salmon
      Milk
  ¼ cup green onion, sliced
  ⅓ cup water chestnuts, chopped
  ½ cup celery, diced
    2 tablespoons butter or margarine
    1 tablespoon flour
  ¼ teaspoon salt
  ¼ teaspoon thyme
  ¼ teaspoon Tabasco sauce
    1 cup sharp Cheddar cheese, shredded

OMELETS:

    8 eggs
    1 teaspoon salt
  ½ teaspoon marjoram
      Pepper
      Butter
    1 cup alfalfa sprouts
      Orange slices and parsley for garnish

SALMON FILLING: Drain and flake salmon, reserving liquid. Add milk to salmon liquid to make ¾ cup. Saute green onion, water chestnuts and celery in butter. Blend in flour. Add combined milk and salmon liquid. Cook, stirring constantly, until thick and smooth. Add salmon, seasonings and cheese; heat until cheese melts and sauce is hot.

FOR EACH OMELET: Beat 2 eggs, ¼ teaspoon salt, ⅛ teaspoon marjoram and dash of pepper. In small omelet pan heat 2 teaspoons butter until sizzling. Pour egg mixture into pan; cook until done, loosening egg around edges to allow uncooked egg to run under cooked portion. Place ½ cup salmon mixture in center of each omelet. Top with 2

tablespoons alfalfa sprouts; fold over. Garnish omelets
with remaining alfalfa sprouts, orange slices and parsley.

Easy Salmon Souffle

375 degrees   4 SERVINGS

  1 can (7¾ oz.) pink salmon
    Milk
  ¼ cup (½ stick) butter or margarine
  2 tablespoons fine dry bread crumbs
  3 tablespoons flour
  4 eggs, separated
    Dill Sauce (p. 211)

Drain liquid from salmon into measuring cup; add
enough milk to make 1 cup. Mash salmon; include bones
and skin, only if desired. Using about 1 teaspoon of the
butter, coat sides and bottom of 6-cup souffle dish or
casserole. Sprinkle with crumbs, rotating dish so that
crumbs coat all areas. In small saucepan melt remaining
butter; blend in flour. Gradually add salmon liquid-milk
mixture. Cook, stirring until thick. Beat egg yolks with
fork. Add small amount of hot sauce to egg yolks. Blend
and stir yolk mixture back into remaining sauce, whipping with wire whisk to blend thoroughly. Add salmon;
cook 2 minutes; remove from heat. Beat egg whites until
stiff. Fold ¼ of egg whites into sauce; fold sauce into
remaining egg whites. Pour into prepared baking dish.
Bake for 25 minutes or until done. Serve at once with Dill
Sauce.

Paella

350 degrees   8 TO 10 SERVINGS

¼ cup Spanish olive oil
1 clove garlic
1 large onion, minced
1 large green pepper, cubed
2 large tomatoes, peeled and cubed
1 tablespoon parsley leaves
1 teaspoon salt
2 cups long grain rice
4 cups boiling water
1 teaspoon saffron or turmeric
¼ teaspoon black pepper
1 teaspoon paprika
½ lb. crabmeat, boned
1 package (10 oz.) frozen peas
½ lb. mushroom caps
1 can (7 oz.) artichoke hearts
½ lb. small cooked fresh shrimp
12 large green shrimp in shells
1 lb. clams in shells
1 can (4 oz.) pimiento, cut into strips

Heat olive oil in large heavy skillet or "paella" pan over medium heat. Add garlic clove, slightly pounded to give more flavor; brown slightly. Add onion and green pepper; brown slowly for 10 minutes. Add tomatoes, parsley and salt; cook slowly for 5 minutes, stirring occasionally. Add rice; turn with spatula a few times. Add boiling water; stir. Add saffron or turmeric, black pepper and salt to taste. At this point, mixture may be put into 3-quart baking dish or dripping pan (preferably shallow and large), or it may be kept in large skillet atop range. Sprinkle crab meat and frozen peas over top of rice. Do not stir any more. If cooking on range, watch for an even boiling point, neither too brisk nor too slow. If using oven, cover pan; bake for 45 to 60 minutes. Arrange mushroom caps, rounded side up, and artichoke hearts evenly over top. Add shrimp, large and small, and clams (still in shells), spacing them evenly over the dish. Without disturbing rice, sink them into the liquid with spatula. Turn heat down as liquid is absorbed. Do not stir, just make sure everything is cooking by pushing it down into liquid gently with spatula. If baking, allow another 15 minutes in the oven.

Jellied Salmon Loaf

8 SERVINGS

    2 envelopes (1 T. each) unflavored gelatin
 ½ cup cold water
 ½ cup boiling water
    2 tablespoons vinegar or lemon juice
    1 cup mayonnaise
 ½ teaspoon salt
 ¼ teaspoon ground pepper
    2 tablespoons catsup
    1 can (15 oz.) red or pink salmon
    2 hard cooked eggs, shelled and diced
 12 stuffed olives, sliced

Soften gelatin in cold water; dissolve in boiling water; cool. Add vinegar, mayonnaise, salt, pepper and catsup; chill until mixture begins to thicken. Drain salmon; discard skin and bones; flake. Fold into thickened gelatin mixture along with chopped eggs and sliced olives. Chill until set. Unmold and slice to serve. Garnish with fresh parsley and lemon wedges.

Roast Turkey

325 degrees

TO THAW FROZEN TURKEY: Leave turkey in original bag and use one of the following methods:

a. Place on tray in refrigerator for 3 to 4 days.

b. Place on tray at room temperature in closed grocery bag for 1 hour per pound of turkey. Closed bag prevents skin of turkey from becoming too warm.

c. Cover with cold water, changing water occasionally; allow one-half hour per pound of turkey. Refrigerate or cook turkey as soon as thawed. If turkey is to be stuffed, do so just before roasting.

Follow instructions on bag for commercially-stuffed turkeys. Refreezing uncooked turkey is not recommended.

TO PREPARE FRESH OR FROZEN TURKEY FOR OVEN:

a. Remove plastic bag if used with turkey. Remove neck and giblets from cavities. Rinse turkey and pat dry. Cook neck and giblets for broth to flavor dressing and/or to make giblet gravy.

b. Follow favorite dressing recipe to stuff turkey (p. 133) or bake stuffing in a casserole. Because stuffing expands during roasting, turkey body and neck cavity should be stuffed loosely—approximately ¾ cup stuffing per pound oven-ready weight. If not stuffed, rub turkey cavities generously with salt and, if desired, insert pieces of celery, carrots, onion and/or parsley for added flavor. Neck skin should be skewered to back, and wings should be twisted behind body to lie flat against pan or rack. Fasten legs down by tying or tucking under skin band. Do not fasten down legs for faster cooking.

TO ROAST: Place turkey breast-up on rack in shallow roasting pan. If a roast-meat thermometer is used, insert into thick part of thigh. Bulb must not touch bone. Roast in preheated 325 degree oven. Time chart below is guide to length of roasting time. When thermometer registers 180 to 185 degrees, the turkey is done. To check, move thermometer slightly toward center of bird. If it then registers less than 180 degrees, more cooking is required. A "tent" of foil placed loosely over turkey will delay browning until about last half hour when tent can be removed to allow final browning. Turkey may be basted regularly, if desired, with melted butter.

TURKEY IS DONE WHEN:

a. Roast-meat thermometer inserted in thigh registers 180 to 185 degrees.

b. Thick part of drumstick feels soft when pressed with thumb and forefinger.

c. Drumstick and thigh move easily.

TIME CHART FOR ROASTING STUFFED TURKEY: Because turkeys vary from one to another due to conformation, variety, etc., cooking times can be only approximate. Because of this it would be well to allow an extra half hour of roasting time in case turkey needs extra cooking. Check to see if done during last hour of roasting. All turkeys should be roasted in preheated 325 degree oven.

Ready-To-Cook Weight	Approximate Cooking Time	Thermometer
6 lbs.	3 hours	All
8 lbs.	3½ hours	180 to 185 degrees
12 lbs.	4½ hours	
16 lbs.	5½ hours	
20 lbs.	6¼ hours	

NOTE: Unstuffed turkeys require about ½ hour less roasting time.

Turkey With Soy-Butter Glaze

1 roast turkey (p. 130)
2 tablespoons butter, melted
⅓ cup light corn syrup
1 tablespoon soy sauce
¼ teaspoon garlic salt

Prepare and cook turkey as directed. Just as turkey is done, brush with Soy-Butter Glaze, made by combining remaining ingredients. Bake for 10 to 15 additional minutes. Allow turkey to stand about 30 minutes after removal from oven for easier carving.

Water Chestnut Stuffing

STUFFS 16-LB. TURKEY

¾ cup (1½ sticks) butter or margarine
1 large onion, chopped
3 ribs celery, chopped
12 cups dry bread cubes or bread crumbs
3 tablespoons fresh parsley, chopped
1½ teaspoons salt
2 tablespoons poultry seasoning or ground sage
¼ to ½ teaspoon ground pepper
1 cup water chestnuts, thinly sliced
About ¾ cup broth or water

In skillet, cook butter, onion and celery until tender, stirring occasionally. In large bowl, combine bread cubes, parsley, salt, poultry seasoning and pepper. Mix to combine. Add butter-onion mixture and water chestnuts. Toss, adding as much liquid as desired.

NOTE: Dressing may be stuffed into turkey or baked in 3-quart casserole for 45 minutes or until hot.

NOTE: Broth can be chicken bouillon cube dissolved in water or cooking liquid from giblets.

Bread And Celery Stuffing

STUFFS 14-TO 18-LB. BIRD

    4 cups celery, diced
    1 cup onion, chopped
    1 cup (2 sticks) butter or margarine
    4 quarts dry bread cubes
    1 tablespoon salt
1½ teaspoons poultry seasoning
    ½ teaspoon sage
    ½ teaspoon pepper
       Hot broth or water

Cook celery and onion in butter or margarine over medium heat until onion is transparent but not brown; stir occasionally. Combine with bread cubes and seasoning; toss lightly. Add enough broth to moisten as desired.

GIBLET STUFFING: Add chopped, cooked giblets; use giblet broth as liquid.

RAISIN STUFFING: Add 2 cups seedless raisins; add 1 cup chopped nuts, also, if desired.

CHESTNUT STUFFING: Add 4 cups boiled chestnuts, chopped; use milk for liquid.

MUSHROOM STUFFING: Add 2 cans (6 oz. each) broiled, sliced mushrooms, drained, or cook 2 cups sliced fresh mushrooms in part of butter.

Hot Turkey Salad

350 degrees   6 SERVINGS

  2 cups cooked turkey breast, diced
  2 cups celery, sliced
  1 cup unseasoned croutons
  1 cup mayonnaise
  ½ cup slivered almonds, toasted
  1 tablespoon lemon juice
  2 teaspoons onion, grated
  ½ teaspoon salt
    Dash paprika
  ½ cup nippy Cheddar cheese, shredded
  1 cup potato chips, crushed

Combine all ingredients but cheese and potato chips. Spoon into six individual baking dishes. Sprinkle top with shredded cheese and potato chips. Bake for 20 to 30 minutes or until bubbling hot.

Lucky Seven Sandwich

8 SANDWICHES

  8 slices rye bread
  8 slices Swiss cheese
  8 large lettuce leaves
 16 tomato slices
  8 slices cooked breast of turkey
 16 slices bacon, cut in half and fried crisp
    Thousand Island Dressing (p. 202)

For each sandwich, place 1 slice rye bread on luncheon plate. Top with slice of Swiss cheese, then lettuce, tomato slices, breast of turkey and bacon slices. Smother with Thousand Island Dressing

NOTE: For Quick Thousand Island Dressing, combine 1 quart thick commercial thousand island dressing with 1 cup buttermilk; blend thoroughly and refrigerate.

Parmesan Fried Chicken

4 SERVINGS

1 broiler-fryer chicken (3 lbs.), cut up
⅓ cup flour
1 teaspoon paprika
¾ teaspoon salt
    Dash pepper
1 egg, beaten
2 tablespoons water
⅔ cup fine dry bread crumbs
⅔ cup grated Parmesan cheese
½ cup (1 stick) butter or margarine
    Shortening

Wash and dry chicken pieces. Combine flour, paprika, salt and pepper in paper sack. Drop chicken into flour mixture; coat thoroughly. In shallow dish blend egg and water. Dip chicken pieces into egg mixture; then roll in combined bread crumbs and Parmesan cheese. If desired, allow chicken pieces to dry on rack for 30 minutes. In hot butter (to which extra shortening may be added, if needed) saute chicken, uncovered, until golden on all sides, using tongs to turn. Lower heat; cook, uncovered, turning occasionally, for 30 to 45 minutes or until tender and brown. Drain thoroughly. Serve hot or cold.

Hot Turkey Salad Rolls

350 degrees   6 SERVINGS

>   2 cups cooked turkey, diced
> 1½ cups celery, diced
>   ¼ cup slivered almonds, toasted or blanched
>   1 tablespoon lemon juice
>   1 tablespoon onion, grated
>   ⅛ teaspoon ground pepper
>   1 teaspoon salt
>   ½ cup mayonnaise
>   6 hard rolls
> 1½ cups Cheddar cheese, shredded

Combine turkey, celery, almonds, lemon juice, seasoning and mayonnaise. Cut small slice from top of each hard roll; scoop out inside (saving for bread crumbs). Fill rolls with turkey salad. Pack cheese on top of each roll, pressing down a bit. Bake for 25 minutes. Serve immediately.

HOT CHICKEN SALAD ROLLS: Use 2 cups cooked diced chicken in place of turkey.

Chicken Cordon Bleu

400 degrees   8 SERVINGS

>   8 chicken breast halves
>   4 oz. thinly sliced boiled or proscuitto ham
>   4 oz. Swiss cheese
>   Leaf thyme or rosemary
>   ¼ cup (½ stick) butter or margarine
>   ½ cup fine dry bread crumbs or cornflake crumbs

Bone chicken breasts; remove skin. Place breast halves one at a time between pieces of plastic wrap. Using rolling pin or flat side of meat mallet, flatten each until about ⅛-inch thick. Peel off wrap. For each chicken piece allow 2 or 3 thin ham slices and 1 stick cheese of 1½-inch length. Place cheese on ham, sprinkle with pinch of crushed thyme or rosemary leaves and wrap up. Roll up chicken breasts with one ham and cheese bundle inside, tucking in ends and fastening with toothpicks. Dip each chicken roll in melted butter, then in crumbs. Arrange in 9 x 13-inch baking dish. Top with any remaining butter or crumbs. Bake 40 minutes, until chicken is tender and golden brown.

Sesame Baked Chicken Breasts

400 degrees   12 SERVINGS

   2 eggs, slightly beaten
   2 tablespoons water
   2 tablespoons soy sauce
   2 teaspoons salt
   ⅛ teaspoon pepper
   12 large chicken breast halves, boned and skinned
   ½ cup flour
   ¾ cup sesame seeds
   ¾ cup (1½ sticks) butter or margarine
      Mushroom Sauce (p. 211)

Blend eggs, water, soy sauce, salt and pepper. Dip chicken into flour, then into egg mixture; sprinkle on both sides with sesame seeds. Divide butter between two 8 x 12-inch baking dishes; melt in oven. Arrange half the chicken breasts in each baking dish, turning to coat with butter. Bake for 40 to 50 minutes. Serve with Mushroom Sauce.

Chicken Smetane

350 degrees   8 SERVINGS

    2 broiler-fryer chickens (2½ to 3 lbs. each)
    1 small clove garlic, finely minced
1½ cups dairy sour cream
    2 tablespoons lemon juice
    1 teaspoon seasoned salt
    1 teaspoon salt
    1 teaspoon paprika
      Dash pepper
    1 cup fine dry bread crumbs
½ cup (1 stick) butter, melted

Disjoint chickens. Set wings, necks and giblets aside for another use. Rinse chicken pieces in cold water; pat dry. Combine minced garlic with sour cream, lemon juice and seasonings. Coat chicken pieces with mixture; let stand, covered, in refrigerator for several hours or overnight. Remove chicken from cream, allowing as much as possible to adhere to pieces. Roll gently in crumbs; arrange in single layer in buttered baking dish. Drizzle with melted butter. Bake 50 to 60 minutes.

Easy Oven Fried Chicken

425 degrees   3 SERVINGS

    1 broiler-fryer chicken (2½ to 3 lbs.), cut up
⅓ cup flour
    1 teaspoon paprika
    1 teaspoon salt
⅛ teaspoon pepper
¼ cup (½ stick) butter

Wash and dry chicken. Combine flour and seasonings in paper bag. Shake 2 or 3 pieces chicken at a time in flour mixture. In shallow pan in oven melt butter; remove pan from oven. Arrange chicken in pan in single layer, with skin side down. Bake, uncovered, 30 minute; turn chicken pieces with tongs; bake 15 minutes or until brown and fork tender.

CREAM GRAVY: Pour drippings from baking pan into measuring cup. Measure ½ cup fat (fat rises to top of cup) into skillet; add 6 tablespoons flour (left over from coating chicken plus more flour as needed). Stir over low heat, loosening brown bits from baking pan, till smooth. Stir in 1 cup chicken broth and 1½ cups half-and-half cream. Cook, stirring until thickened. Season. If gravy becomes too thick, stir in a little water. Serve with chicken.

Ginger Chicken

6 SERVINGS

  6 chicken breast halves
½ teaspoon powdered ginger
¼ teaspoon garlic powder
½ teaspoon salt
  Pepper
  2 tablespoons oil
½ lb. sugar peas
  1 can (8 oz.) water chestnuts, sliced
  2 cups (8 oz.) almonds, toasted
  3 cups chicken stock
¼ cup cornstarch
  2 tablespoons cold water
  4 teaspoons soy sauce

Bone chicken; cut into 1-inch cubes. Toss chicken pieces in mixture of powdered ginger, garlic powder, salt and pepper. Saute in hot oil. Add sugar peas, water chestnuts, toasted almonds and chicken stock. Blend together cornstarch, cold water and soy sauce; stir into chicken mixture. Cook and stir until thick. Serve over hot rice.

Chicken With Golden Rice

400 degrees   10 SERVINGS

      1 stewing hen (about 5 lbs.)
      1 large onion, sliced
      1 tablespoon salt
      1 cup long grain rice
  2½ cups boiling water
      1 teaspoon salt
      1 tablespoon butter
      2 cans (4 oz. each) mushroom stems and pieces
   ½ cup chicken fat or butter or margarine
   ½ cup flour
      1 teaspoon salt
         Dash pepper
   ¼ teaspoon turmeric
      1 cup evaporated milk
   ¼ teaspoon ground oregano
      2 tablespoons green onion, finely chopped
   ½ to 1 cup Cheddar cheese, shredded

Wash hen, disjoint, and cook in water to barely cover with onion and 1 tablespoon salt until chicken is tender. Drain, saving broth; cut chicken from bone and into pieces. Put dry rice into 3-quart casserole. Pour 2½ cups boiling water over it; add 1 teaspoon salt and 1 tablespoon butter; cover and bake for 20 to 30 minutes or until tender. In meantime, drain mushrooms, saving juice. Melt chicken fat in heavy saucepan; blend in flour, 1 teaspoon salt, pepper and turmeric. Measure mushroom juice; add enough chicken broth to make 3 cups. Add to flour-fat mixture along with evaporated milk; stir and cook until thick and smooth. Add oregano and mushrooms. When rice is cooked to tender, remove casserole from oven; place pieces of chicken over top of cooked rice. Sprinkle with chopped green onion; then pour sauce over top. Sprinkle with ½ to 1 cup shredded Cheddar cheese. Lower oven temperature to 350 degrees; bake casserole for 20 to 30 minutes.

Cheese Chicken Cache

375 degrees   4 SERVINGS

    4 chicken breast halves, skinned and boned
    4 sticks Monterey Jack or Swiss cheese, 3 x 1½ x ¼ inches
    4 sprigs fresh sage or ½ teaspoon ground sage
    2 eggs
    2 tablespoons Parmesan cheese
    ¼ teaspoon salt
    ¼ teaspoon ground pepper
    4 teaspoons fresh parsley, minced, or 1 teaspoon dried
      parsley
    ¼ cup clarified butter or oil (below)
      Sprigs fresh parsley, lemon slices

Cut pocket in each chicken piece by holding knife parallel
to breast and making 2-inch deep slit in side, (do not cut
through.) Place piece of cheese and sprig of sage (or ⅛ teaspoon ground sage) in each pocket. In large bowl beat
together eggs, Parmesan cheese, salt, pepper and parsley.
Dip each piece of chicken into egg mixture, coating
thoroughly; then coat each with flour. Heat butter or oil in
skillet. Saute breasts until crisp and golden, turning with
spatula rather than tongs. Transfer to baking dish; bake
for 10 to 12 minutes or until coating begins to brown.
Serve with parsley and lemon slices.

NOTE: To clarify butter, heat until liquified and milk
residue sinks to bottom of pan. The clear yellow liquid at
top is clarified butter. Skim off and use, discarding
residue. (Clarified butter does not burn as easily as regular
butter.)

Soups and Vegetables

Utah's little "melting pot" has changed since the pioneers first entered Salt Lake Valley. One hundred and fifty years ago immigrant Mormons brought with them treasured recipes from their native lands. Before long they were sharing them with each other, and the melting pot became a sort of international cooking pot.

Converts from other countries emigrate to Utah much less frequently now. It is more an exchange of missionaries—foreign ones coming to the states, local ones receiving calls to lands afar. But both groups bring their tastes for foreign dishes to the culture here—such recipes as Minestrone soup from Italy, Vichyssoise from France, Gazpacho from Spain. Each new recipe gives the melting pot a stir.

Lithuanian Cabbage Soup, a frugal but delicious concoction served over hot boiled potatoes, was brought to Utah a few years ago by an investigator of the Mormon Church. His mother, he told us, had used this recipe in Lithuania during World War I to keep her children alive Later he used it during hard times to keep his own motherless children nourished.

"This recipe is a gift for you," he said.

In like manner, all of these recipes have been given to us and now, in turn, we give them back to you.

And once again, the Mormon "melting pot" has had another stir.

Basic Meat Stock

400 degrees   2 QUARTS

> 2 lbs. veal or beef bones
> 2 large carrots
> 2 celery stalks
> 1 unpeeled onion, cut in half and stuck with 3 cloves
> 3 quarts cold water
> 2 bay leaves
>   Salt and several peppercorns
>   Pinch leaf thyme, crushed
> 3 tablespoons tomato puree

Rub meat bones with oil. Place in shallow pan; bake for 20 minutes. Rub carrots, celery and onion with oil. Add to bones; continue roasting another 20 minutes or until vegetables and bones are a rich, dark brown. Remove from oven. Place in large pot with remaining ingredients. Bring to boil, skim off foam and simmer 4 to 5 hours to reduce by one-third. Strain and freeze.

Basic Chicken Stock

                                                               2 QUARTS

> 3 quarts cold water
>   Bones, gizzard and neck of 1 chicken
> 1 onion, peeled, cut in half and stuck with 2 cloves
> 2 carrots
> 2 celery stalks
> 6 parsley stems
> 2 bay leaves
>   Salt and 4 to 6 peppercorns
>   Pinch leaf thyme

Place cold water in large kettle or saucepan. Add remaining ingredients. Bring to boil; skim off foam. Simmer slowly 4 hours to reduce by one-third. Strain and freeze.

Basic Fish Stock

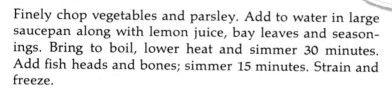

2 QUARTS

2 carrots
2 celery stalks
1 onion
6 parsley stems
2 quarts plus 1 cup water
  Juice of 1 lemon
2 bay leaves
  Salt and several peppercorns
  Pinch of leaf thyme
1 lb. heads and bones of white fish (cod, halibut, sole, haddock, perch, turbot, trout)

Finely chop vegetables and parsley. Add to water in large saucepan along with lemon juice, bay leaves and seasonings. Bring to boil, lower heat and simmer 30 minutes. Add fish heads and bones; simmer 15 minutes. Strain and freeze.

Clarified Soup Stock

  Cold fish, chicken, turkey or meat broth
2 egg whites, whipped frothy
2 egg shells, crushed
2 tablespoons ice, crushed
¼ cup onion, carrot, celery or other vegetables, finely chopped

In large kettle combine cold broth, egg whites, egg shells, crushed ice and vegetables. Slowly bring to boil and cook 20 minutes without stirring or disturbing the gathering crust on top. Strain through several layers of cheese cloth.

French Onion Soup

8 SERVINGS

  4 cans (10 ¾ oz. each) beef broth or consomme
  2 quarts water
12 beef bouillon cubes
  1 stalk celery, cut in pieces
  1 small carrot, cut in pieces
  1 turnip, diced
  6 black peppercorns
  ¼ cup (½ stick) butter (no substitute)
12 large (4 lbs.) onions, thinly sliced
    Parmesan Toast (below)

Combine beef broth, water and bouillon cubes in large kettle. Add celery, carrots, turnips and peppercorns; simmer together about 60 minutes; strain. In heavy saucepan melt butter over medium heat; add onions and cook and stir for about 30 minutes or until onions are a deep golden brown. Add to hot beef stock. Bring to boil. Serve hot with a piece of Parmesan toast floating on each bowl.

PARMESAN TOAST: Toast thick slices of French bread until toasty dry. Generously butter one side; sprinkle generously with parmesan cheese; broil until lightly browned, taking care not to burn.

Tomato Consomme

8 SERVINGS

4 cups tomato juice
2 cans (10 ¾ oz. each) beef broth or consomme
4 whole cloves
8 peppercorns
½ bay leaf
½ teaspoon salt
  Dash ground sweet basil

1 small onion, chopped
A few celery tops
Parsley sprigs

Combine all ingredients in heavy saucepan; simmer 30 minutes. Strain through cheesecloth. Serve with a slice of orange in each bowl of consomme.

Minestrone

10 TO 12 SERVINGS

1 lb. mild bulk pork sausage
6 cups water
2 beef bouillon cubes
2 onions, chopped
2 large carrots, sliced
2 large celery ribs, diced
1 can (28 oz.) tomatoes, pureed
2 cans (8 oz. each) tomato sauce
1 tablespoon dried parsley flakes or 3 tablespoons fresh
  parsley, chopped
½ teaspoon sweet basil, crushed
1 teaspoon leaf oregano, crushed
  Salt, pepper to taste
  Garlic salt to taste
1 can (1 lb.) garbanzo beans, drained
1 can (1 lb.) cut green beans, drained
1 cup egg dumpling macaroni noodles, uncooked

Brown pork sausage in heavy kettle; drain. Dissolve bouillon cubes in water. Add onions, carrots, celery, tomatoes, tomato sauce, parsley and seasonings. Simmer, covered, for 6 hours. Thirty minutes before serving time, add garbanzo beans, green beans and noodles. Simmer until noodles are tender.

NOTE: If desired, use ¾ cup less water and add green beans, undrained.

Vegetable Soup

8 TO 10 SERVINGS

3 to 4-lb. meaty beef soup bone
2 quarts cold water
1 small onion, quartered
1 teaspoon salt
1 bay leaf
2 cups tomatoes
6 sprigs parsley
¼ head young cabbage, chopped
¼ cup rice or barley
5 or 6 carrots, sliced
2 cups cut green beans
1 cup potatoes, diced
½ cup celery, chopped

Cut half the meat from bone; brown in hot fat. Add remaining meat and bone to cold water. Add browned meat, onion, salt and bay leaf; cook slowly for 2 hours. Add vegetables; continue to cook for 1 hour.

Lithuanian Cabbage Soup

6 SERVINGS

1 quart cold water
1 onion, chopped
1 bay leaf
1½ teaspoons salt
1 tablespoon vinegar
1 tablespoon sugar
2 tomatoes, chopped, or 1 can (1 lb.) whole tomatoes
1 medium cabbage, coarsely chopped
1 cup carrots, diced or thinly sliced
2½ lbs. soup bones or chicken parts (necks, wings, gizzards)
    or 3 beef or chicken bouillon cubes
    Freshly grated pepper
6 to 10 boiled potatoes

Combine all ingredients but potatoes in large kettle. Bring to boil; simmer for 60 minutes or until all vegetables are tender. Serve in bowls over hot boiled potatoes.

NOTE: For Lithuanian Borscht, add raw beets, peeled and cut in strips, along with other vegetables and cook until tender.

Easy Danish Soup

6 SERVINGS

6 medium carrots
4 medium potatoes
1 medium onion
2 stalks celery
½ teaspoon salt
½ lb. lean ground beef
½ teaspoon salt
¼ teaspoon sage
¼ teaspoon pepper
1 egg
½ slice bread
1 tablespoon cream or evaporated milk
1½ tablespoons flour
1½ cups boiling water
1 can (10¾ oz.) beef broth or bouillon
2 tablespoons parsley, minced

Peel and cube carrots, potatoes, onion and celery; place in pressure cooker with prescribed amount of water (according to manufacturer's instructions) to which has been added ½ teaspoon salt. Cook 3 minutes at 15 lbs. pressure. Reduce pressure under cold water. Remove cover; set pan aside. Make meat balls by thoroughly combining ground beef, ½ teaspoon salt, sage, pepper, egg, bread, cream and flour. Chill, if desired; form into very small balls with wet hands. Cook meat balls in boiling water for 8 minutes. Add undiluted beef bouillon; heat. Pour over cooked vegetables. Gently stir in minced parsley.

Clam Chowder

8 SERVINGS

   1 cup onion, finely chopped
   1 cup celery, finely diced
   2 cups potatoes, finely diced
   2 cans (6½ oz. each) clams, undrained
  ¾ cup butter
  ¾ cup flour
   1 quart half-and-half cream
1½ teaspoons salt
  ¼ teaspoon pepper

Combine vegetables in small saucepan. Drain clams; pour juice over vegetables; add enough water to barely cover. Cook, covered, until tender—about 15 minutes. In meantime, melt butter in large heavy saucepan. Stir in flour until blended and bubbly. Remove from heat; stir in cream until smooth and blended. Return to heat; cook and stir with wire whip until thick and smooth. Add undrained vegetables and clams; heat through. Season with salt and pepper.

Tuna Broccoli Soup

4 TO 6 SERVINGS

  2 tablespoon butter or margarine
  1 cup (¼ lb.) fresh mushrooms, sliced
  3 cups (½ lb.) broccoli flowerettes
  1 large onion
  1 clove garlic
  3 tablespoons butter
¼ cup flour
  1 teaspoon salt
  1 teapsoon sweet basil, crumbled
  4 cups milk
  1 can (14½ oz. or 1⅞ cups) chicken broth
  2 cans (6½ or 7 oz. each) tuna fish, drained
  1 tablespoon lemon juice

In large heavy saucepan, melt 2 tablespoons butter. Cook washed and sliced mushrooms until tender; remove with slotted spoon; set aside. In same pan in drippings saute broccoli, onion and garlic until crisp-tender; remove with slotted spoon. Melt remaining 3 tablespoons butter in pan. Stir in flour, salt and sweet basil until blended. Remove from heat. Gradually stir in milk and broth. Return to heat; cook and stir until thickened. Add mushrooms, broccoli, onion, garlic, tuna fish and lemon juice. Heat and serve, seasoning further, if necessary.

Fish Chowder

4 TO 6 SERVINGS

1 *quart fish stock (p. 145)*
2 *large (2 cups) onions, chopped*
4 *large carrots, pared and cubed*
4 *large potatoes, pared and cubed*
1 *bay leaf*
  Pinch of leaf thyme, crumbled
  Pinch parsley or dill
1 *lb. white fish (cod, halibut, sole, haddock, perch, turbot, trout) or fresh or frozen shellfish, peeled*
1 *cup heavy cream*
¼ *cup (½ stick) butter*

In large saucepan bring fish stock to boil. Add vegetables and herbs. Continue to simmer, skimming off foam, until vegetables are nearly tender. Add shellfish or skinned fish in chunks; cook until fish just flakes with fork—7 to 10 minutes (a little longer if fish chunks are thick). Stir in cream and butter. Season to taste with salt and pepper. Serve immediately.

NOTE: Two cups clam juice and two cups water may be substituted for fish stock.

NOTE: If desired, canned fish, crab or shrimp may be used in place of fresh or frozen fish, but it should be added at last minute so it isn't overcooked.

Avocado Soup

1 large avocado, peeled and pitted
1 can (14½ oz.) clear chicken broth
½ cup dairy sour cream
⅛ teaspoon chili powder
1 teaspoon onion, chopped
  Fresh lemon slices

Combine all ingredients in blender or food processor; blend until smooth. Cover and refrigerate several hours or until chilled. Stir well just before serving. Garnish with fresh lemon slices and a bit of parsley.

Cream Of Tomato Soup

4 SERVINGS

2 cups tomato juice
2 slices onion
1 bay leaf
1 teaspoon salt
¼ teaspoon pepper
3 allspice berries
2 tablespoons butter or margarine
2 tablespoons flour
2 cups milk

Combine tomato juice, onion and seasonings; simmer 10 minutes; strain. Meanwhile, melt butter in heavy large saucepan; stir in flour; then add milk; stir and cook until thick. Just before serving, slowly add hot, strained tomato juice to white sauce, stirring constantly. Serve immediately.

Mushroom And Potato Soup

14 CUPS

3 tablespoons butter or margarine
2 leeks or green onions , chopped
2 large carrots, sliced (1½ cups)
8 cups boiling chicken broth or water
1 tablespoon fresh dill, chopped, or 2 teaspoon dill weed or
  seed
2 teaspoons salt
½ teaspoon ground black pepper
1 bay leaf
2 lbs. (5 cups) potatoes, diced
1 lb. fresh mushrooms or 2 cans (8 oz. each)
  sliced mushrooms
2 tablespoons butter
1 cup light cream
¼ cup flour

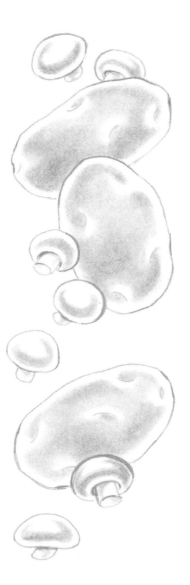

In 4-quart kettle melt 3 tablespoons butter. Add leeks and carrots; saute for 5 minutes. Add broth or water, dill, salt, pepper, bay leaf and potatoes. Simmer, covered, until potatoes are just tender, about 20 minutes. Remove bay leaf. Meanwhile, rinse, pat dry and slice fresh mushrooms (5 cups) or drain canned mushrooms. In large skillet melt 2 tablespoons butter. Add mushrooms; saute until golden, about 5 minutes. Combine cream with flour until smooth. Stir into soup along with mushrooms. Cook and stir until hot and slightly thickened. Garnish with fresh dill, if desired.

Cheesy Potato Soup

4 medium potatoes, diced
1 large onion, chopped
1 quart water
¼ cup (½ stick) butter or margarine
3 tablespoons flour
½ cup milk
1½ cups (6 oz.) shredded sharp cheese
1 teaspoon salt
¼ teaspoon seasoned salt
¼ teaspoon paprika
⅛ teaspoon ground pepper
   Chopped chives

Combine potatoes, onion and water in heavy saucepan. Bring to boil, reduce heat and simmer until tender, about 20 minutes. In heavy skillet melt butter; add flour; cook and stir until mixture bubbles. Remove from heat; stir in milk. Return to heat; cook and stir until thickened. Stir mixture slowly into potatoes; cook and stir until thick. Add cheese and seasonings. Serve topped with chopped chives.

Vichyssoise

6 CUPS

3 cups sliced potatoes
3 cups water
3 chicken bouillon cubes
1 teaspoon onion salt
¼ cup (½ stick) butter
2 cups half-and-half cream
¼ teaspoon celery salt
¼ teaspoon white pepper
   Chopped chives

Wash, peel and slice potatoes (about 2 large ones). Add water and bouillon cubes. Bring to boil; cook until potatoes are very tender. Force potatoes and cooking liquid through fine sieve; or puree in blender or food processor. Combine with remaining ingredients except chives. Heat 10 minutes, but do not allow to boil. Chill. Serve in chilled bowls placed in crushed ice, if desired. Top each serving with chives.

NOTE: Potato soup may also be served hot.

Cheese Soup

4 SERVINGS

½ cup carrot, finely diced
¼ cup celery, finely diced
¼ cup thinly sliced green onion, including green tops
½ tablespoons butter
¼ cup flour
2 cups milk
1½ cups chicken broth
    Dash paprika
1½ cups (6 oz.) shredded sharp cheddar cheese
    Sour cream (optional)

In heavy saucepan cook vegetables in melted butter over low heat until crisp-tender, stirring frequently. Blend in flour. Remove from heat; stir in milk and chicken broth gradually, until liquid and roux are well blended. Return to heat; cook and stir until thick and bubbly. Add cheese; stir until melted. Serve soup immediately, topped with dollop of sour cream, if desired.

Cream Of Corn Soup

4 SERVINGS

½ cup (2 slices) bacon, diced
¼ cup onion, minced
⅓ cup flour
4 cups milk
1 teaspoon salt
¼ teaspoon pepper
¼ teaspoon celery salt
1 can (17 oz.) cream style corn.

Cook bacon in heavy saucepan over medium heat until almost crisp. Add onion; cook until soft but not brown. Blend in flour and milk; cook and stir until thick and smooth. Season. Add corn; bring to boiling point. Season to taste and serve.

NOTE: If desired, top with spiced whipped cream made by combining ½ cup heavy cream, whipped, and ½ teaspoon cinnamon.

Wilted Lettuce Soup

6 SERVINGS

⅓ lb. (7 slices) bacon
6 green onions, thinly sliced
1½ cups heavy cream
¾ cup milk
3 eggs, unbeaten
3 tablespoons vinegar
¾ cup boiling water
½ teaspoon salt
⅛ teaspoon freshly ground pepper
4 to 6 cups leaf lettuce, shredded and loosely packed
8 to 12 small hot boiled potatoes

Fry bacon until crisp. Remove bacon from pan; saute onions in bacon fat until tender. With fork, lightly beat together cream, milk, and eggs. Stir in vinegar. When onions are transparent, add boiling water, salt and pepper; stir. Remove from heat. Add cream mixture and lettuce leaves. Place over medium low heat; cook and stir with fork until mixture thickens and becomes creamy. Do not boil. Season to taste with vinegar, salt and pepper. Serve over boiled white potatoes in soup bowl; sprinkle with crumbled bacon.

Cream Of Zucchini Soup

6 TO 8 SERVINGS

  2 cups (2 medium) onions
  2 tablespoons butter or margarine
3¾ cups (4 medium) zucchini squash
  3 cups chicken broth
⅛ teaspoon freshly ground black pepper
⅛ teaspoon nutmeg
⅛ teaspoon salt
    Pinch cayenne pepper
½ cup half-and-half cream
    Cheddar cheese, shredded

Clean, chop and cook onion in butter until soft and transparent but not browned. Wash and slice zucchini. Combine onion, zucchini and chicken broth in large saucepan. Bring to boil; simmer 15 minutes or until squash is tender. Add seasonings. Puree mixture in blender or food processor until smooth; return to saucepan. Add half-and-half cream; adjust seasonings to taste. Reheat but do not boil. Serve hot, garnished with shredded Cheddar cheese.

Vegetables With Dill Dressing

8 SERVINGS

½ lb. fresh mushrooms, cleaned and halved
¼ cup (½ stick) butter
1½ cups carrots, thinly sliced diagonally
1½ cups pearl onions or onion wedges
1½ cups zucchini, thinly sliced
2 tablespoons lemon juice
¼ teaspoon salt
⅛ teaspoon freshly ground pepper
¼ teaspoon leaf marjoram, crushed
  Dill Dressing (below)

Saute fresh mushroom halves in butter. Add carrots, onions, zucchini, lemon juice and seasonings. Cover; simmer gently for 15 minutes or until vegetables are tender crisp. Turn into serving bowl, spoon juices over vegetables and top with Dill Dressing.

DILL DRESSING:

⅔ cup mayonnaise
⅔ cup sour cream
3 tablespoons onion, chopped
1 teaspoon dried dill weed
1 teaspoon Beau Monde seasoning (below)

Combine ingredients thoroughly. Refrigerate. Serve cold over hot vegetables.

NOTE: In place of Beau Monde seasoning, you may use ¼ teaspoon salt, ¼ teaspoon onion powder, ¼ teaspoon monosodium glutemate and ¼ teaspoon crushed celery seed.

Mixed Vegetables Italian

6 SERVINGS

2 tablespoons oil
1 cup stewed tomatoes

1 beef bouillon cube
 2 cups zucchini, unpared, cut in 1-inch cubes
 ¾ cup green pepper, cut in 1-inch pieces
 ½ cup fresh, frozen or canned corn
 ½ cup carrots, sliced
 ½ cup potatoes, diced
 ½ cup onion, coarsely chopped
 ½ teaspoon oregano leaves
 1 teaspoon salt
 ⅛ teaspoon freshly ground pepper

Place all ingredients in 10-inch skillet. Cover; simmer until crisp done, about 20 minutes. Serve with slotted spoon.

NOTE: If desired, eggs may be poached in vegetable juice and served with vegetables to make complete meal.

Vegetables In German Pancake

400 degrees   6 SERVINGS

 1 recipe German Pancake (p. 44)
 1 lb. fresh mushrooms, quartered
 3 medium (½ lb.) carrots, pared and sliced thinly
 1 medium zucchini, washed, trimmed and sliced thinly
 2 tablespoons oil
 ½ teaspoon dill weed
 1 teaspoon summer savory
 ½ teaspoon salt
 1 cup (4 oz.) Gouda or Gruyere cheese, shredded
   Additional cheese, shredded

Bake German Pancake in 9-inch pie dish. In meantime, saute mushrooms, carrots and zucchini in hot oil in large skillet about 5 minutes. Add seasonings. Lower heat; stir in 1 cup cheese. Cook, stirring, until cheese melts and coats vegetables, about 2 minutes. Spoon vegetable mixture into baked pancake, top with additional shredded cheese. Broil until cheese melts. Cut in wedges; serve immediately.

Stir Fried Vegetables

6 SERVINGS

   3 *full strips lean bacon*
   2 *cups cabbage, finely sliced*
   1 *cup celery, thinly sliced diagonally*
   1 *small onion, finely sliced*
   1 *carrot, cut into very thin strips*
  ½ *green pepper, cut into thin strips*
   1 *can (2 oz.) sliced mushrooms, drained*
1½ *teaspoons sugar*
    Salt and pepper to taste

Prepare all vegetables, working quickly. Cut bacon into ½-inch pieces; fry quickly in hot skillet until barely crisp. Immediately add all vegetables, sprinkle with sugar, salt and freshly grated pepper. Stir-fry until barely tender, 4 or 5 minutes. Serve immediately.

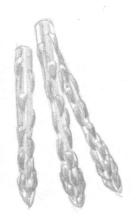

Asparagus Almandine

6 SERVINGS

  2 *cups Cheese Sauce (p. 212)*
  1 *cup slivered blanched almonds, toasted*
  2 *lbs. fresh asparagus or 2 cans (2 lbs.) or 2 packages (10 oz. each) frozen asparagus*

Make Cheese Sauce, using cooking water of asparagus as part of liquid, if desired. Add almonds to cheese sauce. Wash fresh asparagus; cut into short lengths. Cook in small amount boiling salted water until tender, 10 to 12 minutes. Drain. (Or drain canned asparagus and cut into short lengths. Or cook frozen asparagus according to package directions; cut into short lengths.) Add asparagus to cheese sauce and heat thoroughly. Stir very gently so as not to mash asparagus. Serve in patty shells or crisp toast.

Broccoli Onion Casserole

325 degrees   6 SERVINGS

1 *lb. fresh broccoli or 1 package (10 oz.) frozen cut broccoli*
3 *medium (¾ lb.) onions, quartered, or 8 to 10 small onions*
2 *tablespoons butter or margarine*
2 *tablespoons flour*
¼ *teaspoon salt*
   Freshly ground pepper
1 *cup milk*
1 *package (3 oz.) cream cheese*
1 *cup (4 oz.) Cheddar cheese, shredded*
½ *cup buttered bread crumbs*

Slit fresh broccoli spears lengthwise; cut in 1-inch pieces. Cook in small amount boiling, salted water until barely tender, about 15 minutes. Or cook frozen broccoli according to package directions. Drain. Cook onions in boiling salted water until tender; drain. In saucepan melt butter; blend in flour, salt and pepper. Remove from heat. Add milk, stir till smooth. Then stir in cream cheese until melted. Place well drained vegetables in 1½-quart casserole. Pour sauce over. Top with shredded cheese. Bake, covered, for 30 minutes. Remove lid; sprinkle around edges with crumbs. Continue to bake 15 minutes longer or until heated through.

Saucy Red Beets

6 SERVINGS

1 can (1 lb.) sliced beets
¼ cup onion, sliced
2 tablespoons butter
¼ cup sugar
½ teaspoon salt
⅛ teaspoon pepper
1 tablespoon lemon juice
⅓ cup beet liquid or water

Pour off liquid from beets; reserve. Saute onion in butter until tender. Stir in sugar, salt, pepper, lemon juice and ⅓ cup beet liquid. Add beets; cook until thoroughly heated, about 5 minutes, stirring occasionally.

Party Broccoli

6 TO 8 SERVINGS

2 packages (10 oz. each) frozen broccoli
2 tablespoons onion, minced
2 tablespoons butter
1½ cups dairy sour cream
2 teaspoons sugar
¾ teaspoon white vinegar
½ teaspoon poppy seeds
½ teaspoon paprika
¼ teaspoon salt
⅛ teaspoon cayenne pepper
⅓ cup cashews, chopped

Cook broccoli according to package directions, taking care not to overcook; drain. Saute onion in butter until tender. Remove from heat; stir in sour cream, sugar, vinegar, poppy seeds, paprika, salt and cayenne pepper. Arrange broccoli on heated platter; pour sour cream sauce over it. Garnish with cashews.

NOTE: If vegetable is not to be served immediately, re-heat sour cream sauce just to serving temperature. Do not boil as sauce will curdle.

Scalloped Spring Cabbage

350 degrees   4 TO 6 SERVINGS

    2 cups Cheese Sauce (p. 212)
    1 to 2 tablespoons vinegar
    1 medium green cabbage
    ½ cup soda cracker crumbs, buttered

Add vinegar to cheese sauce. Cut cabbage into small wedges. Cook in small amount boiling salted water until crisp-tender, 7 to 10 minutes. Drain thoroughly. Arrange in buttered 1½-quart casserole. Top with cheese sauce. Cover with buttered crumbs. Bake 20 minutes or until crumbs are browned lightly and sauce is bubbling.

NOTE: Drained cooked cabbage may be mixed with hot sauce, sprinkled with buttered bread crumbs and served immediately.

Cauliflower With Almonds

6 SERVINGS

    1 medium head cauliflower
    ½ cup blanched slivered almonds, toasted
    1 cup Cheese Sauce (p. 212)
      Paprika or fresh parsley, chopped

Trim leaves from cauliflower, leaving 1 inch of stem Steam, tightly covered, using enough water to cover stem but not to touch head. Cook until tender, about 25 minutes. To serve, cut off stalk and place cauliflower, stem side down, in serving dish. Stick blanched almonds into cauliflower; pour Cheese Sauce over top. Sprinkle with paprika or chopped parsley.

Carrots With Bacon

8 SERVINGS

2 lbs. fresh carrots
⅛ teaspoon salt
3 slices bacon
   Freshly ground pepper and salt
3 tablespoons fresh parsely, chopped

Peel and coarsely shred carrots. In medium saucepan combine with 3 tablespoons water and ⅛ teaspoon salt. Cover; simmer for 5 minutes. Remove from heat; drain, if necessary, and set aside. In meantime, fry bacon in large skillet until crisp; remove bacon strips. Drain, crumble and set aside. Toss 2 tablespoons bacon drippings lightly into carrots; heat; season to taste. Spoon into serving bowl; sprinkle with bacon bits and fresh parsley.

Sweet And Sour Green Beans

4 SERVINGS

2 strips bacon
1 cup onion, finely chopped
1 tablespoon flour
½ cup bean liquid
¼ cup cold water
¼ cup vinegar
1 tablespoon sugar
1 teaspoon salt
¼ teaspoon ground pepper
1 package (10 oz.) frozen cut green beans, cooked according to package directions, saving liquid or 1 lb. fresh beans, cleaned, trimmed and cooked, saving liquid or 1 can (16 oz.) cut green beans, drained, saving liquid.

Brown bacon in skillet until crisp; remove bacon and crumble; set aside. Saute onion in bacon fat. Stir in flour, then all liquids. Add seasonings and cook, stirring, until mixture boils. Add beans. Heat and serve with crisp bacon bits.

Green Bean Casserole

350 degrees   8 TO 10 SERVINGS

    2 lbs. fresh green beans, trimmed and cut French style
    1 can (8 oz.) water chestnuts, drained and sliced
    ⅓ cup (⅔ stick) butter
    1 small onion, diced
    1 can (4 oz.) mushroom stems and pieces, drained
    3 tablespoons flour
    2 cups milk
1⅓ cups sharp Cheddar cheese, shredded
    ¾ teaspoon salt
    ⅛ teaspoon pepper
       Few drops Tabasco sauce
1½ teaspoons soy sauce
    ⅓ cup sliced almonds, toasted

Cook beans in small amount of salted water until crisp tender. Drain. Combine in baking dish with sliced water chestnuts. Melt butter in heavy fry pan. Add onions; saute until golden. Add drained mushrooms. Blend in flour; add milk; stir and cook until thick. Blend in cheese and seasonings. Pour over beans in casserole; top with sliced almonds. Bake for 20 to 30 minutes or until slightly brown and bubbly.

NOTE: Two packages (10 oz. each) frozen French cut green beans may be used in place of fresh beans. Cook according to package directions, drain and continue as above.

Green Beans With Cheese Sauce

8 SERVINGS

2 lbs. green beans, trimmed and cut into 1-inch pieces
½ cup Cheese Sauce (p. 212)
½ teaspoon Dijon mustard
¼ teaspoon paprika
    Pimiento pieces

Wash beans and trim ends. Cut into 1-inch lengths. Cook in small amount of boiling salted water until crisp-tender, about 20 minutes. Drain. In meantime, make Cheese Sauce; season with mustard and paprika. Serve hot beans with mustard sauce poured over them. Garnish with pimiento.

NOTE: Two packages (10 oz. each) frozen cut green beans, cooked according to package directions may be used in place of fresh beans.

Stuffed Green Peppers

5 SERVINGS

1 lb. lean ground beef
1 large onion, chopped
1 can (12 oz.) whole kernel corn, drained
2 slices white bread, crumbled
1 teaspoon salt
⅛ teaspoon ground black pepper
5 large green peppers
2 cups tomato juice
1½ tablespoons sugar
½ teaspoon salt
½ teaspoon chili powder
2 tablespoons cornstarch
¼ cup cold water

Cook ground beef and onion in skillet until meat is browned and onion is transparent. Combine with drained corn, bread crumbs, 1 teaspoon salt, and pepper. Cut off tops of green peppers, clean out seeds, wash and drain. Stuff generously with mixture. (At this point, peppers may be packed carefully into plastic bags, sealed and frozen, then recipe continued when frozen peppers are taken from freezer.) Place green peppers, top side up, in one layer in large skillet or saucepan. Pour tomato juice into pan; add sugar, remaining salt and chili powder. Cover pan; bring juice to boil and then reduce heat; simmer for 45 minutes (or longer if peppers are frozen). When done, remove peppers to serving dish. Combine cornstarch and cold water until blended; add to tomato juice; cook and stir until thick and clear. Serve over hot stuffed peppers.

NOTE: 1 large potato, coarsely grated, may be substituted for whole kernel corn, if desired.

Marinated Mushrooms

4½ CUPS

1 lb. medium-sized fresh mushrooms or 2 cans (6 to 8 oz. each) whole mushrooms
¼ cup oil
3 tablespoons cider vinegar
1 envelope (1⅜ oz.) dried onion soup mix
¼ cup fresh parsley, chopped

Rinse, pat dry and halve fresh mushrooms to make about 5 cups; or drain canned mushrooms. Place mushrooms in large bowl. Combine oil, vinegar and onion soup mix; blend. Pour over mushrooms, tossing to coat completely. Cover and marinate for at least 6 hours. Stir in parsley just before serving.

Mushroom Eggplant Main Dish

350 degrees   6 SERVINGS

  1 *lb. fresh mushrooms or 2 cans (8 oz. each) sliced*
    mushrooms
1¼ *lbs. eggplant*
  2 *tablespoons flour*
  1 *teaspoon salt, divided*
 ⅛ *teaspoon ground black pepper, divided*
  8 *tablespoons oil, divided*
  1 *cup onion, chopped*
  1 *clove garlic, minced*
  2 *tablespoons butter or margarine*
  1 *can (8 oz.) tomato sauce*
  1 *teaspoon Italian Seasoning (p. 221)*
  1 *lb. creamed cottage cheese*
  2 *eggs, lightly beaten*
  4 *oz. mozzarella cheese, sliced*

Rinse, pat dry and slice fresh muchrooms, or drain canned mushrooms; set aside. Remove eggplant stem. Pare eggplant, if desired; cut eggplant into ¼-inch slices. Combine flour with ½ teaspoon of the salt and $^{1}/_{16}$ teaspoon black pepper. Coat eggplant slices with flour mixture. In large skillet heat 6 tablespoons oil. Add eggplant, a few slices at a time; fry until golden on both sides. Remove and set aside. In same skillet heat remaining 2 tablespoons oil. Add onion and garlic; saute for 2 minutes. Add butter; heat until butter melts. Add reserved mushrooms; saute for 3 minutes. Stir in tomato sauce, Italian seasoning, remaining ½ teaspoon salt and $^{1}/_{16}$ teaspoon black pepper. Bring to boiling point. Reduce heat and simmer; uncovered, for 2 minutes. In 13 x 9 x 2-inch casserole arrange half of fried eggplant in a layer. Mix cottage cheese with eggs. Spread half over eggplant. Spoon half of mushroom sauce mixture over cheese. Repeat layering once more. Arrange mozzarella cheese on top. Bake, uncovered, until bubbly and hot, about 30 minutes. Let stand 10 minutes before serving.

Mushroom Patties

8 PATTIES

1 lb. fresh mushrooms
2 cups soft bread crumbs
½ cup walnuts, chopped
¼ cup onion, chopped
¼ cup fresh parsley, chopped
4 eggs, lightly beaten
¾ teaspoon salt
¼ teaspoon ground black pepper
¼ cup oil

Rinse, pat dry and finely chop mushrooms to make about 4 cups. In large bowl combine mushrooms with all remaining ingredients except oil; mix well. Shape into patties about 4 inches in diameter. In large skillet heat oil. Add patties; fry over medium low heat until patties are set and golden, about 5 minutes on each side.

Honey Onions

400 degrees   **8 SERVINGS**

8 medium or 12-16 small onions
  Salt and pepper
⅓ cup honey
¼ cup (½ stick) butter or margarine
  Ground cloves

Cook whole onions in small amount of salted water, covered, until barely tender, about 20 minutes. Arrange in well buttered baking dish; season with salt and pepper. Heat together honey and butter; pour over onions. Sprinkle lightly with ground cloves. Bake for 20 to 25 minutes or until golden brown.

NOTE: May be assembled a day ahead, then refrigerated until time to bake.

Gourmet Peas

3 TO 4 SERVINGS

2 cups fresh peas, shelled or 1 package (10 oz.) frozen peas
¼ to ½ cup undiluted beef consomme
¼ cup dairy sour cream

Cook peas, covered, in boiling consomme until barely tender. Remove lid and cook consomme down quickly, taking care not to cook dry. Stir in sour cream, heat through and serve immediately.

Potato Pancakes

20 MEDIUM PANCAKES

  2 tablespoons flour
1½ teaspoons salt
  ¼ teaspoon baking powder
  ⅛ teaspoon pepper
  3 cups (2 lb.) potatoes, grated
  2 eggs, well beaten
  2 tablespoons onion, chopped
  1 tablespoon fresh parsley, minced, or 1 teaspoon dried

Combine flour, salt, baking powder and pepper; set aside. Wash, pare and finely grate potatoes; set aside. Combine flour mixture with eggs, onion and parsley. Drain potatoes thoroughly; add to batter and beat. In skillet heat enough fat to make ¼-inch deep. Spoon 2 tablespoons batter into fat for each pancake, leaving 1-inch space between pancakes. Cook over medium heat until golden brown and crisp; turn carefully and brown other side. Drain on absorbent paper. Keep warm in oven (200 degrees) until all pancakes are cooked. Serve with sauerbraten or as main dish with applesauce.

Potatoes Au Gratin

8 SERVINGS

  4 cups boiled potatoes, finely diced
  1 cup Cheddar cheese, shredded
  2 tablespoons onion, finely chopped
  2 tablespoons butter
  2 eggs, slightly beaten
  1 cup milk
  2 teaspoons salt
    Freshly grated pepper
½ cup cheese, shredded

Arrange alternate layers of potatoes and cheese in buttered 1½-quart baking dish. Sprinkle each layer with
onion; dot with butter. Mix eggs, milk and seasonings.
Pour over potato mixture. Sprinkle with additional shredded cheese. Bake for 45 minutes.

New Potatoes With Sesame

3 TO 4 SERVINGS

  1 lb. small new potatoes
⅓ cup green onions, including green ends, sliced
¼ cup (½ stick) butter or margarine
  2 tablespoons sesame seeds, toasted

Cook unpeeled new potatoes in small amount of boiling
salted water in covered saucepan for 20 to 30 minues or
until just tender; peel. Cook onions in butter until soft.
Drain potatoes; coat gently with butter-onion mixture.
Spoon into hot serving dish; sprinkle with toasted sesame
seeds. Serve immediately.

NOTE: To toast sesame seeds, spread seeds thinly in
small baking dish. Bake at 350 degrees for 15 to 20
minutes. Take care not to burn. Sesame seeds may be
toasted ahead of time and used in tossed green salads or
as garnish for other vegetables.

Sweet Potato Balls

325 degrees   12 POTATO BALLS

    2 lbs. sweet potatoes or yams
    ⅓ cup (⅔ stick) butter
    3 tablespoons brown sugar
    ¼ teaspoon salt
    12 large marshmallows
    4 cups uncrushed cornflakes

Scrub sweet potatoes thoroughly. Cook, covered, in small amount of boiling salted water until tender, 30 to 40 minutes. Drain, peel and mash to make 4 cups. Season with butter, brown sugar and salt. Cool slightly. With tablespoon scoop up about ¼ cup of mixture; shape around marshmallow, using more potato as needed to make ball. Roll each ball in uncrushed corn flakes. Place on buttered baking dish when all balls are made; cover with foil and refrigerate or freeze. Bake 20 to 30 minutes or until hot and marshmallow begins to ooze out. If potato balls are frozen, allow about 40 minutes for baking.

Tomato Casserole

350 degrees   4 TO 6 SERVINGS

    8 large tomatoes
    ½ cup bread crumbs
    ½ cup Cheddar cheese, grated
    ¼ cup onion, chopped, if desired
       Salt, pepper, garlic salt
       Sugar
    2 tablespoons butter

Peel and slice tomatoes. Arrange alternate layers of tomatoes, crumbs, cheese and chopped onion in greased 1½-quart baking dish. Sprinkle each layer of tomatoes with salt, pepper, sugar and garlic salt. Dot top with butter. Bake 45 minutes.

Surprise Turnip Casserole

350 degrees   8 SERVINGS

6 medium (2½ lbs.) white turnips
½ cup chicken broth
2 teaspoons onion, finely chopped
2 tablespoons parsley, chopped
¾ cup applesauce
2 tablespoons butter or margarine, melted
⅛ teaspoon freshly ground pepper
1 cup croutons
2 tablespoons butter or margarine, melted

Pare and dice turnips. Cook until tender in chicken broth. Allow turnips to absorb as much liquid as possible and add more liquid, if needed. Drain; mash turnips. Combine with onion, parsley, applesauce, 2 tablespoons butter and pepper. Toss croutons with remaining butter; sprinkle over top of casserole. Bake 20 minutes or until casserole is heated and croutons are lightly browned.

Zucchini Squash Au Gratin

                                     6 SERVINGS

2 cups Cheese Sauce (p. 212)
½ teaspoon Worcestershire sauce
2 lbs. unpeeled young zucchini squash
Paprika

Add Worcestershire sauce to cheese sauce. Wash unpeeled squash; slice in ½-inch slices. Cook in small amount boiling salted water until crisp-tender, about 5 minutes. Drain thoroughly. Place in serving dish; pour sauce over. Sprinkle with paprika. Serve immediately.

Baked Stuffed Zucchini

350 degrees   6 TO 8 SERVINGS

    4 medium zucchini
 1½ lbs. lean ground beef
    1 onion, chopped
    1 clove garlic, minced
 ½ green pepper, chopped
    1 quart whole tomatoes
    1 can (8 oz.) tomato sauce
    1 can (6 oz.) tomato paste
 ¼ teaspoon thyme
 ½ teaspoon rosemary
       Parmesan cheese
       Cheddar cheese, shredded

Parboil whole zucchini about 10 minutes. Drain; slice in half and scoop out middle. Mash zucchini pulp and set aside. Saute ground beef, onion, garlic and green pepper until vegetables are tender and meat loses color. Add tomatoes, tomato sauce, tomato paste, thyme, rosemary and mashed zucchini. Simmer until of proper consistency. Stuff scooped out zucchini shells with mixture. Sprinkle generously with both cheeses. Bake for 45 minutes.

Zucchini Bake

350 degrees   10 SERVINGS

 1¼ lbs. young zucchini
    4 eggs
 ½ cup milk
    3 tablespoons flour
 ½ teaspoon baking powder
 ½ lb. Monterey Jack cheese, cubed
 ¼ cup fresh parsley, chopped
 ¼ cup green pepper, diced

Wash and trim zucchini. Cut in ½-inch pieces. Cook, covered, in small amount of boiling salted water for 5 minutes; drain. Beat eggs with milk, flour and baking powder. Combine with cheese, parsley and green pepper. Spoon into buttered 2-quart casserole. Bake 40 minutes. Remove from oven; allow to stand 10 minutes, then serve immediately.

Skillet Zucchini

6 SERVINGS

2 tablespoons oil
1 small onion, sliced
4 medium zucchini, cut into 1-inch slices
2 fresh tomatoes, peeled and cut up
1 tablespoon sweet red pepper, chopped
1 teaspoon salt
½ teaspoon basil, crushed
¼ teaspoon fresh ground pepper
1 bay leaf

Heat oil in skillet. Add onion; saute until lightly browned. Add remaining ingredients. Cover; simmer until zucchini is barely tender, about 13 minutes. Remove bay leaf and serve.

NOTE: Chopped pimiento may be used in place of sweet red pepper.

Salads and Dressings

The old farmer's market is gone. A large hotel has taken over its spot, and wholesale produce houses have scattered. As for the farmers who arrived at daybreak each morning to sell their garden products, they too have scattered—into other businesses.

Furrowed farmlands of Davis County have given way to condominiums. And the state's last commercial rhubarb field was recently "turned under."

But there are compensations. Refrigerated trucks in California load up with fresh garden produce right at the harvesting site and then roll through the night to get their wares to Salt Lake markets by early morning. Bringing produce from Bountiful could not beat that time by much!

Recipes in this chapter provide direction for combining those fresh food items with appropriate seasonings and dressing. Make Ahead Green Salad that stays fresh and crisp in the refrigerator for 24 hours is a boon to those with full schedules and pinched time allotments. The sophisticated Buffet Salad is another you'll want to try.

Other salad offerings are the classics like Emerald, Frozen Fruit, Raw Cranberry and Molded Tuna Salads. Newcomers include Chicken and Mushroom Salad, Corned Beef and Potato Salad, Shrimp Salad with Herbs and the Lebanese Taboola salad.

The blessing of our time and place is that there are foodstuffs available to make all of these salads.

Hot Picador Salad

6 SERVINGS

  1 lb. lean ground beef
¼ cup onion, chopped
  2 cups cooked or 1 can (1 lb.) kidney beans, drained
½ cup Clear French Dressing (p. 202)
½ cup water
  1 tablespoon chili powder
  4 cups lettuce, shredded
½ cup green onions, sliced
  2 cups (8 oz.) sharp Cheddar cheese, shredded
     Crisp tortillas

Brown ground beef in skillet. Add ¼ cup onion; cook until tender. Stir in kidney beans, French dressing, water and chili powder; simmer 15 minutes. Combine lettuce and green onions in large salad bowl. Add beef mixture and 1½ cups of the cheese; toss lightly. Sprinkle with remaining cheese. Serve with crisp tortillas.

Chicken and Mushroom Salad

4 TO 6 SERVINGS

     1 lb. fresh mushrooms
  ¼ cup salad oil
     2 tablespoons fresh lemon juice
1¼ teaspoons salt
     1 teaspoon sugar
  ¼ teaspoon ground black pepper
     2 cups cooked chicken, diced
     1 green pepper, cut into ¾-inch chunks
  12 cherry tomatoes
  ½ cup bean sprouts

Rinse, pat dry and slice mushrooms to make about 5 cups; place in large bowl. Mix together oil, lemon juice, salt, sugar and black pepper; pour over mushrooms. Toss well to coat mushrooms completely with dressing. Stir in chicken, green pepper, tomatoes and bean sprouts; toss gently. Chill for 30 minutes. Serve on lettuce leaves.

Shrimp Salad With Herbs

8 SERVINGS

2 *cans (6½ oz. each) small deveined shrimp*
2 *tablespoons lemon juice*
¾ *cup mayonnaise*
2 *tablespoons tarragon vinegar*
2 *tablespoons cream*
2 *tablespoons parsley, finely chopped*
2 *tablespoons onion, finely minced*
½ *teaspoon celery seed*
½ *teaspoon sweet basil*
½ *teaspoon salt*
½ *teaspoon monosodium glutemate*
¼ *teaspoon pepper*
2 *cups cabbage, shredded*
1 *cup celery, diced*
8 *avocado halves or tomato cups*
Crisp greens

Drain shrimp, rinse. Place in bowl; cover with ice-filled water; add lemon juice; chill for 20 minutes. In meantime, blend mayonnaise, vinegar and all herbs and spices; refrigerate in covered jar. To serve combine drained shrimp, cabbage, celery and herb dressing. Toss to mix evenly. Serve in avocado halves or tomato cups on crisp greens.

Ann's Favorite Salad

6 SERVINGS

¾ large head iceberg lettuce, shredded
2 medium tomatoes, diced
1 small dill pickle, chopped
½ cup (2 oz.) Cheddar cheese, shredded
½ cup (2 oz.) Monterey Jack cheese, shredded
½ can (12 oz.) luncheon meat
   French dressing
1 can (3 oz.) dried onion rings

Toss together all ingredients except onion rings, using any
kind and amount of French dressing desired. Sprinkle
dried onion rings over the top; serve.

Corned Beef And Potato Salad

4 TO 6 SERVINGS

4 cups (1½ lbs.) pared cooked potatoes, cubed
1 can (12 oz.) corned beef, cubed
½ cup celery, finely diced
¼ cup onion, chopped
¼ cup salad oil
2 tablespoons vinegar
½ teaspoon salt
¼ teaspoon garlic powder
¼ teaspoon freshly ground pepper
⅔ cup dairy sour cream
2 tablespoons mayonnaise
2 tablespoons fresh horseradish
½ teaspoon Dijon mustard
   Crisp salad greens
   Dill pickles and tomato wedges, if desired

Combine potatoes, corned beef, celery and onion in large bowl. In jar shake together oil, vinegar, salt, garlic powder and pepper until well mixed. Pour over potato mixture; toss lightly. Cover and chill several hours. Just before serving, mix sour cream and mayonnaise with horseradish and mustard. Toss carefully into salad. Season to taste. Serve on salad greens, garnished with dill pickles and tomato wedges, if desired.

Fresh Garden Salad

10 SERVINGS

    1 small head cauliflower, separated
1½ lbs. fresh peas or 1 package (10 oz.) frozen peas
  ½ lb. snap green beans or 1 package (10 oz.) frozen cut
       green beans
  ¼ lb. fresh spinach leaves, washed and torn
    1 cup cherry tomatoes, cut up
    1 cup celery, thinly sliced
  ½ cup unpared cucumber, thinly sliced
    1 medium avocado, peeled and sliced
      Zesty Dressing (p. 201)

Cook cauliflowerets in 1 inch of salted water for 10 minutes; drain. Shell and wash peas; cook in small amount boiling water for 3 or 4 minutes; drain. Or cook frozen peas according to package directions; drain. Wash green beans; remove ends and strings; break into 1-inch pieces. Cook in small amount boiling salted water 20 to 30 minutes or until barely tender; drain. Or cook frozen beans according to package directions; drain. Chill cooked vegetables for at least 1½ hours. Just before serving combine all vegetables but avocado in large bowl. Toss Zesty Dressing into vegetables very gently. Serve in lettuce cups, garnished with avocado slices.

Wilted Spinach Salad

4 GENEROUS SERVINGS

2½ lbs. fresh spinach (1½ lbs. cleaned and stemmed)
 2 tablespoons granulated sugar
 1 cup vinegar
10 slices (½ lb.) bacon
   Salt and pepper

Break spinach stems just under leaves. Wash spinach well in several waters. Dry; drain on a towel. Place leaves in large salad bowl. Put sugar in pan over very low heat, watching carefully until sugar turns a light blond carmel color. Do not stir sugar, but occasionally tilt pan in different directions. When sugar is melted, add vinegar and increase heat. Vinegar must boil until all sugar is dissolved. While sugar is cooking, cut bacon slices across into ¼-inch strips. Place bacon pieces in skillet; cook until bacon is cooked but not crisp. Pour vinegar and sugar solution into bacon and fat. Shake pan well so fat can absorb vinegar solution; bring to boil. While sugar and bacon are cooking, season spinach leaves with salt and pepper. Pour fat and vinegar solution over spinach leaves; toss thoroughly. Serve as a separate course on dinner plates.

Make-Ahead Green Salad

12 SERVINGS

  2 heads iceberg lettuce
1½ cups green pepper, diced
1½ cups red onion, chopped
  2 packages (10 oz. each) frozen peas
  2 cups mayonnaise
  2 tablespoons sugar
1¼ cups Parmesan cheese
  8 slices bacon, cut into ½ inch slices

Wash, drain and chill lettuce. In large broad-base crystal salad bowl arrange lettuce that's been cut into bite-size pieces. Sprinkle with green pepper, then red onion, and finally cooked and chilled green peas. Spread mayonnaise over top of salad, sealing to salad bowl on all sides. Sprinkle with sugar, then with Parmesan cheese, and finally with bacon that's been cooked crisp and drained. Refrigerate salad bowl for at least 8 hours or overnight.

Buffet Salad

8 TO 10 LARGE SERVINGS

½ head lettuce
1 small bunch chicory leaves or endive
1 head romaine
½ bunch water cress
2 medium tomatoes, peeled
1 medium avocado, peeled
3 hard cooked eggs
½ lb. bacon, cooked crisp
2 cups cooked chicken breast, finely diced
½ cup bleu cheese, crumbled, or Cheddar cheese, finely shredded
2 tablespoons chives, finely chopped, or green onion tops
1 cup Garlic French Dressing (below)

With sharp knife, chop each of the greens very fine. Spread in layers in large salad bowl, heaping up slightly in center. Finely chop tomatoes, avocado, eggs and bacon. Arrange along with the chicken, cheese and chives in rows of pretty contrasting colors over top of greens. For example, arrange tomato and avocado in two wide rows, side by side, across center of greens. Next to tomato, place row of cheese, then eggs. Next to avocado, place row of chicken, then chives. Sprinkle bacon along edges of tomato and avocado. To keep salad looking attractive while serving, sprinkle part of dressing across only one end at a time, mix lightly, and serve from that section.

NOTE: To make Garlic French Dressing, put cut clove garlic into recipe of Clear French Dressing (p. 202); allow to stand, covered, for several hours. Remove garlic before using.

Sour Cream Fruit Salad

10 SERVINGS

2 cans (11 oz. each) mandarin oranges, drained
1 can (1 lb. 13 oz.) pineapple chunks or tidbits, drained
1 pint (16 oz.) dairy sour cream
2½ cups (7 oz.) coconut
2 cups small or cut up marshmallows

Combine all ingredients. Chill in covered container for several hours. Serve on crisp greens.

Oriental Bean Salad

6 TO 8 SERVINGS

1 can (1 lb.) cut green beans, drained
1 can (1 lb.) cut yellow wax beans, drained
1 can (5 oz.) water chestnuts, drained and sliced thinly
½ cup onion rings
¼ cup sugar
⅓ cup vinegar
2 tablespoons salad oil
2 tablespoons soy sauce
½ teaspoon salt
¼ teaspoon pepper

In large bowl, combine beans, water chestnuts and onion rings. In pint jar with tightly fitting lid, combine remaining ingredients; cover and shake to blend, stirring to dissolve sugar, if necessary. Pour dressing over vegetables. Cover; chill several hours or overnight, stirring now and then. Drain vegetables before serving.

Caesar Salad

12 SERVINGS

  1 clove garlic
¾ cup olive or salad oil
  2 cups croutons (below)
  6 quarts salad greens (2 to 3 heads romaine, red lettuce,
    butter lettuce, etc.)
  1 tablespoon Worcestershire sauce
    Freshly ground black pepper
½ cup hard Cheddar or Parmesan cheese, freshly grated
  2 small eggs, raw or cooked 1 minute
½ cup lemon juice (2 lemons)
  6 to 8 anchovy fillets, snipped, or ½ cup bleu cheese,
    crumbled (optional)

Crush garlic, add to oil; allow to stand several hours or overnight. Prepare croutons ahead of time as described below. Wash, dry and chill salad greens until time to use. To make salad, tear or break clean dry greens into bite-size pieces in large bowl. Strain oil, discarding garlic. Pour ½ cup garlic-flavored oil over greens. Add Worcestershire sauce, a generous amount of black pepper, grated cheese, unbeaten eggs and lemon juice in that order. Toss and mix gently but thoroughly until there is a thick creamy look to the lettuce. Add anchovies or bleu cheese, if desired, and toss. Adjust seasonings. Pour remaining ¼ cup garlic-flavored oil over croutons and toss; add to salad. Serve immediately while croutons are crisp.

CROUTONS: Cut bread (preferably stale sourdough French bread) into tiny cubes; toast in slow oven (300 degrees), stirring frequently, till dry and golden brown. If desired, brown cut garlic in butter or oil in skillet; remove garlic and add croutons, tossing until coated with oil. May be stored in covered refrigerator jar until time to use.

Potato Salad

8 SERVINGS

6 medium potatoes
½ medium onion, chopped
8 hard cooked eggs
3 to 4 tablespoons prepared mustard
1 cup salad dressing
1 tablespoon sugar
1 teaspoon salt
½ to 1 teaspoon celery seed (optional)

Cook, peel and dice potatoes; combine with chopped onion. Shell eggs; separate yolks and whites. Dice egg whites; set aside. Mash yolks with mustard; stir into salad dressing along with sugar and salt. Combine dressing with potatoes and onions. Fold in egg whites carefully. Adjust seasoning. Cover and chill for several hours before serving.

Sicilian Salad

10 SERVINGS

1 large or 2 small heads red lettuce
½ head iceberg lettuce
1 package (0.7 oz.) garlic cheese dressing mix
2 flat jars or cans (4 to 6 oz. each) marinated artichoke hearts, drained
½ cup pecans, broken
2 tablespoon dry bleu cheese, crumbled
2 cans (11 oz. each) mandarin oranges, chilled and drained

Wash, drain and dry greens; chill. In large bowl tear greens into bite size pieces. Make up dressing according to package directions; pour over greens and toss. Add remaining ingredients. Toss very gently and serve immediately.

Sesame Spinach Salad

6 SERVINGS

1 package (10 oz.) fresh spinach
2 tablespoons (or more) sesame seeds
1 tablespoon butter
¾ cup Sweet Sour French Dressing (p. 203)
1 cup croutons (p. 185)

In large bowl tear into bite-size pieces spinach that's been rinsed, dried, stemmed and chilled. Brown sesame seeds in butter in small skillet. Toss into spinach along with dressing. Add croutons and serve immediately.

Salad Monterey

6 SERVINGS

½ cup olive or salad oil
1 tablespoon chives or green onions, snipped
1 teaspoon dill weed
½ teaspoon garlic salt
2 cups (6 oz.) fresh mushrooms, thinly sliced
2 quarts crisp salad greens, torn
2 tablespoons lemon juice
   Salt, freshly ground pepper

Combine olive oil, chives, dill weed and garlic salt in large salad bowl. Add mushroom slices; toss to coat well. Toss into salad greens. Sprinkle with lemon juice; toss lightly. Season to taste with salt and pepper. Serve immediately.

Taboola (Lebanese Salad)

8 SERVINGS

1 head romaine lettuce
1 small bunch parsley
½ to 1 cup Bulgur wheat (p. 80)
1 large tomato, finely diced
1 large cucumber, peeled and finely diced
1 medium onion, very finely chopped
¼ cup salad oil
½ cup lemon juice (2 lemons)
Salt and pepper

Wash lettuce; drain thoroughly and dry; cover and chill. Wash, stem and shake parsley dry; cover and chill. Thirty minutes before assembling salad, set bulgur wheat to soak in water that measures a little more than measurement of wheat. (For example, soak ½ cup bulgur in a little more than ½ cup water.) Set aside. Wrap parsley in leaves of lettuce; chop as finely as possible. (The secret of Taboola is in the finely chopped vegetables.) Combine greens with bulgur, which should have absorbed all water. At this point salad may be covered tightly and refrigerated. When time to serve, add finely diced vegetables, salad oil and lemon juice. Toss until well mixed, using hands as the Lebanese do, if desired. Season with salt and pepper. Be sure to add enough lemon juice and salt to get characteristic flavor.

NOTE: To double recipe, use 1 head iceberg lettuce, 1 head romaine and 1 large bunch parsley; double other ingredients.

Mexicali Salad

1 large head iceberg lettuce, shredded
4 cups (1 lb.) sharp Cheddar cheese, shredded
1 can (1 lb.) chili beans without meat, undrained
½ cup green onions, sliced
½ cup Catalina Dressing (p. 204)
1 medium package corn chips

Toss together all ingredients but corn chips until well mixed. Toss in corn chips and serve.

Tomato Aspic

8 SERVINGS

4 cups tomato juice
⅓ cup onion, chopped
¼ cup fresh celery leaves, chopped
2 tablespoons brown sugar
1 teaspoon salt
1 teaspoon sweet basil
2 envelopes (1 T. each) unflavored gelatin
¼ cup cold water
3 tablespoons lemon juice
1 cup celery, finely diced

In large saucepan combine tomato juice, onion, celery leaves, brown sugar, salt and sweet basil; simmer 5 minutes. Strain. Soften gelatin in cold water; add to hot juice along with lemon juice; stir until dissolved. Chill until partially set. Stir in celery. Pour into 5-cup ring mold. Chill until firm. Unmold on lettuce greens. Fill center, if desired, with Shrimp Salad With Herbs (p. 179) or Lentil Salad (p. 90).

Mustard Ring

8 SERVINGS

4 eggs
¾ cup sugar
1 envelope (1 T.) unflavored gelatin
1½ tablespoons dry mustard
½ teaspoon turmeric
¼ teaspoon salt
1 cup water
½ cup cider vinegar
1 cup heavy cream, whipped

Beat eggs. In top of double boiler thoroughly combine sugar and gelatin; stir in seasonings. Add water and vinegar to eggs; stir into sugar mixture. Cook over boiling water, stirring constantly, until mixture is slightly thickened. Cool until thick. Fold in whipped cream. Pour carefully into 5-cup ring mold. Chill until firm. Unmold; fill center with cole slaw. Garnish with crisp greens. Especially good served with ham.

Molded Tuna Fish Salad

6 SERVINGS

1 package (3 oz.) lemon flavor gelatin
½ cup boiling water
1 can (6½ oz.) tuna fish, drained
1 can (10¾ oz.) chicken gumbo soup
2 tablespoons green pepper, chopped
1 tablespoon onion, chopped
2 tablespoons celery, chopped
½ cup heavy cream, whipped
½ cup mayonnaise

Dissolve gelatin in boiling water; cool slightly. Fold in remaining ingredients. Pour into 5-cup salad mold or into six individual molds. Chill until set. Serve on fresh greens.

Cucumber Salad Ring

2½ packages (2½ T.) unflavored gelatin
2½ cups water
  3 chicken bouillon cubes
  ½ cup white wine vinegar
  2 tablespoons sugar
  ½ teaspoon salt
1½ tablespoons fresh lemon juice
  2 medium unpared cucumbers
  3 tablespoons celery, finely chopped
  3 tablespoons onion, finely chopped
  3 stuffed olives, sliced

Soften gelatin in water. Stir in bouillon cubes, vinegar, sugar and salt; heat and stir until bouillon cubes are dissolved. Stir in lemon juice. Cool in refrigerator until slightly thickened (about 45 minutes). Cut one cucumber in half crosswise; reserve one half. Dice or coarsely chop remaining cucumbers; set aside. Slice reserved cucumber half into 14 to 16 slices. In 5-cup salad mold arrange sliced stuffed olives decoratively, then spoon carefully some of the gelatin mixture over it; arrange sliced cucumbers in decorative pattern in gelatin. Stir chopped cucumbers, celery and onion into remaining gelatin. Spoon carefully over cucumbers in mold. Refrigerate until set, at least one hour. Unmold on endive or red lettuce. (Use within 2 days.)

NOTE: If desired, one stuffed olive slice and one cucumber slice may be arranged in bottom of individual molds, then topped with gelatin.

Jellied Spring Salad

6 SERVINGS

1 envelope (1 T.) unflavored gelatin
¼ cup cold water
1½ cups hot water
1 tablespoon lemon juice
1 tablespoon vinegar
1 teaspoon salt
1 cup peeled cucumber, diced
½ cup green onions, sliced
½ cup radishes, sliced
1 cup celery, diced

Soften gelatin in cold water; dissolve in hot water. Add lemon juice, vinegar and salt. Chill until partially set. Add remaining ingredients; chill until firm. Serve on crisp lettuce with mayonnaise.

Lemon Fruit Ring

6 TO 8 SERVINGS

1 teaspoon (⅓ envelope) unflavored gelatin
¼ cup cold water
1 cup pineapple juice
1 package (3 oz.) lemon flavor gelatin
1 cup orange juice (2 oranges)
2 teaspoons sugar
1 cup heavy cream, whipped
1 cup pineapple tidbits, drained
1 can (11 oz.) mandarin oranges, drained
½ cup slivered almonds
  Fresh strawberries
  Avocado slices

Soften unflavored gelatin in cold water. Bring pineapple juice to boil; add both unflavored and lemon flavor gelatin to dissolve. Add orange juice and sugar. Chill until partially set. Fold in whipped cream, pineapple, mandarin oranges and nuts. Pour into 5-cup ring mold; chill until firm. Unmold onto fresh romaine leaves. Fill center with fresh strawberries and avocado slices.

NOTE: Recipe may be doubled and set to mold in 10-cup bundt pan.

Raw Cranberry Salad

8 SERVINGS

    4 cups (1 lb.) raw cranberries
    1 orange
1½ cups sugar
    1 package (3 oz.) lemon or orange flavor gelatin
    1 cup boiling water
 ½ cup pecans, coarsely chopped
 ½ cup celery, diced

Chop or grind cranberries and whole orange to medium degree of coarseness, catching all juice and pouring back into cranberries. Add sugar to fruit; set aside. Dissolve gelatin in boiling water. Stir in cranberry-orange mixture, nuts and celery. Pour into salad mold. Chill until set. Serve on lettuce.

Hasty Tasty Orange Salad

8 SERVINGS

    2 or 3 large bananas
    1 can (8 oz. or 1 cup) crushed pineapple, undrained
    1 package (6 oz.) orange flavor gelatin
    2 cups boiling water
  12 ice cubes
 ½ pint (1 cup) heavy cream

Dice bananas into crushed pineapple; allow to stand while preparing gelatin. Dissolve gelatin in boiling water. Add ice cubes; stir until gelatin begins to thicken; remove any remaining ice cubes. Stir pineapple and bananas into gelatin. Whip cream; fold into gelatin mixture. Pour into 6-cup salad mold, cover and chill. Serve on crisp greens.

Molded Shrimp Salad

8 SERVINGS

1 package (3 oz.) lemon flavor gelatin
1 cup boiling water
½ teaspoon salt
1 teaspoon onion, grated
1 cup celery, diced
1 can (6½ oz.) shrimp, drained and cleaned
3 hard-cooked eggs, diced
2 tablespoons green pepper, diced
1 cup Cheddar cheese, shredded
½ cup mayonnaise
½ cup heavy cream, whipped

Dissolve gelatin in boiling water; chill until partially set. Prepare remaining ingredients. Fold into gelatin. Pour into 6-cup mold. Chill until set. Unmold on crisp salad greens. Garnish with a little mayonnaise and whole shrimp.

Raspberry Salad Mold

6 SERVINGS

1 package (3 oz.) raspberry flavor gelatin
1¼ cups boiling water
1 package (10 oz.) frozen raspberries (not thawed)
1 cup crushed pineapple, drained
1 large banana, sliced
½ cup pecans, broken

Dissolve gelatin in hot water. Add frozen raspberries; stir until raspberries are thawed and separated. Stir in pineapple, banana and pecans. Pour into 1-quart mold or into individual molds. Chill until set. Unmold onto crisp lettuce leaves. Serve with mayonnaise, if desired.

NOTE: If desired, ½ small (3 oz.) package cream cheese may be rolled into small balls, then rolled into pecans that have been more finely chopped; place at regular intervals in the soft gelatin after it has been poured into the mold.

Boysenberry Salad

10 SERVINGS

  2 cans (1 lb. each) boysenberries
  1 package (6 oz.) wild cherry or wild raspberry flavor
    gelatin
15 ice cubes
  1 cup sunflower seeds, shelled

Drain juice from boysenberries; heat juice to boiling. In large bowl pour hot juice over gelatin; stir to dissolve. Add ice cubes; stir until gelatin begins to thicken. Remove undissolved ice cubes. Stir in drained boysenberries; add sunflower seeds. Pour into 6-cup salad mold or individual molds. Chill until set. Serve on bibb or butter lettuce. Top with dairy sour cream.

Grenadine Grapefruit Mold

12 SERVINGS

1½ cups pineapple juice
  1 package (3 oz.) lemon flavor gelatin
  1 package (3 oz.) cherry flavor gelatin
 ⅔ cup grenadine syrup
 ¾ cup orange juice
 ⅓ cup lemon juice
  2 large fresh grapefruit, sectioned and well drained, or 2
    cans (1 lb. each) grapefruit sections, well drained

In small saucepan, heat pineapple juice to boiling point. Immediately remove from heat; stir in lemon flavor and cherry flavor gelatin. Stir in grenadine syrup and juices. Chill until gelatin mixture just begins to thicken and set up. In bottom of oiled 9-inch ring mold or other decorative mold arrange part of grapefruit sections, then pour layer of thickened gelatin over top. Arrange another layer of grapefruit over top of gelatin; pour remaining gelatin over top; chill for several hours or until set. Unmold on curly endive. Serve with dairy sour cream.

Molded Cherry Salad

8 SERVINGS

1 package (3 oz.) cherry flavor gelatin
1 cup hot water
1 quart or 1 can (1 lb. 13 oz.) dark sweet cherries
1 package (3 oz.) cream cheese, softened

Dissolve gelatin in hot water; set aside to cool. Drain cherries, saving 1 cup juice; pit cherries. Arrange cherries in 5-cup salad mold. Soften cream cheese with electric beater or in food processor. Add cherry juice, a little at a time, to cream together smoothly. Combine cheese-juice mixture and cooled gelatin; pour over cherries. Chill. Serve on romaine lettuce.

Jellied Coleslaw

8 SERVINGS

1 package (3 oz.) lemon flavor gelatin
½ teaspoon salt
¾ cup boiling water
½ cup cold water
½ cup mayonnaise
½ cup dairy sour cream
1 teaspoon onion, grated
1 tablespoon prepared mustard
2 tablespoons vinegar
1 teaspoon sugar
2 cups cabbage, finely shredded
½ cup green pepper, chopped

Dissolve gelatin and salt in boiling water. Add cold water; chill until syrupy. Fold in remaining ingredients except cabbage and green pepper. Chill until slightly thick; fold in vegetables. Pour into 6-cup mold. Chill until firm. Unmold and garnish with greens and radish roses.

NOTE: Recipe may be doubled and set in 9 x 13-inch pan; cut into squares to serve.

Harvest Fruit Ring

10 SERVINGS

1½ envelopes (1½ T.) unflavored gelatin
⅓ cup cold water
¼ teaspoon ground ginger
⅓ cup lemon juice
⅓ cup canned pineapple juice
⅓ cup sugar
¼ teaspoon salt
2 cups ginger ale
1 cup green grapes or Tokay grapes, halved and seeded
1 can (11 oz.) mandarin oranges, drained
⅔ cup pineapple tidbits, drained
Curly endive
Honey Lemon Dressing (p. 207)

Soften gelatin in cold water; dissolve over hot water. Stir in ginger. Add lemon juice, pineapple juice, sugar and salt; stir until sugar is dissolved. Add ginger ale. Arrange grapes (cut side up, if using Tokay grapes) evenly around bottom of 5-cup ring mold; pour just enough gelatin mixture into mold to cover grapes. Chill until set. Chill remaining ginger ale mixture until it barely begins to thicken. Stir in remaining fruit. Spoon into ring mold. Allow to set several hours. Unmold on serving plate, garnish with greens and serve with Honey Lemon Dressing.

Molded Horseradish Salad

1 package (3 oz.) lemon flavor gelatin
¼ teaspoon salt
1½ cups hot water
½ teaspoon paprika
½ cup mayonnaise
3 tablespoons fresh horseradish
15 stuffed olives, sliced
½ cup heavy cream, whipped
Avocado slices, watercress

Dissolve gelatin and salt in hot water; stir in paprika. Chill until thick but not set. Blend in mayonnaise and horseradish. Fold in sliced stuffed olives and whipped cream. Pour into 5-cup mold. Refrigerate until set. Unmold onto salad greens; garnish with avocado slices and watercress. Especially good served with ham.

Emerald Salad

1 package (3 oz.) lemon flavor gelatin
1 package (3 oz.) lime flavor gelatin
2 cups liquid (pineapple juice plus water), heated
1 cup crushed pineapple, drained
1 cup mayonnaise
1 cup cottage cheese, drained
1 cup evaporated milk
1 cup nuts, coarsely chopped

In large bowl dissolve gelatins in hot liquid. Chill until partially set. Whip until fluffy with electric beater; blend in remaining ingredients. Pour into 8-cup mold or individual molds. Chill until set. Nice when set in ring mold so center can be filled with fruit cocktail.

Frozen Fruit Salad

8 SERVINGS

1 package (3 oz.) cream cheese
1 cup crushed pineapple, undrained
1 cup heavy cream, whipped
½ lb. marshmallows, cut up
4 large bananas, diced
1 small bottle maraschino cherries
   Salad greens

Whip cream cheese until soft, adding pineapple juice until smooth and creamy. Stir into pineapple. Combine with whipped cream. Fold in remaining ingredients; freeze in freezer until firm. Cut and serve on crisp salad greens.

Cherry Ring Salad

6 SERVINGS

1 quart or 1 can (1 lb. 13 oz.) dark sweet cherries
1 package (3 oz.) cherry flavor gelatin
1 cup boiling water
1 cup cherry juice
1 jar (3 oz.) stuffed green olives, drained and sliced
½ cup pecans, broken

Drain cherries, saving juice; remove pits. Dissolve gelatin in boiling water; stir in cherry juice. Chill until gelatin begins to set. Stir in pitted cherries, sliced olives and pecans. Pour into 5-cup ring mold. Chill until firm. Unmold on crisp salad greens; top with mayonnaise.

NOTE: Especially good for Christmas.

Salad Savory

1¾ CUPS

  1 cup (4 oz.) Parmesan cheese, freshly grated
  6 tablespoons sesame seeds
4½ teaspoons salt
  2 teaspoons monosodium glutemate
  1 teaspoon garlic powder
  1 teaspoon celery seed
  2 tablespoons paprika
1½ teaspoons chili powder
  1 tablespoon dried parsley, crushed

Be certain all utensils are free from moisture. In medium container, combine all ingredients; blend thoroughly. Pack into one large or several small shakers. Cap tightly; refrigerate. Sprinkle on salad greens, garlic bread or hot buttered popcorn. May also be mixed with sour cream or cream cheese for dip.

Mayonnaise

2 CUPS

  1 teaspoon salt
  ¼ teaspoon paprika
  ½ teaspoon dry mustard
    Dash cayenne pepper
  2 egg yolks
  2 tablespoons vinegar
  2 cups salad oil
  2 tablespoons lemon juice

Combine dry ingredients; add egg yolks and blend. Add vinegar and mix well. Add salad oil, 1 teaspoon at a time, beating with rotary beater, until ¼ cup has been added. Add remaining salad oil in increasing amounts, alternating last ½ cup with lemon juice. If desired, 1 tablespoon hot water may be added to take away oily appearance.

Modified Mayonnaise

1 PINT

1 egg, unbeaten
2 tablespoons sugar
1½ teaspoons salt
2 teaspoons prepared mustard
⅛ teaspoon paprika
¼ cup vinegar
¾ cup salad oil
¼ cup cornstarch
1 cup water

Put egg, sugar, seasonings, vinegar and salad oil in mixing bowl; do not stir. In small saucepan make a paste by mixing cornstarch with ½ cup water; add additional water. Cook over low heat, stirring constantly, until it boils and becomes clear. Add hot cornstarch mixture to ingredients in mixing bowl; beat briskly with electric beater. Cool before serving. Use as boiled dressing in potato salad or cole slaw.

Zesty Dressing

¾ CUP

½ cup mayonnaise
2 tablespoons tarragon vinegar
2 tablespoons chili sauce
1 teaspoon Worcestershire sauce
½ teaspoon garlic salt
¼ teaspoon freshly ground pepper

Blend together all ingredients and pour over vegetable salad.

Thousand Island Dressing

4½ CUPS

    2 eggs
    ½ teaspoon dry mustard
    ¼ teaspoon salt
    3 tablespoons sugar
    2 tablespoons vinegar
      Few grains paprika
      Few grains red pepper
    2 cups salad oil
  1½ cups catsup
    1 small onion, finely grated
    5 to 7 sweet gherkin pickles, chopped
    1 small can pimientos, drained and chopped

Beat eggs until thick; add mustard, salt, sugar, vinegar, paprika and red pepper. Gradually add oil, beating constantly. Add catsup gradually. Stir onion, pickles and pimientos into salad dressing. Store in covered jar in refrigerator for several hours before using.

Clear French Dressing

¾ CUP

    ½ cup salad oil
    2 tablespoons vinegar
    2 tablespoons lemon juice
    1 teaspoon sugar
    ½ teaspoon salt
    ½ teaspoon dry mustard
    ½ teaspoon paprika
      Dash cayenne pepper

Put all ingredients in jar; cover and shake well. Shake again before using.

Creamy French Dressing

1⅔ CUPS

1 teaspoon sugar
1 tablespoon paprika
1 teaspoon salt
   Dash cayenne pepper
⅓ cup vinegar
1 egg
1 cup salad oil

Combine sugar and seasonings. Add vinegar and egg; beat well. Add salad oil 1 teaspoon at a time until ¼ cup has been added. Add remaining oil in gradually increasing amounts, beating well after each addition.

Sweet Sour French Dressing

1¼ CUPS

½ cup sugar
¼ cup wine vinegar
¼ cup fresh lemon juice
 1 tablespoon onion, grated
⅓ cup salad oil
 1 teaspoon salt
½ teaspoon paprika
¼ teaspoon celery salt

In small saucepan combine sugar and vinegar; cook until sugar dissolves. In pint jar combine sugar-vinegar mixture, lemon juice, onion, oil and seasonings. Cover; shake thoroughly. Shake again before serving. Delicious on melon or fruit salad.

Catalina Dressing

1½ cups

½ cup vinegar
½ cup salad oil
½ cup sugar
½ cup catsup
1 teaspoon salt
½ teaspoon garlic salt
½ teaspoon onion salt

Combine all ingredients in quart jar and shake thoroughly. Chill. Shake again before using. Especially good on raw vegetable salad.

Poppy Seed Dressing

3 cups

1½ cups sugar
2 teaspoons dry mustard
2 teaspoons salt
⅔ cup vinegar
3 tablespoons onion, finely grated
2 cups salad oil
3 tablespoons poppy seeds

Combine sugar, mustard, salt and vinegar; add onion and stir thoroughly. Add oil very slowly while mixing in blender or beating with rotary beater; continue adding until thick. Stir in poppy seeds; store in refrigerator. Good with fruit salads.

Celery Seed French Dressing

1½ CUPS

½ cup sugar
¾ teaspoon salt
1 teaspoon paprika
1 teaspoon celery salt
1 teaspoon prepared mustard
1 teaspoon onion juice or onion salt
¼ cup vinegar or lemon juice or 2 tablespoons of each
1 cup salad oil
1 teaspoon celery seed

Combine all ingredients but salad oil and celery seed in medium mixing bowl; beat together. While continuing to beat, add salad oil almost drop by drop at first; then increase amounts very slowly until all oil is added. Mixture should be thick. Stir in celery seed. Good for both fruit and vegetable salads.

Rich Bleu Cheese Dressing

1 QUART

⅓ cup onion, chopped
2 cups mayonnaise
2 cloves garlic, minced
½ cup fresh parsley, chopped, or 3 T. dried parsley
1 cup dairy sour cream
½ cup vinegar
2 tablespoons lemon juice
½ lb. bleu cheese, crumbled
   Salt and pepper

Combine all ingredients but bleu cheese; blend. Crumble cheese into dressing; season to taste. Refrigerate until time to serve. Use within 48 hours; it becomes stronger with age.

Mild Roquefort Dressing

2 CUPS

¾ cup olive or salad oil
4 tablespoons wine vinegar
4 tablespoons cream
½ clove garlic, minced
1 tablespoon onion, grated
1 package (3 oz.) Roquefort or bleu cheese
1 teaspoon salt
½ teaspoon pepper
Dash cayenne pepper
2 packages (3 oz. each) cream cheese

If using blender, put all ingredients in blender jar in order given; blend until thoroughly mixed. If dressing is mixed by hand or electric mixer, mash onion and garlic with fork; add oil, vinegar, salt and pepper. In separate bowl, mash cheeses; add cream and blend. Combine two mixtures; beat hard. May be stored in refrigerator indefinitely.

Summertime Creamy Dressing

1½ CUPS

¼ cup currant jelly
1 package (8 oz.) cream cheese
1 tablespoon lemon juice
½ cup mayonnaise

Gradually add currant jelly to cream cheese, blending until smooth. Add lemon juice and mayonnaise. Stir until blended. Serve with fruit salads.

Mock Bleu Cheese Dressing

4½ CUPS

1 package (8 oz.) cream cheese
2 cups mayonnaise
2 cups buttermilk
1 teaspoon garlic salt
1 teaspoon onion salt
1 teaspoon monosodium glutemate
½ teaspoon ground black pepper

Cream cheese; gradually add mayonnaise and then buttermilk; beat constantly. Stir in seasonings. Store in closed
jar in refrigerator. May also be used as vegetable dip.

Honey Lemon Dressing

1½ CUPS

2 tablespoons strained honey
2½ tablespoons lemon juice
1 package (3 oz.) cream cheese
½ teaspoon grated lemon rind (½ lemon)
¾ cup salad oil
Dash cayenne pepper
Salt to taste

Gradually add honey and lemon juice to cream cheese,
blending until smooth. Add lemon rind. Gradually add
oil, beating well. Season to taste. Chill. Serve with molded
fruit salad.

Sauces and Seasonings

Our sauce recipes were chosen for specific reasons, because they enhance particular garden vegetables or favorite fruit puddings. Included, too, are ice cream sauces (Royal Chocolate Sauce and Quick Caramel Sauce) because dairying is such an important industry in Utah and Mormons seem to enjoy ice cream.

Simple as it is, one of the most versatile and popular items in the chapter is the Cheese Sauce (Mornay Sauce to the French). By itself it is a delicious Cheese Rabbit to be served over rice, toast or crackers. But with the addition of a tablespoon of vinegar or a dash of Worcestershire sauce or a soupcon of mustard, it evolves into a savory dressing for 7-minute cabbage or crisp-tender young zucchini or fresh cut green beans. The Cheese Sauce recipe is good to keep in one's head!

Not to be overlooked is a little group of recipes for popular seasoning mixes—dried onion soup, Italian and French herb seasonings and seasoned salt; also a handy recipe for Salad Savory is found in another chapter. These little aromatics can be made in quantity for a fraction of the supermarket price and are excellent for seasoning food storage dinners.

And when packaged attractively, seasoning mixes make charming and welcome gifts!

Easy Hollandaise Sauce

¾ CUP

2 egg yolks
¼ teaspoon salt
Dash cayenne pepper
½ cup butter, melted
1 tablespoon lemon juice

In small bowl beat egg yolks until thick and lemon-colored. Add salt and cayenne pepper. Add half the butter, about 1 teaspoon at a time, beating constantly. Combine remaining melted butter with lemon juice. Add slowly, about 1 teaspoon at a time, to yolk mixture, beating constantly. Serve immediately.

Pesto Sauce

¾ CUP

¼ cup (½ stick) butter at room temperature
¼ cup Parmesan cheese
½ cup fresh parsley, finely chopped
1 clove garlic, crushed
1 teaspoon dried basil leaves
½ teaspoon dried marjoram leaves
¼ cup olive or salad oil
¼ cup pine nuts or walnuts, chopped

In blender or food processor combine all ingredients and blend until a thick paste. Store, covered tightly, in refrigerator or freezer until ready to use. Makes enough sauce for 1 lb. hot, drained pasta (linguine, spaghetti, etc.).

Dill Sauce

1 CUP

½ cup mayonnaise
½ cup dairy sour cream
½ teaspoon prepared mustard
⅛ teaspoon salt
1 teaspoon onion, grated
1 teaspoon vinegar
  Pinch tarragon
1 teaspoon dill weed

Combine all ingredients until blended. Chill in covered container. Excellent with cucumbers and other raw vegetables.

Mushroom Sauce

4 CUPS

½ cup (1 stick) butter or margarine
½ cup plus 2 tablespoons flour
2 cans (10 ¾ oz. each) chicken broth
1 cup heavy cream
½ teaspoon salt
  Few grains white pepper
1 can (8 oz.) button mushrooms, drained
¼ cup fresh parsley, chopped

Melt butter in medium saucepan. Stir in flour. Remove from heat; add chicken broth; stir until smooth. Cook and stir until thick. Add cream, salt, pepper, drained mushrooms and parsley. Serve hot.

NOTE: Save mushroom juice to use in gravy, soup or as substitute for red or white wine.

Bearnaise Sauce

1½ CUPS

3 tablespoons white wine vinegar
1 teaspoon crushed tarragon
1 teaspoon green onion, chopped
2 whole eggs
2 tablespoons fresh lemon juice
1 cup (2 sticks) butter, melted and hot

In small saucepan combine vinegar, tarragon and green onion. Simmer until liquid is reduced to about 2 teaspoons. Remove from heat; set aside. Combine eggs and lemon juice in blender. Add vinegar mixture; blend. While still blending, slowly add hot butter. When blended, turn mixture into small saucepan. Cook over very low heat until slightly thickened, taking care not to boil as it will curdle. Serve with broiled steak.

Cheese Sauce

2 CUPS

2 tablespoons butter or margarine
2 tablespoons flour
1 cup milk
1 cup sharp Cheddar cheese, shredded
Salt and pepper

Melt butter or margarine in small saucepan; blend in flour. Remove from heat. Stir in milk until smooth and blended. Return to heat; cook and stir until thick. Remove from heat; add cheese. Allow to stand until cheese is partially melted; stir to blend. Season to taste.

Catsup Sauce

½ CUP

3 tablespoons brown sugar, packed
¼ cup catsup

¼ teaspoon nutmeg
1 teaspoon Dijon mustard

Combine all ingredients. Delicious when spread over meat loaf before baking.

Orange Sauce

6 SERVINGS

1 tablespoon butter or margarine
1 tablespoon flour
½ cup orange juice (1 orange)
½ teaspoon grated orange rind (½ orange)
    Dash salt

Melt butter in small saucepan. Stir in flour; cook until well blended. Add orange juice; cook and stir until thick and smooth. Add orange rind and salt to taste. Serve over hot cooked broccoli.

NOTE: Grapefruit juice may be substituted for orange juice, if desired.

Raisin Sauce

1¼ CUPS

1 cup raisins
1 cup water
3 tablespoons sugar
1 tablespoon cornstarch
    Dash salt
1 teaspoon butter
½ teaspoon prepared mustard

Wash raisins; cover with water; cook for 5 minutes. Combine sugar and cornstarch; add to raisins, stirring and cooking until thick. Remove from heat. Add remaining ingredients, mixing well. Serve with baked ham or ham loaf.

Autumn Sunshine Sauce

1½ CUPS

½ cup brown sugar, packed
2 egg yolks, unbeaten
  Dash salt
2 egg whites, unbeaten
½ cup heavy cream, whipped
1 teaspoon vanilla

Sift sugar; add half the sugar to egg yolks; beat until light. Add salt to egg whites; beat until foamy. Add remaining sugar, 1 tablespoon at a time, beating after each addition, until sugar is blended; continue beating until stiff. Combine egg yolks and egg whites. Fold in whipped cream and vanilla. Serve over steamed pudding.

Hard Sauce

2 CUPS

½ cup (1 stick) butter or margarine
1 cup confectioners' sugar
¼ teaspoon nutmeg

With spoon or electric mixer, beat butter with sugar until fluffy and creamy; beat in nutmeg. Place in serving dish. Refrigerate until firm. Serve over hot steamed pudding, allowing 2 tablespoons each.

Hot Butter Sauce

1½ CUPS

½ cup butter (no substitute)
1 cup sugar
½ cup heavy cream
1 teaspoon vanilla

Combine all ingredients but vanilla in small heavy saucepan. Bring to boil; reduce heat and simmer for 10 minutes. Remove from heat. Add vanilla. Serve hot over hot pudding or plain cake.

Spiced Pudding Sauce

1¼ CUPS

  1 *cup sugar*
¼ *teaspoon cinnamon*
¼ *teaspoon nutmeg*
1½ *tablespoons cornstarch*
  1 *cup boiling water*
  2 *tablespoons butter*
1½ *teaspoons vanilla*

In small saucepan combine sugar, spices and cornstarch; mix thoroughly. Add water and butter; stir and cook over medium heat until thick and clear. Add vanilla. Serve hot over steamed pudding.

Cherry Sauce

4 CUPS

  2 *cans (1 lb. each) sour cherries*
¼ *cup sugar*
  3 *tablespoons cornstarch*
½ *cup cold water*
½ *teaspoon almond extract*

Combine undrained sour pitted cherries and ¼ cup sugar; allow to stand 30 to 60 minutes so cherries absorb sweetness. Drain juice into small saucepan. Blend cornstarch and cold water; stir into cherry juice. Cook over medium heat, stirring, until mixture is thick and clear. Reduce heat to simmer; cook another 15 minutes over low heat. Stir in cherries and flavoring; cool, then chill. Serve over ice cream, plain cake or Norwegian Rice In Cream (p. 230).

Sweet Cherry Sauce

2 CUPS

   1 *can (1 lb. or 2 cups) dark sweet cherries*
   1 *cup cherry juice and water*
  ¼ *cup sugar*
   2 *tablespoons cornstarch*
     Dash salt
   1 *tablespoon butter*
  ¾ *teaspoon vanilla or brandy extract*

Drain and pit cherries, reserving juice. Measure reserved cherry syrup; add water to equal 1 cup liquid. Combine sugar, cornstarch and salt in medium saucepan. Gradually stir in syrup; bring to boil over medium heat, stirring constantly. Add pitted cherries; boil 1 minute. Remove from heat. Blend in butter and extract. Delicious over ice cream.

Raspberry Sauce

3 CUPS

   2 *packages (10 oz. each) frozen red raspberries*
   1 *cup water*
   3 *tablespoons cornstarch*
     Dash salt
     Sugar
     Lemon juice

Add water to frozen raspberries; bring to boil. Put through sieve, extracting all juice. (Use raspberry pulp in tapioca.) Add enough water to make 3 cups juice. Combine a little cold water with cornstarch; stir into juice; cook until mixture is thick and clear. Add salt, sugar and lemon juice to taste. Chill. Serve over ice cream, plain cake or Norwegian Rice In Cream (p. 230).

Royal Chocolate Sauce

2 CUPS

¾ cup cocoa
1 cup sugar
1 cup light corn syrup
½ cup light cream
2 tablespoons butter
¼ teaspoon salt
1 teaspoon vanilla

In medium saucepan combine cocoa and sugar; blend. Stir in corn syrup and cream. Add butter and salt, bring to boil and simmer 5 minutes. Remove from heat; stir in vanilla. Store in tightly covered jar in refrigerator. If desired, reheat to serve.

Light Chocolate Sauce

1 CUP

1 square (1 oz.) unsweetened chocolate
1 tablespoon butter or margarine
⅓ cup boiling water
1 cup sugar
   Few grains salt
2 tablespoons light corn syrup
½ teaspoon vanilla

In small saucepan melt chocolate and butter over very low heat. Gradually add boiling water, stirring. Bring to boil. Add sugar, salt and corn syrup. Boil 5 minutes or until desired consistency. Remove from heat; add vanilla.

Quick Caramel Sauce

1 CUP

     2 tablespoons butter or margarine
1¼ cups brown sugar, packed
     2 tablespoons dark corn syrup
     ½ cup light cream
     ½ teaspoon vanilla

In small saucepan melt butter or margarine. Remove from
heat. Add brown sugar and corn syrup; blend well. Stir in
cream until smooth. Return to heat. Bring to boil, stirring;
simmer 1 minute. Remove from heat; add vanilla. Cool
and dilute with cream, if necessary.

Rich Caramel Sauce

3½ CUPS

2¼ cups (1 lb.) brown sugar, firmly packed
     ½ cup (1 stick) butter
     1 cup cream

Combine all ingredients in top of double boiler. With
wooden spoon blend until smooth. Cook over simmering
water for 1 hour.

Whipped Dry Milk Topping

2 CUPS

     ½ cup nonfat dry milk
     ½ cup ice water
     2 tablespoons lemon juice
     2 to 4 tablespoons sugar

Sprinkle nonfat dry milk on top of ice water in chilled
bowl. With cold beaters, beat until stiff enough to stand in

peaks. Add lemon juice; continue beating until stiff. (If necessary, set in pan of crushed ice.) Beat in sugar. This will take 5 minutes or more of beating.

Baked Cranberry Walnut Relish

350 degrees   1 QUART

1 lb. fresh cranberries
2½ cups sugar
1 cup walnuts, broken and toasted
1 cup orange marmalade
¼ cup lime juice (2 limes)

Wash cranberries and drain. In shallow pan, stir cranberries with sugar. Cover tightly with aluminum foil. Bake at 350 degrees F. for 60 minutes. Spread walnuts in separate shallow pan; toast in oven until light golden brown, about 12 minutes. Stir together baked cranberries, walnuts, marmalade and lime or lemon juice until well mixed. Chill.

Curried Fruit Bake

350 degrees   12 SERVINGS

1 can (1 lb.) peach halves
1 can (20 oz.) pineapple slices
1 can (16 oz.) pear halves
8 maraschino cherries
⅓ cup butter
¾ cup light brown sugar, packed
2 teaspoons curry powder

Drain fruit well; pat dry with paper towel. Arrange in 1½-quart casserole. Melt butter; blend with brown sugar and curry. Spoon over fruit. Bake 45 minutes. Delicious served with ham.

NOTE: Casserole may be baked for 1 hour, then refrigerated several hours or overnight. To serve, heat at 350 degrees, for 30 minutes.

Dried Onion Soup Mix

EQUIVALENT TO 1⅜ OZ. PACKAGE

¼ cup instant minced onion
2 tablespoons instant beef bouillon
½ teaspoon onion powder

To make soup, stir mix into 4 cups boiling water; reduce heat. Cover; simmer 5 minutes.

French Herb Seasoning

1 CUP

¼ cup tarragon
¼ cup chervil
1 tablespoon leaf sage
¼ cup thyme
1 tablespoon rosemary
2½ tablespoons dried chopped chives
1 tablespoon dried orange rind
1 tablespoon ground celery seed

Combine tarragon, chervil, sage, thyme, rosemary, chives, orange rind and celery seed in small bowl; stir until well blended. Pack into crocks or small jars; seal and label. Store in cool, dry place. Crumble in hand when using. Use along with salt and pepper to season meat, poultry, salad dressings and vegetables.

Italian Seasoning

1⅔ CUPS

½ cup leaf oregano
½ cup leaf basil
2 tablespoons leaf sage
1 teaspoon thyme
1 jar (3¼ oz.) seasoned salt
2 tablespoons lemon pepper
2 tablespoons garlic powder

Combine oregano, basil, sage, thyme, seasoned salt, lemon pepper and garlic powder in small bowl; stir to blend. Pack into small crocks, jars or clear plastic containers. Seal and label. Store in cool, dry place. Crumble in hand before using in salads, salad dressings, sauces, meat and vegetable casseroles.

Seasoned Salt

¾ CUP

½ cup salt
1 tablespoon celery salt
1 tablespoon garlic salt
1 tablespoon paprika
1 teaspoon dry mustard
1 teaspoon onion powder
1 teaspoon pepper

Place all ingredients in blender container; cover and blend on high speed for 20 seconds. Store in tightly covered container.

Desserts and Pastries

The social calendar of a Mormon ward (parish) is dotted with events. And for each event there are refreshments.

If the men have anything to say about it, they'll choose fruit pies made by the ward's best cooks. Their preferences include Sweet Cherry Pie, Sour Cream Raisin, Pineapple Meringue or Butterscotch Peach Pie.

On the other hand Boy Scouts go for ice cream. They take their electric freezers filled with ice cream mix to the ward building; then all join together for the freezing. They have more ice cream to eat that way!

And they compete to see whose ice cream is the best. Honors might go to refreshing Lemon Ice Cream with Banana Bavarian running a close second. A lot of interest is shown in the Caramel Ice Cream, especially if filled with pecans or cashews.

However, weight consciousness has pervaded the monthly Relief Society luncheons, so the women look askance upon desserts . . . except, that is, when it comes to the annual Relief Society birthday party, usually held in March. On that occasion the ladies have delicious food beautifully served. For dessert they might serve Chocolate Pastry Cake or nut-studded Chocolate Roll, with one at each table to be cut and served with elegance.

Such occasions not only provide food for the ward members, but also food for our newspaper column. Some of our best stories about some of our best cooks and their recipes have been discovered at such occasions as these.

Frozen Strawberry Squares

350 degrees   12 SERVINGS

  1 cup flour
¼ cup brown sugar, packed
½ cup (1 stick) butter
½ cup pecans or walnuts, broken
  2 egg whites
  1 package (10 oz.) frozen strawberries, partially defrosted
  1 cup sugar
  2 tablespoons lemon juice
  1 cup heavy cream, whipped

Combine flour and brown sugar. Cut in butter as for pastry until mixture forms crumbs; stir in nuts. Spread in large shallow pan. Bake 15 minutes, stirring 3 or 4 times to keep from burning. Remove from oven. Cool and crush into crumbs. In large bowl combine egg whites, strawberries and sugar; beat until stiff and thick—about 5 minutes. Stir in lemon juice. Fold in whipped cream. In bottom of 9 x 13 x 2-inch baking pan or dish, spread all but 1 cup of crumbs. Pour strawberry filling evenly over crumbs. Sprinkle remaining crumb mixture over top, cover with foil or plastic wrap and freeze for several hours. Will not freeze hard. Cut into squares to serve. If desired, each piece may be garnished with dollop of whipped cream and a fresh strawberry with its stem.

MILE HIGH STRAWBERRY PIE: Strawberry mixture may be piled high into 9-inch baked pastry shell with ½ recipe of crumb mixture sprinkled over top, then frozen.

Fresh Lemon Ice Cream

                                       20 SERVINGS

  3 quarts milk
1½ cups heavy cream

1 cup plus 2 tablespoons fresh lemon juice (5 lemons)
1 tablespoon lemon extract
6 cups sugar

Blend ingredients together. Freeze in 6-quart ice cream freezer, according to manufacturer's directions, using 8 parts ice to 1 part salt. Pack; allow to ripen 2 to 3 hours.

NOTE: For 4-quart freezer use following ingredients and proceed as above. Makes 14 servings.

2 quarts milk
1 cup heavy cream
¾ cup lemon juice (3 lemons)
2 teaspoons lemon extract
4 cups sugar

NOTE: If desired, ice cream may be served in hollowed out lemons, garnished with fresh mint.

Frosty Fruit Freeze

4 QUARTS

4 cups sugar
4 cups water
¾ cup lemon juice (3 lemons)
2 packages (10 oz. each) frozen raspberries
1 can (1 lb.) pineapple slices, drained and cut into tidbits
1 bag (20 oz.) frozen blueberries
4 to 6 bananas, sliced

In medium saucepan combine sugar and water; boil together for 5 minutes. Cool. Add lemon juice. Freeze. About 1 hour before serving, combine all ingredients except bananas in large punch bowl. Empty frozen lemon ice over top. Allow to thaw. Mix gently with fork while still partially icy. Stir in sliced bananas. Serve immediately. Makes enough for 20 sherbet glasses.

Banana Bavarian Ice Cream

20 SERVINGS

4 cups sugar
4 cups milk
4 cups cream (part evaporated milk, if desired)
2 cups orange juice (4 oranges)
1 cup lemon juice (4 lemons)
4 bananas, mashed
1 can (15½ oz.) crushed pineapple, undrained

Combine chilled ingredients in 6-quart ice cream freezer, filling no more than ¾ full. Freeze according to manufacturer's directions, using 8 parts ice to 1 part salt. Pack and ripen.

NOTE: For 4-quart freezer use following ingredients and proceed as above. Makes 14 servings.

3 cups sugar
3 cups milk
3 cups heavy cream
1½ cups orange juice (3 oranges)
¾ cup fresh lemon juice
3 bananas, mashed
1 can (8½ oz.) crushed pineapple, undrained

NOTE: For other variations omit banana and pineapple; add 3 cups mashed strawberries, raspberries, apricot puree or fresh peaches.

Cranberry Sherbet

2 cups (½ lb.) fresh cranberries
1½ cups water
1 cup sugar
½ envelope (½ T.) unflavored gelatin
¼ cup cold water
¼ cup lemon juice (1 lemon)

Cook washed cranberries in 1½ cups water until skins pop. Press through sieve; add sugar; stir until sugar dissolves. Soften gelatin in cold water; add to cranberries. Cool; add lemon juice. Freeze firm in shallow tray. Break into chunks; beat smooth with electric beater. Return quickly to freezer; freeze firm.

Caramel Ice Cream

20 SERVINGS

1 cup sugar
¾ cup water
2 tablespoons flour
3 cups cold milk
2 eggs, slightly beaten
2¼ cups sugar
1 quart heavy cream
2 cans (13 oz. each) evaporated milk

In medium skillet heat 1 cup sugar over medium heat until it caramelizes, shaking skillet often to keep from burning. Add water; cook until sugar is dissolved. Combine flour with 1 cup cold milk; then combine with beaten eggs, sugar and remaining fresh milk. Cook and stir until slightly thick. Add caramelized sugar; chill. Combine with whipping cream and evaporated milk. Freeze in a 6-quart freezer and pack according to manufacturer's directions.

Apricot Souffle

350 degrees   6 SERVINGS

    1 quart or 1 can (1 lb. 13 oz.) apricot halves
    3 tablespoons butter or margarine
    ¼ cup flour
    1 cup milk, scalded
    4 egg yolks
    ¼ cup sugar
    ⅛ teaspoon salt
    4 egg whites
      Whipped cream

Drain apricots, reserving syrup. Arrange fruit halves close together in bottom of buttered 2-quart casserole. In medium saucepan melt butter, blend in flour and gradually add hot milk. Cook and stir until mixture thickens and comes to boil; remove from heat. In small bowl beat egg yolks with sugar and salt until thick. Stir a little hot white sauce into yolks; then stir all of yolk mixture back into white sauce. In large bowl beat egg whites until stiff but not dry. Fold into white sauce mixture. Pour over apricots. Set casserole into shallow pan; pour hot water around casserole to depth of 2 inches. Bake 55 to 60 minutes until souffle is lightly browned and cooked through. Serve souffle warm. Serve with cold apricot syrup and with slightly sweetened whipped cream.

Fresh Pineapple With Honey Sauce

                                               4 TO 6 SERVINGS

    1 fresh pineapple
    ½ cup honey
    1 tablespoon lime juice
    1 cup heavy cream
    ½ cup Macadamia nuts

Peel, core and slice fresh pineapple; cut into chunks. Cover; chill. (If desired cut whole pineapple in half; scoop out each half, cubing pineapple meat, saving pineapple shells for serving.) In medium bowl beat honey with electric mixer until foamy, about 1 minute. Stir in lime juice. Whip cream until stiff. Fold in chilled honey mixture; cover and refrigerate for at least 1 hour. When ready to serve, stir nuts into whipped cream mixture. Serve over chilled pineapple chunks.

NOTE: Although not as exotic, almonds or cashews may be used in place of Macadamia nuts.

Old Fashioned Fruit Cobbler

350 degrees   6 TO 8 SERVINGS

  3 cups fresh fruit (rhubarb, apricots, peaches, apples, plums or cherries)
  2 tablespoons butter
  ⅔ cup sugar (use 1 cup for rhubarb)
  2 tablespoons flour
  ½ teaspoon cinnamon
  1 cup flour, stirred and measured
  2 tablespoons sugar
  1½ teaspoons baking powder
  ½ teaspoon salt
  ⅓ cup oil
  3 tablespoons milk
  1 egg, slightly beaten

Arrange fruit in greased 11½ x 7½-inch baking pan. Cut butter into mixture of ⅔ cup sugar, 2 tablespoons flour and cinnamon until fine crumbs. Sprinkle over fruit. Sift together 1 cup flour, 2 tablespoons sugar, baking powder and salt. Combine oil, milk and egg; stir into dry ingredients with fork until just blended. Dot over top of fruit. Bake 25 to 30 minutes or until done. Serve hot with cream, whipped cream or ice cream.

Norwegian Rice In Cream

12 SERVINGS

2¼ cups boiling water
1 teaspoon salt
1 cup long grain rice
⅔ cup milk (approximately)
⅓ cup sugar (approximately)
½ teaspoon almond extract
2 cups heavy cream, whipped

Bring water to boil in 1½-quart saucepan; add salt. Stir in rice slowly so water keeps boiling. Cover; turn heat to simmer; allow rice to cook 30 minutes or until just tender. Add enough milk to barely fill in rice and be level with top of rice. Cover pan; simmer another 30 minutes or until all milk is absorbed. Stir in sugar to taste and almond extract. Chill. Just before serving, fold in whipped cream. Served with chilled Raspberry Sauce (p. 215) or Cherry Sauce (p. 216).

NOTE: In Scandinavia during the holidays it is traditional to stir one whole blanched almond into pudding. The one who gets the almond is given a marzipan candy in the shape of a Christmas pig.

Apple Crisp

350 degrees   6 SERVINGS

3 large cooking apples, peeled, cored and thinly sliced
¾ cup brown sugar, packed
½ cup flour
½ cup (1 stick) butter or margarine
¾ cup rolled oats

Arrange sliced apples in buttered 9-inch round baking dish. Combine brown sugar and flour; cut butter into mixture as for pastry. Toss in rolled oats. Spoon over apples, pressing down lightly. Bake for 35 to 40 minutes

NOTE: 1 quart home canned or 2 cans (1 lb. each) canned apple slices may be used in place of fresh apples.

PEACH CRISP: Slice 3 large fresh peaches or thoroughly drain 1 quart or 1 can (29 oz.) sliced peaches. Place in baking dish, sprinkle with lemon juice and top with above flour-butter mixture. Bake as directed.

Chocolate Roll

375 degrees   8 SERVINGS

5 egg yolks
1 cup sifted confectioners' sugar
¼ cup flour, stirred and measured
½ teaspoon salt
3 tablespoons cocoa
1 teaspoon vanilla
5 egg whites, stiffly beaten
1 cup heavy cream
8 to 12 large marshmallows, cut up
½ recipe Chocolate Butter Cream Frosting (p. 263)
¼ cup nuts, chopped

In small bowl beat egg yolks until thick and lemon-colored. Sift together confectioners' sugar, flour, salt and cocoa 3 times; beat into egg yolks until well blended. Add vanilla. Fold in stiffly beaten egg whites. Bake 15 to 20 minutes in jelly roll pan (10 x 15 x 1-inch) that's been greased, lined with waxed paper and greased again. Turn out onto towel sprinkled with confectioners' sugar. Remove waxed paper. Roll chocolate sponge and towel up together to cool. Unroll. Whip cream and sweeten slightly. Fold in marshmallows. Spread over chocolate sponge. Roll as for jelly roll. Frost top with ½ recipe Chocolate Butter Cream Frosting; sprinkle with chopped nuts. Chill. Slice to serve.

Lemon Torte

275 degrees   10 TO 12 SERVINGS

  6 *egg whites (room temperature)*
  ¼ *teaspoon cream of tartar*
1½ *cups sugar*
  6 *egg yolks*
  1 *cup sugar*
  6 *tablespoons lemon juice (1½ lemons)*
1½ *tablespoons grated lemon rind (3 lemons)*
  2 *cups heavy cream*
  ¼ *cup sugar*

Generously butter a 9 x 13 x 2-inch baking dish; set aside. In large bowl beat egg whites with cream of tartar until frothy. Add 1½ cups sugar gradually, continuing to beat until stiff meringue is formed. Spoon meringue into prepared pan; spread over pan evenly, pushing meringue up sides. Bake for 1 hour. (Meringue shell will extend above pan's edge.) Cool. In large bowl, beat egg yolks until creamy and thick. Gradually add 1 cup sugar, then lemon juice and grated rind. When thoroughly beaten, cook in top of double boiler over boiling water until very thick, stirring constantly. Remove from heat; cool. Whip cream and sweeten with ¼ cup sugar. Fold half of whipped cream into cooled lemon mixture. Spread over meringue; top with remaining whipped cream. Cover; chill for 24 hours.

NOTE: A 9- or 10-inch pie may be made exactly as above, by using only two-thirds of each ingredient. Butter pie pan well; spread meringue in it to form crust, pushing meringue up sides. Continue as above.

Gable House Cheesecake

400 degrees   12 SERVINGS

CRUST:

   1 cup sifted flour
   ¼ cup sugar
   1 teaspoon grated lemon rind
   ½ cup (1 stick) butter
   1 egg yolk, slightly beaten
   ¼ teaspoon vanilla

FILLING:

   3 packages (8 oz. each) cream cheese at room temperature
   5 eggs
   1 cup sugar
   1½ teaspoons vanilla

TOPPING:

   1 pint dairy sour cream
   ½ cup sugar
   1½ teaspoons vanilla

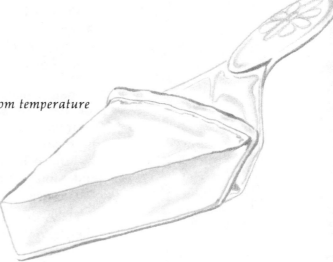

CRUST: Combine flour, sugar and lemon peel in medium mixing bowl. Cut in butter with pastry cutter. Add egg yolk and vanilla; stir together to make dough. Put ⅓ of dough on bottom of ungreased 9½-inch spring form pan (with sides removed), using fingers to press dough evenly. Bake for 6 minutes. Cool. Attach sides of pan to bottom; pat remaining dough evenly around sides. Set aside. Lower oven heat to 325 degrees.

FILLING: Beat cream cheese in large mixing bowl until soft. Add eggs, one at a time, beating well after each addition. Add sugar and vanilla; blend. Pour into crust. Bake for 1 hour. Remove from oven.

TOPPING: Combine sour cream with ½ cup sugar and 1½ teaspoons vanilla. Return to oven to bake 5 minutes longer. Chill.

Rhubarb Cream Mold

6 SERVINGS

    1 cup (⅓ lb.) rhubarb, sliced
    1 cup sugar
    ½ cup water
    ½ cup pineapple juice
    1 envelope (1 T.) unflavored gelatin
    ¼ cup cold water
    1 cup crushed pineapple, drained
    1 cup heavy cream, whipped

In small saucepan combine rhubarb, sugar and water; cook until rhubarb is tender, about 5 minutes. Stir in pineapple juice. Soften gelatin in cold water; stir into hot fruit mixture to dissolve. Chill until mixture thickens. Stir in whipped heavy cream and pineapple. Pour into 4-cup mold. Chill. Unmold and garnish, if desired, with fresh strawberries.

NOTE: A drop or two of red food coloring can be added to heighten the pink color.

Lemon Surprise Pudding

325 degrees

6 SERVINGS

    2 tablespoons butter
    1 cup sugar
    ¼ cup flour, stirred and measured
      Dash salt
    ⅓ cup lemon juice (1½ lemons)
    1½ teaspoons grated lemon rind (1 lemon)
    3 eggs, separated
    1½ cups milk, scalded

In large bowl cream together butter and sugar. Stir in flour, salt, lemon juice and grated rind. Add beaten egg yolks and milk. Blend well. Fold in stiffly beaten egg whites. Pour into greased 1½-quart casserole. Bake in pan of hot water for 1 hour or until done. Serve hot or chilled.

Caramel Custard Ring

325 degrees   6 SERVINGS

½ cup granulated sugar
5 eggs
½ cup sugar
¼ teaspoon salt
1 teaspoon vanilla
3¼ cups milk

Sprinkle ½ cup granulated sugar over bottom of small heavy skillet. Cook over low heat, stirring with wooden spoon every minute for 4 minutes, then every half minute, until sugar turns to a golden syrup. Remove from heat immediately; pour into bottom of 5-cup ring mold, turning mold to coat sides. Cool. In large bowl lightly beat eggs with ½ cup sugar, salt and vanilla. Gradually stir in milk. Pour into caramel-lined mold. Place a baking pan on middle rack of oven; set ring mold in it. Pour 1-inch hot water in baking pan. Bake custard 55 to 60 minutes or until set. Remove mold immediately from hot water. Chill for 3 to 24 hours before serving. Remove from mold.

Carrot Pudding

8 TO 10 SERVINGS

1 cup sugar
½ cup (1 stick) butter or margarine
3 eggs
1 cup raw carrot, grated
1 cup raw potato, grated
1½ cups flour, stirred and measured
1 teaspoon soda
½ teaspoon baking powder
½ teaspoon cinnamon
½ teaspoon cloves
½ teaspoon nutmeg
1 cup raisins
1 cup nuts, coarsely chopped

Cream together sugar and butter until creamy. Beat in eggs. Add grated carrot and potato. Mix well. Add flour sifted with soda, baking powder and spices. Add nuts and raisins; mix. Put batter into greased 1½-quart pudding mold or pan. Cover with lid or with double thickness of waxed paper tightly tied over top. Place on trivet in deep kettle. Add enough boiling water to come halfway up sides of mold or pan. Steam, covered, for 3 hours. Serve hot with whipped cream or Hard Sauce (p. 214), Spiced Pudding Sauce (p. 215) or Autumn Sunshine Sauce (p. 214).

Cranberry Pudding/Butter Sauce

350 degrees

8 SERVINGS

3 tablespoons butter or margarine
1 cup sugar
2 cups sifted flour
2 teaspoons baking powder
½ teaspoon salt
1 cup evaporated milk
2 cups (½ lb.) whole cranberries

Cream together butter and sugar. Add sifted dry ingredients alternately with milk, beating after each addition. Fold in washed whole cranberries. Pour into greased 8 x 8 x 2-inch baking dish. Bake 25 to 30 minutes. Serve with Hot Butter Sauce (p. 214).

NOTE: Recipe may be doubled; bake in 9-inch springform pan using tube center.

Pumpkin Cake Roll

375 degrees

9 SERVINGS

FILLING:

1 cup confectioners' sugar
2 packages (3 oz. each) cream cheese
¼ cup (½ stick) butter or margarine
½ teaspoon vanilla

CAKE:

3 eggs
1 cup sugar
⅔ cup canned pumpkin
1 teaspoon lemon juice
¾ cup flour, stirred and measured
1 teaspoon baking powder
2 teaspoons cinnamon
1 teaspoon ginger
½ teaspoon nutmeg
½ teaspoon salt
1 cup walnuts, chopped

Combine all ingredients for Filling. Beat smooth and set aside. Beat eggs on high speed for at least 5 minutes, then gradually beat in sugar. Stir in pumpkin and lemon juice. Sift together dry ingredients; fold into pumpkin mixture. Generously grease a 15 x 10 x 1-inch jelly roll pan; sprinkle well with flour. Spread batter in baking pan; then sprinkle nuts evenly over top. Bake for 15 minutes. Turn cake onto terry towel that's been sprinkled with confectioners' sugar. Starting at narrow end, roll towel and cake up together. Cool. Unroll and spread with cake filling. Roll up cake roll without towel, wrap in plastic wrap or waxed paper; chill. Slice and serve.

Danish Almond Puff

350 degrees   12 SERVINGS

½ cup (1 stick) butter or margarine
1 cup flour, stirred and measured
2 tablespoons water
1 cup water
½ cup (1 stick) butter or margarine
1 cup flour, stirred and measured
1 teaspoon almond extract
3 large eggs
   Confectioners' Sugar Icing (below)
   Sliced almonds

Cut ½ cup butter into 1 cup flour as for pastry. Add 2 tablespoons water; mix with fork until ball forms. Divide. On ungreased baking sheet (12 x 16 inches) pat each portion of dough with hands into strip 12 x 3 inches, spacing strips about 3 inches apart. In saucepan bring 1 cup water to boil; add butter; cook until butter is melted. Add 1 cup flour all at once, cooking and stirring with wooden spoon until mixture pulls away from sides of pan to gather into smooth ball. Remove pan from heat; stir in almond extract. Add eggs, one at a time, beating after each until smooth. Divide dough in half; spread each half evenly over one pastry strip. Bake 1 hour or until golden brown. While still warm, frost with Confectioners' Sugar Icing; sprinkle generously with sliced almonds. Cool; slice diagonally to serve. For tea table, cut pastries in half lengthwise before slicing diagonally to make finger puffs.

CONFECTIONERS' SUGAR ICING:

1½ cups confectioners' sugar
2 tablespoons soft butter or margarine
½ teaspoon almond extract
1 to 2 tablespoons water

Mix together all ingredients until smooth and spreadable.

Double Chocolate Pastry Cake

425 degrees   12 SERVINGS

2 bars (4 oz. each) German sweet chocolate
½ cup sugar
½ cup water
¼ teaspoon cinnamon
2 teaspoons vanilla
1 package (9 oz. or 10 oz.) pie crust mix or 2 cups
   Pastry Mix (p. 252)
2 cups heavy cream
   Chocolate curls (below)

Reserve 1 square chocolate for chocolate curls. Place remaining chocolate, sugar, water and cinnamon in small saucepan. Stir over low heat until sauce is smooth. Remove from heat. Add vanilla; cool to room temperature. Blend ¾ cup sauce into pie crust mix. Divide into 4 parts. Using spatula or hands, press or spread each part over bottom of inverted round 9-inch cake pan to within ¼ inch of edge. Bake 8 to 10 minutes, until firm, taking care not to burn. If necessary, trim edges to make layers even. Cool. Run tip of knife under edges to loosen from pans. Lift carefully as layers are fragile. Whip cream just to soft peaks. Fold in remaining chocolate sauce. Spread mixture between layers and over top, but not around sides. Garnish with chocolate curls and chill at least 8 hours.

NOTE: To make chocolate curls, hold 1 square of the chocolate inside closed fist until chocolate softens. Peel into curls with vegetable peeler.

Dainty Tarts

325 degrees   2 DOZEN

PASTRY:

  ½ cup (1 stick) butter or margarine, softened
  1 package (3 oz.) cream cheese, softened
  1 cup flour, sifted
  ¼ teaspoon salt

In bowl blend together all ingredients with fork to make pastry. Divide dough into 24 equal balls. With fingertips or end of wooden spoon, press each ball to fit ungreased 1¼-inch tart pans. Fill each tart with 1 teaspoon filling (see below). Bake 25 minutes. Cool 5 minutes; remove from pan.

PECAN FILLING:

  1 large egg, beaten
  ¾ cup brown sugar, packed
  ½ teaspoon vanilla
  ½ cup pecans, chopped

Combine ingredients; proceed as above.

CURRANT COCONUT FILLING:

  ¾ cup currants
  ¾ cup brown sugar, packed
1½ tablespoons butter
  1 small egg
  ½ teaspoon vanilla
  ¼ teaspoon nutmeg
  ⅓ cup coconut

Combine ingredients; proceed as above.

Angel Pie

4½ tablespoons cornstarch
¾ cup sugar
1½ cups boiling water
¼ teaspoon salt
3 egg whites
3 tablespoons sugar
1½ teaspoons vanilla
1 baked 9-inch pastry shell
1 cup Caramel Sauce (p. 218)
1 cup heavy cream, whipped and slightly sweetened
½ square (½ oz.) unsweetened chocolate shaved into chocolate curls

In medium saucepan combine cornstarch and sugar; blend thoroughly. Add boiling water, stirring constantly. Cook and stir until thick and clear, 10 to 12 minutes. In large clean glass or stainless bowl combine salt and egg whites. Beat until stiff, gradually adding sugar and vanilla. Pour hot cornstarch mixture over egg whites, beating constantly. Cool mixture slightly; pour into pastry shell. Chill. Shortly before serving, pour enough Caramel Sauce in thin layer to cover entire filling. Cover with whipped cream; garnish with chocolate curls (see p. 239).

NOTE: Caramel Sauce should be thin enough that when pie is cut, sauce slightly runs down sides of cut pieces.

Plum Kuchen
375 degrees   TWO 9-INCH KUCHENS

PASTRY:

2½ cups flour, sifted
 1 cup shortening
 1 teaspoon salt
⅓ cup cold water
 1 teaspoon vinegar

Combine flour and salt in medium mixing bowl. Cut in shortening with pastry cutter. Add combined water and vinegar; mix until ball forms. Divide dough in half; roll each to fit a 9-inch pie dish, shaping crust and fluting edges but keeping them thin and low. Makes 2 pastry shells.

PLUM KUCHEN:

 1 9-inch unbaked pastry shell
⅓ cup nuts, finely ground
 4 cups fresh plums, quartered
¼ cup sugar
½ to 1 teaspoon cinnamon
 1 tablespoon flour

Spread ground nuts evenly over bottom of unbaked pastry shell. Arrange plums close together in orderly fashion, skin side down, in circle around outer edge of bottom of pastry shell; then arrange another circle inside that and another until entire pastry is covered. Combine sugar, cinnamon and flour; sprinkle evenly over fruit. Bake 40 to 45 minutes or until fruit is tender and cooked. Serve warm, topped with whipped cream.

PLUM ZWETSCHGEN KUCHEN (Plum Pie with Custard)

 1 9-inch unbaked pastry shell
 4 cups plums, quartered
 2 eggs
   Pinch salt

3 tablespoons cream or milk

3 to 4 tablespoons sugar

Arrange plums in bottom of pastry shell as for plum ku-chen. Combine eggs, salt, cream and sugar; beat together with fork. Pour over plums. Bake for 40 to 45 minutes or until fruit is tender.

NOTE: Any fresh fruit may be used in either pie. Apri-cots, apples and sour cherries are especially good.

Chocolate Almond Chiffon Pie

ONE 9-INCH PIE

1 9-inch baked pastry or crumb shell

⅓ cup blanched, slivered almonds, toasted

1 envelope (1 T.) unflavored gelatin

¼ cup cold water

2 squares (1 oz. each) unsweetened chocolate

¼ teaspoon almond extract

⅔ cup sugar

¼ teaspoon salt

½ cup hot milk

1 teaspoon vanilla

2 cups heavy cream

3 tablespoons blanched almonds, ground

Sprinkle toasted almonds over bottom of chilled pastry or crumb crust. Soften gelatin in cold water. In small sauce-pan over very low heat melt chocolate. Add almond ex-tract, sugar, salt and hot milk. Cook and stir for about 4 minutes. Stir in gelatin mixture; allow to cool. Beat chocolate mixture until light colored and fluffy. Add vanilla. Fold in heavy cream that's been whipped; stir in ground almonds. Pour into pie shell; chill. Serve with dollops of whipped cream.

Traditional Pumpkin Pie

425 degrees   ONE 9-INCH PIE

    2 eggs, slightly beaten
1½ cups cooked or canned pumpkin or banana squash
    ¾ cup sugar
    ½ teaspoon salt
    1 teaspoon cinnamon
    ½ teaspoon ginger
    ¼ teaspoon cloves
1⅔ cups evaporated milk or half-and-half cream
    1 9-inch unbaked pastry shell with high fluted rim

In large bowl combine all filling ingredients in order given. Pour into pastry shell. Bake at 425 degrees for 15 minutes. Reduce temperature to 350 degrees; continue baking for 45 minutes or until knife inserted into center of pie filling comes out clean. Cool. Garnish with whipped cream, if desired.

Sour Cream Raisin Pie

300 degrees   ONE 8-INCH PIE

    2 tablespoons cornstarch
    ¾ cup sugar
    ¼ teaspoon salt
    1 teaspoon cinnamon
    ½ teaspoon nutmeg
    ¼ teaspoon cloves
    2 egg yolks, well beaten
    1 cup dairy sour cream
    1 cup raisins
    1 baked 8-inch pastry shell
    2 egg whites
    ¼ cup sugar

In top of double boiler mix together cornstarch, sugar, salt and spices. Add egg yolks; mix well. Stir in sour cream and raisins. Cook over hot water until thick. Cool. Pour into baked pastry shell. Make meringue by beating egg whites until stiff, gradually adding sugar. Spread meringue over pie filling, sealing meringue to pastry on all sides. Bake 20 to 30 minutes, until meringue is lightly browned. Cool to serve.

Pineapple Meringue Pie

350 degrees   ONE 9-INCH PIE

1 can (1 lb. 4 oz.) *crushed pineapple, undrained*
½ cup sugar, divided
2½ *tablespoons cornstarch*
¼ *teaspoon salt*
¼ *teaspoon nutmeg*
3 *egg yolks*
1 *tablespoon lemon juice*
  9-inch baked pastry shell
3 *egg whites*
  Dash salt
6 *tablespoons sugar*

In medium saucepan heat pineapple. Mix ¼ cup sugar with cornstarch, salt and nutmeg; add to hot pineapple. Cook, stirring until thick and clear. Beat egg yolks with remaining ¼ cup sugar; stir into hot mixture. Cook, stirring, for 1 minute. Remove from heat, stir in lemon juice; cool. Pour into baked pie shell. Make meringue by beating egg whites with salt until stiff, then gradually beating in 6 tablespoons sugar. Spread over pineapple filling, making sure to seal meringue to pastry shell. Bake 12 to 15 minutes until meringue is lightly browned. Chill to serve.

Lemon Meringue Pie

350 degrees   ONE 9-INCH PIE

   1 *cup sugar*
1¼ *cups water*
   1 *tablespoon butter*
 ¼ *cup cornstarch*
   3 *tablespoons cold water*
   6 *tablespoons lemon juice (1½ lemons)*
   1 *teaspoon grated lemon rind (½ lemon)*
   3 *egg yolks*
   2 *tablespoons milk*
   1 *9-inch baked pastry shell (p. 252)*

Before making the pie filling, assemble all ingredients. Combine sugar, water and butter in medium saucepan; heat until sugar is dissolved. Add cornstarch that has been dissolved in cold water. Cook, stirring, over medium heat until mixture thickens and becomes quite clear, about 8 minutes. Add lemon juice and peel; cook, stirring for 2 more minutes. Remove from heat. Combine egg yolks with milk; beat thoroughly. Very slowly add egg yolk mixture to lemon sauce, stirring constantly. Return to heat; bring mixture just to boil. Remove from heat; cool and pour into baked 9-inch pastry shell. Spread meringue over pie filling, sealing it to edges of pastry shell on all sides. Bake 13 to 15 minutes or until meringue is slightly browned. Cool in draft-free spot for 2 to 3 hours.

MERINGUE:

   3 *egg whites*
   6 *tablespoons sugar*
   1 *teaspoon lemon juice*

Beat egg whites until stiff. Add sugar gradually; beat until all sugar granules are dissolved. Add lemon juice; mix well.

NOTE: To keep crust from becoming soggy, brush bottom of baked shell with slightly beaten egg yolk; then proceed as in recipe.

NOTE: Lemon Meringue Pie is best eaten without refrigeration. But it must be refrigerated after 3 hours.

NOTE: Meringue pies are most easily cut with knife that has been dipped in hot water.

Sweet Cherry Pie

400 degrees   ONE 9-INCH PIE

  3 cups pitted fresh sweet dark cherries
  ¾ cup sugar
  ¼ cup flour
  ½ teaspoon almond extract
  2 tablespoons butter
    Pastry for two-crust pie

Combine pitted cherries, sugar, flour and almond extract. Pour into pastry-lined 9-inch pie dish. Dot with butter. Adjust top crust; flute edges and cut vents. Bake 45 minutes or until pastry is golden brown.

APPLE PIE: Use 6 cups sliced apples in place of cherries; add 1 teaspoon cinnamon and ¼ teaspoon nutmeg in place of almond extract.

PEACH OR APRICOT PIE: Use 5 cups fresh peach slices or apricot halves in place of cherries; add 1 tablespoon lemon juice in place of almond extract.

PLUM PIE: Use 4 cups sliced fresh plums in place of cherries. Use ½ teaspoon cinnamon and 1 tablespoon lemon juice in place of almond extract.

Butterscotch Peach Pie

425 degrees   ONE 9-INCH PIE

    Pastry for 2 crust pie
1 *quart or 1 can (1 lb. 13 oz.) peaches, drained and sliced,*
    reserving juice
½ *cup brown sugar, firmly packed*
2 *tablespoons flour*
⅛ *teaspoon salt*
½ *cup peach syrup*
¼ *cup (½ stick) butter or margarine*
2 *teaspoons lemon juice*

Place peaches in pastry-lined 9-inch pie pan. Combine sugar, flour, salt and peach syrup; add butter. Cook until thick, stirring. Remove from heat; add lemon juice. Pour over peaches. Adjust top crust, flute edges and cut vents. Bake for 30 minutes or until delicately browned. If desired, 10 minutes before pie is finished, brush lightly with milk and sprinkle with 1 teaspoon granulated sugar.

Glazed Fresh Strawberry Pie

ONE 9-INCH PIE

1 *package (3 oz.) cream cheese, softened*
    Milk
1 *baked 9-inch pastry shell*
1 *quart fresh strawberries, washed and hulled*
1 *cup sugar*
3 *tablespoons cornstarch*
    Whipped cream

Whip together cream cheese and enough milk to make fluffy. Spread cream cheese over bottom of cooled pastry shell. Separate out the choicest half of strawberries; arrange in pie shell covering the cream cheese. Mash

remaining berries; strain to extract juice. Combine strawberry juice with enough water to make 1½ cups. Bring
juice mixture to boil. Stir in sugar and cornstarch which
have been thoroughly combined. Cook over low heat, stirring until mixture boils. Cook 1 minute. Pour over berries
in pie shell. Chill 2 hours. Just before serving garnish with
whipped cream.

Pear Pie

425 degrees   ONE 8-INCH PIE

  1 *quart or 1 can (1 lb. 13 oz.) pear halves*
½ *cup sugar*
  2 *tablespoons cornstarch*
¼ *teaspoon cinnamon*
½ *teaspoon nutmeg*
½ *cup light cream*
  1 *tablespoon orange juice*
  1 *tablespoon lemon juice*
   Pastry for two-crust 8-inch pie
  1 *tablespoon butter*

Drain pear halves thoroughly; cut into pieces. Combine
with mixture of sugar, cornstarch, cinnamon and nutmeg.
Carefully stir in cream and fruit juices. Line an 8-inch pie
pan with favorite pastry. Add pear mixture; dot with butter. Adjust top crust; flute edges and cut vents. Brush crust
with cream; sprinkle with sugar. Bake 30 to 35 minutes or
until golden brown. Serve warm or cold.

NOTE: Pears must be thoroughly drained or pie will be
runny.

Canned Sweet Cherry Pie

400 degrees ONE 9-INCH PIE

   1 quart or 2 cans (16 oz. each) dark sweet cherries
2½ tablespoons cornstarch
   3 tablespoons butter
   1 tablespoon lemon juice
      Pastry for two crust pie

Drain juice from cherries. Mix ¼ cup juice with corn-starch until smooth. Stir into remaining pie juice. Cook over medium heat, stirring, until mixture thickens and comes to full boil. Remove from heat. Stir in lemon juice, butter and pitted cherries. Pour into pastry-lined 9-inch pie dish. Adjust top crust. Flute edges; cut vents. Bake 45 minutes or until pastry is golden brown.

Frosty Lemon Pie

ONE 9-INCH PIE

   1 9-inch baked pastry shell
1¼ cups applesauce
   1 package (3 oz.) lemon flavor gelatin
½ cup sugar
   1 tablespoon lemon juice
⅛ teaspoon mace
   1 tablespoon grated lemon rind, if desired
   4 cups Whipped Dry Milk Topping (p. 218, double recipe)

Heat applesauce in double boiler; stir in gelatin and sugar until dissolved. Add lemon juice, mace and lemon rind; chill until stiff. Combine with 3 cups of the whipped dry milk topping; blend with beater. Spoon into pastry shell. Chill until firm, about 30 minutes. Garnish with additional topping and sprinkling of grated lemon rind.

Fresh Peach Pie

ONE 9-INCH PIE

2 cups fresh peaches, sliced
1 tablespoon lemon juice
¼ cup sugar
3 tablespoons cornstarch
1 tablespoon butter or margarine
    Dash salt
½ teaspoon almond extract
1 baked 9-inch pastry shell
    Whipped cream

In medium-size mixing bowl sprinkle peaches with lemon juice and sugar; allow to stand for 1 hour. Drain off juice; should measure about 1 cup. Combine peach juice and cornstarch. Cook and stir in small saucepan over medium heat until thick. Stir in butter, salt and almond extract. Cool. Place peaches in baked pastry shell. Pour cooled mixture over top. Chill. Serve with whipped cream.

Huckleberry Pie

400 degrees   ONE 8-INCH PIE

2⅔ cups Canned Huckleberries and juice (p. 311)
1 cup sugar
¼ cup flour
    Dash salt
¼ teaspoon nutmeg
1 tablespoon lime or lemon juice
1 tablespoon butter

Drain berries, saving juice. Bring juice to boil. Combine sugar, flour, salt and nutmeg; stir into juice. Cook until thick, stirring constantly. Add lime juice and drained berries. Pour into pastry-lined 8-inch pie dish. Dot with butter. Adjust top crust; flute edges and cut vents. Bake 30 to 40 minutes or until pastry is golden brown.

Pastry Mix

6 cups flour, sifted
2 teaspoons salt
2 cups (1 lb.) lard or shortening

Combine flour and salt in mixing bowl. Cut shortening into flour with pastry cutter or two knives until mixture is as coarse as small peas. Store in refrigerator in covered containers. This will keep up to 6 weeks. Makes 8 cups mix.

SINGLE CRUST: With fork stir 2 to 3 tablespoons ice water into 1½ cups chilled pastry mix until ball gathers in center of mixing bowl. Turn onto lightly floured board; knead once or twice. Roll into crust and fit into 9-inch pie dish; crimp edges. With 4-tined fork, prick bottom and sides of crust frequently. (Use 1¼ cups mix for 8-inch pastry shell.)

DOUBLE CRUST: Use 2½ cups pastry mix with ⅓ cup ice water or enough water to barely hold dough together in a ball. Proceed as for single crust. Divide dough in half. Roll out one-half and fit into pie dish; trim edge of pastry at edge of dish. Place pie filling in shell. Roll out second half of pastry. Arrange on top of filling; trim crust ⅜-inch beyond edge of dish. With fingers tuck extended pastry back underneath lower crust, making a seal. Crimp edges and cut vents in pastry.

BAKED PASTRY SHELL: Prepare pastry for single crust; arrange pastry in pie dish, trim edges and crimp. Prick entire surface evenly with 4-tined fork. Bake at 450 degrees for 10 to 15 minutes or until lightly browned. If desired, to keep pastry shell from shrinking, fit a square of waxed paper loosely into unbaked shell, allowing edges of paper to extend outside of shell. Pour any kind of dry beans over waxed paper to fill pastry shell. Bake at 450 degrees for about 8 minutes or until edges of pastry first begin to brown. Remove pie dish from oven, remove

beans and waxed paper, and return pastry to oven. Continue baking until lightly browned—about 7 minutes. Save dry beans to re-use in making other baked crusts.

Rich Flaky Pastry

ONE TWO-CRUST PIE

1 cup vegetable shortening (do not use lard or butter)
¾ teaspoon salt
2 cups flour, stirred and measured
¼ cup cold water

Measure shortening into bowl. Add salt and half of flour. Stir with spoon until it creams together and is smooth and satiny. Add water and remaining flour. Stir with spoon until mixture clings together in ball. Roll out as desired. do not be afraid to handle.

NOTE: Recipe may be doubled or tripled.

Baked Whole Wheat Pie Shells

425 degrees   THREE 9-INCH PASTRY SHELLS

½ cup (1 stick) butter or margarine
½ cup sugar
2 cups sifted finely ground whole wheat flour
1 teaspoon cinnamon
4 dashes salt

Combine all ingredients; mix in electric mixer until crumbly. Pat into three 9-inch pie tins. Bake 8 to 10 minutes or until lightly browned. Cool. Fill as desired.

Cakes and Frostings

Cakes are for celebrating—birthdays, anniversaries, holidays, missionary farewells and reunions. And cakes are also for soothing—illnesses, deaths, disasters and defeats.

Mormon women, who are members of the Mormon Relief Society, have learned to live by their creed, "Charity Never Faileth." They can stir up a cake at a moment's notice practically with one hand. And cakes are sent out of the house on missions of mercy or triumph about as often as they are set onto their own tables.

One of the standbys, 30-Minute Cocoa Cake is just that—a 30-minute production, frosting and all! And the tempting cake stays moist for days.

Golden Sponge Cake is easy and elegant. Lemon Butter Fluff Icing goes well with it, but the cake is about as delicious when served plain—and lower caloried besides.

Poundcakes don't always bake well at Utah's high altitude, but Sour Cream Poundcake is an exception.

Other favorites among cake recipes use the bounties of the garden and orchard: Pumpkin Cake, Chocolate Zucchini Country Cake, Bing Cherry Cake and Whole Wheat Carrot Cake. Add to them Oatmeal Cake topped with broiled icing, and you have a parade of cakes not only fit for celebrating and soothing, but also for nourishing!

Mother's Ginger Cakes

350 degrees   18 LARGE CUPCAKES

⅓ cup melted shortening or salad oil
½ cup sugar
½ cup molasses
1 egg
1 teaspoon soda
2 cups flour, stirred and measured
1 teaspoon ground ginger
½ teaspoon ground cinnamon
¼ teaspoon ground cloves
½ cup sour milk or buttermilk
½ cup nuts, coarsely chopped
½ cup raisins

In large mixing bowl combine melted shortening, sugar, molasses, egg and soda; beat until well blended and light. Add sifted dry ingredients and sour milk or buttermilk; mix until well blended. Stir in nuts and raisins. Spoon batter into muffin tins that have been greased or lined with cupcake liners, filling about ⅔ full. Bake for 20 to 25 minutes. If desired, frost with Caramel Frosting.

Caramel Frosting

FROSTS 18 LARGE CUPCAKES

2 tablespoons granulated sugar
2 tablespoons water
2 tablespoons butter
2 cups confectioners' sugar
Pinch salt

In small heavy skillet place granulated sugar over medium heat until sugar melts and is caramel brown in color, shaking skillet as needed to keep sugar from burning. Add water; heat and stir until sugar is dissolved. Remove from heat. Cream together butter, confectioners' sugar, salt and enough caramel syrup to make spreadable.

Whole Wheat Carrot Cake

350 degrees   12 TO 14 SERVINGS

2 cups brown sugar, packed
1 cup oil
3 eggs
2 cups (½ lb.) carrots, finely grated
1 cup crushed pineapple, drained
3 cups whole wheat flour, stirred and measured
1 teaspoon salt
1 teaspoon soda
1 teaspoon cinnamon
2 teaspoons vanilla
1 cup raisins
1 cup nuts, broken
1 cup coconut (optional)

Grease and flour 9 x 13-inch baking pan or spray 10-inch bundt pan with vegetable cooking spray; then sprinkle with granulated sugar. Beat together brown sugar, oil and eggs. Stir in carrots and pineapple. Blend together dry ingredients; stir into batter thoroughly. Add vanilla, raisins, nuts and (optional) coconut. Pour into prepared pan. Bake 9 x 13-inch cake for 30 to 35 minutes or until done when tested. For bundt cake, bake 1 hour or until done. Frost with Rosalie's Cream Cheese Frosting (below).

Rosalie's Cream Cheese Frosting

FROSTS 9-INCH LAYER CAKE

2 packages (3 oz. each) cream cheese, softened
3 cups confectioners' sugar
1 teaspoon vanilla

In large bowl cream the cream cheese until smooth. Gradually beat in confectioners' sugar and vanilla. Beat until of spreading consistency, adding a little evaporated milk, if necessary.

Oatmeal Cake

350 degrees   9 x 13-INCH CAKE

1¼ cups boiling water
1 cup quick cooking rolled oats
½ cup (1 stick) butter or margarine
¾ cup granulated sugar
¾ cup brown sugar, packed
2 eggs, slightly beaten
1½ cups sifted flour
1 teaspoon soda
½ teaspoon salt
1 teaspoon cinnamon
½ teaspoon nutmeg
Broiled Coconut Topping (below)

Pour boiling water over rolled oats; let stand 20 minutes (Makes 1½ cups thick oatmeal). Cream together butter and sugars. Add eggs. Stir in oatmeal, then sifted dry ingredients. Bake in greased 9 x 13-inch pan for 40 to 45 minutes or until done. Spread with Coconut Topping; broil until frosting bubbles, taking care not to burn.

Broiled Coconut Topping

FROSTS 9 x 13-INCH CAKE

6 tablespoons (¾ stick) butter or margarine
½ cup brown sugar, packed
¼ cup cream or evaporated milk
¾ cup nuts, coarsely chopped
1 cup coconut

Combine all ingredients. Spread over spice, oatmeal or carrot cake. Broil until frosting bubbles and browns slightly. (Take care not to burn.)

Favorite Spongecake

375 degrees   10-INCH TUBE CAKE

6 eggs, separated
¾ teaspoon cream of tartar
½ cup plus 2 tablespoons sugar
1½ cups flour, stirred and measured
½ cup plus 2 tablespoons sugar
¾ teaspoon baking powder
½ teaspoon salt
½ cup orange juice, apricot nectar or water
1 tablespoon grated orange rind (1 orange)
1 teaspoon lemon extract
½ teaspoon vanilla

Separate eggs, placing whites in large mixing bowl, yolks in small mixing bowl. (If egg whites are brought to room temperature before beating, they will give greater volume.) Add cream of tartar to egg whites. Beat at high speed until foamy. Gradually add ½ cup plus 2 tablespoons sugar, continuing to beat until stiff peaks form. To egg yolks, add flour, remaining sugar, baking powder, salt, orange juice or water, orange rind and flavorings. Blend at low speed until moistened; beat 1 minute at medium speed, scraping bowl occasionally. Pour over egg whites. By hand, fold carefully just until well blended. Pour batter into ungreased 10-inch tube pan. Bake for 35 to 40 minutes or until top springs back when lightly touched. Invert and cool thoroughly. Remove cooled cake from pan. If desired, frost with Lemon Butter Fluff Frosting (p. 261).

Pumpkin Cake

350 degrees 8-INCH LAYER CAKE

¾ cup shortening
1¼ cups sugar
2 eggs
1 cup canned or cooked pumpkin
¾ cup milk
1 teaspoon soda
2¼ cups sifted flour
Pinch salt
3 teaspoons baking powder
1 teaspoon cinnamon
½ teaspoon cloves
½ teaspoon nutmeg
1 cup broken nuts

Cream together shortening and sugar. Add eggs; beat until light and fluffy. Combine pumpkin, milk and soda; add alternately with sifted dry ingredients. Stir in nuts. Pour into two 8-inch layer cake pans that have been lined with waxed paper, then greased and floured. Bake 25 minutes or until done. Frost, if desired, with Rosalie's Cream Cheese Frosting (p. 257).

NOTE: Cake may be baked in 9 x 13-inch pan for 40 to 45 minutes or until done.

Gussie's Fruitcake

250 degrees 4 FRUIT CAKES (2 LBS. EACH)

MIXTURE I:

1 lb. raisins
1 package (11 oz.) currants
1 lb. walnuts, coarsely chopped
½ lb. candied fruit cake mix
2 tablespoons flour

MIXTURE II :

3 cups brown sugar, lightly packed
1 lb. butter (no substitute)
6 large or 8 small eggs
½ cup molasses
½ cup buttermilk
1 cup grape (or other fruit) juice
2 tablespoons vanilla

MIXTURE III :

4 cups sifted flour
1 tablespoon cinnamon
1 teaspoon cloves
1 teaspoon nutmeg
1 teaspoon soda

Combine each of the three above mixtures in separate containers. Add Mixture III to Mixture II; blend thoroughly. Stir in Mixture I thoroughly. Spoon batter into four loaf pans (9½ x 5½ x 2½ inches) that have been lined with pan liners or with greased heavy brown paper. Bake for 2 hours. Cool thoroughly. Remove from pans; moisten top of each cake with pastry brush dipped into grape juice. Wrap cold cakes in plastic wrap, then in aluminum foil. Store in cool place.

Lemon Butter Fluff Frosting

FROSTS 10-INCH ANGEL FOOD CAKE

1 package (3 oz.) cream cheese, softened
½ cup (1 stick) butter or margarine, softened
4 cups confectioners' sugar
2 tablespoons cream
1 tablespoon lemon juice
2 teaspoons grated lemon rind (1 lemon)

Cream together cheese and butter. Add sugar, cream, lemon juice and lemon rind; beat until fluffy and smooth.

Orange Raisin Cake

375 degrees   9 x 13-INCH CAKE

1 large orange
1 cup raisins
⅓ cup walnuts
2 cups flour, stirred and measured
1 cup sugar
1 teaspoon soda
¾ teaspoon salt
½ cup shortening
1 cup milk
2 eggs
⅓ cup sugar
1 teaspoon cinnamon
¼ teaspoon nutmeg
¼ cup walnuts, chopped

Lightly grease and flour 9 x 13 x 2-inch pan. Squeeze orange, saving juice. In food processor or food chopper, coarsely chop pulp and rind of orange with raisins and nuts; set aside. In large bowl sift together flour, 1 cup sugar, soda and salt. Add shortening and milk; beat on low speed for 1½ minutes. Add eggs; beat 1½ minutes. Fold in orange-raisin-nut mixture. Pour batter into prepared pan. Bake 35 to 40 minutes or until cake tests done. Spoon reserved orange juice over warm cake; sprinkle with mixture of ⅓ cup sugar, 1 teaspoon cinnamon, ¼ teaspoon nutmeg and ¼ cup chopped walnuts.

NOTE: Orange glaze and cinnamon sugar topping may be omitted and cake frosted with Rosalie's Cream Cheese Frosting (p. 257).

Mace Poundcake

350 degrees   10-INCH BUNDT CAKE

 1 cup (2 sticks) butter or margarine
 2 cups sugar
 5 large eggs
 2 cups flour, stirred and measured
 1 tablespoon ground mace
 1 cup nuts, broken

Cream butter; add sugar gradually, creaming together until light and fluffy. Add eggs, one at a time, beating 1 minute after each addition. After last egg is added, beat batter 1 additional minute. Sift flour and mace into batter and blend; stir in nuts. Grease bundt pan very heavily, using 2 or 3 tablespoons shortening, or spray generously with liquid shortening. Sprinkle with granulated sugar. Spoon batter into pan. Bake for 45 to 50 minutes or until done. Turn out of pan immediately.

Chocolate Butter Cream Frosting

1 CUP

 2 tablespoons butter or margarine, room temperature
 2 cups confectioners' sugar
⅛ teaspoon salt
 1 square (1 oz.) unsweetened chocolate, melted
 1 teaspoon vanilla
 2 tablespoons warm cream or evaporated milk

In small mixing bowl cream butter. Add confectioners' sugar, salt, melted chocolate, vanilla and enough warm cream to make of spreadable consistency.

NOTE: For rich, more satiny icing increase butter to ¼ cup (½ stick).

Chocolate Chip Cake

375 degrees   8-INCH LAYER CAKE

½ cup shortening
½ cup granulated sugar
1 cup brown sugar, packed
2 eggs
1 cup evaporated milk
1 teaspoon vanilla
2¾ cups flour, stirred and measured
1 teaspoon soda
½ teaspoon salt
1 cup chocolate chips or broken nuts, dates, raisins or any
combination
Brown Sugar Frosting (p.271)

Cream together shortening and sugars. Add eggs; beat
well. Add evaporated milk and vanilla alternately with
sifted dry ingredients. Stir in chocolate chips (or alternate
ingredients.) Bake for 25 to 30 minutes in two 8-inch layer
cake pans that have been lined with waxed paper, then
greased and floured. Frost with Brown Sugar Frosting.

Party Meringue Cake

300 degrees   9 SERVINGS

4 large egg whites (room temperature)
1 cup sugar
2 cups sifted cake flour
2½ teaspoons baking powder
½ teaspoon salt
1 cup sugar
½ cup shortening
⅔ cup milk
½ teaspoon vanilla
½ teaspoon lemon extract
4 egg yolks
½ cup slivered almonds
2 cups fresh fruit
1 cup heavy cream

Beat egg whites until foamy. Gradually add 1 cup sugar; continue beating until mixture holds a stiff peak. Set aside. Sift flour, baking powder, salt and 1 cup sugar into mixing bowl. Add shortening, milk, vanilla and lemon extract. Beat at medium speed for 2 minutes. Add egg yolks and continue beating for 2 minutes longer. Pour into two greased 8-inch square or 9-inch round cake pans. Top with meringue and sprinkle with almonds. Bake for 40 to 45 minutes or until cake tests done. Cool 10 minutes. Loosen meringue from sides of pan; cool cake completely before removing from pan. Serve separately or in two layers topped with fruit and slightly sweetened whipped cream.

Spicy Applesauce Cake

375 degrees   10-INCH TUBE CAKE

   1 cup (2 sticks) butter or margarine
   2 cups sugar
   2 eggs
   1 teaspoon vanilla
3¾ cups sifted all-purpose flour
   1 teaspoon baking powder
   ½ teaspoon soda
   1 teaspoon ground allspice
   1 teaspoon ground cinnamon
   ½ teaspoon ground nutmeg
   ¼ teaspoon ground cloves
   3 tablespoons cocoa
   1 can (1 lb.) or 2 cups applesauce
   1 cup seedless raisins

Cream butter and sugar together until light and fluffy. Add eggs and vanilla; beat until smooth. Sift together flour, baking powder, soda, spices and cocoa. Add alternately with applesauce. Stir in raisins. Pour into greased and floured 10-inch tube pan. Bake for 75 minutes or until cake tests done. Cool slightly before removing from pan. Frost with Cream Cheese Frosting (p. 257).

Chocolate Zucchini Country Cake

350 degrees   10-INCH TUBE CAKE

¾ cup (1½ sticks) butter or margarine
2 cups sugar
3 eggs
2½ cups flour, stirred and measured
1 teaspoon salt
2 teaspoons cinnamon
2½ teaspoons baking powder
½ teaspoon soda
⅓ cup cocoa
½ cup milk
2 teaspoons vanilla
2 cups peeled or unpeeled zucchini, grated
1 cup nuts, broken

Prepare 10-inch tube pan by lining bottom of pan with waxed paper, then greasing paper and dusting with flour. Cream together butter and sugar. Add eggs; beat well. Sift together dry ingredients and add to batter alternately with combined milk, vanilla and grated zucchini. Beat well. Stir in nuts. Bake for 1 hour. If desired, drizzle with Butter Cream Frosting (below) or Chocolate Butter Cream Frosting (p. 263).

NOTE: Coconut or grated orange rind may be added to batter before baking.

Butter Cream Frosting

FROSTS 10-INCH TUBE CAKE

¼ cup (½ stick) butter or margarine
3½ cups (1 lb.) confectioners' sugar
¼ teaspoon salt
1 teaspoon vanilla
4 tablespoons cream or evaporated milk

In mixing bowl cream butter. Add confectioners' sugar, salt, vanilla and cream. Beat until smooth and of spreading consistency. If necessary, thin with additional cream.

30-Minute Cocoa Cake

400 degrees   9 x 13 INCH CAKE

  2 cups sugar
  2 cups flour, stirred and measured
  1 teaspoon soda
  1 teaspoon cinnamon
  1 cup (2 sticks) butter or margarine
  ¼ cup cocoa
  1 cup water
  ½ cup buttermilk
  2 eggs, slightly beaten
  1 teaspoon vanilla
     Quick Cocoa Frosting (p. 269)
  ½ cup nuts, chopped

In large mixing bowl stir together sugar, flour, soda and cinnamon. In medium saucepan combine butter, cocoa and water; bring to boil over medium heat, cooking until butter is melted. Add to sugar-flour mixture; blend. Whip together buttermilk and eggs; blend into batter thoroughly. Stir in vanilla. Pour into ungreased 9 x 13-inch baking pan. Bake for 20 minutes. Five minutes before cake is done, begin to make Quick Cocoa Frosting. Frost cake as soon as it comes from oven. Sprinkle immediately with chopped nuts. Cool.

NOTE: If desired, stir 1 cup broken nuts and/or 1 cup raisins into icing before spreading over cake.

Bing Cherry Cake

375 degrees   9-INCH LAYER CAKE

1 quart or 1 can (29 oz.) dark sweet cherries
¾ cup (1½ sticks) butter or margarine
1½ cups sugar
3 eggs
1 teaspoon vanilla
2½ cups flour, stirred and measured
1 teaspoon ground cinnamon
½ teaspoon ground cloves
½ teaspoon ground nutmeg
1 teaspoon baking soda
1 cup sour milk
1 cup walnuts, coarsely chopped

Prepare two 9-inch layer cake pans by greasing generously and dusting with flour or lining with waxed paper. Drain cherries; pit and set aside. Cream together butter and sugar until fluffy. Beat in eggs one at a time; then add vanilla. Sift together flour and spices; stir ½ cup of flour mixture gently into cherries. Stir soda into sour milk; add along with dry ingredients to cake batter; blend. Stir in cherries and nuts. Pour batter into prepared pans. Bake for 30 to 40 minutes or until cake tests done. Cool 10 minutes; turn out of pans. Ice with Ivory Frosting (below).

Ivory Frosting

FROSTS 9-INCH LAYER CAKE

2 egg whites, unbeaten
¼ cup brown sugar (packed)
1¼ cups granulated sugar
5 tablespoons water
⅛ teaspoon ground nutmeg
1 teaspoon vanilla

Combine all ingredients except vanilla in top of double boiler. Beat until thoroughly mixed. Place over boiling

water; beat until frosting stands in peaks, about 7 minutes. Remove from heat; add vanilla.

Quick Cocoa Frosting

FROSTS 9 x 13-INCH CAKE

½ cup (1 stick) butter or margarine
¼ cup cocoa
⅓ cup milk
3½ cups (1 lb.) confectioners' sugar
1 teaspoon vanilla

In medium saucepan combine butter, cocoa and milk. Bring to boil; simmer about 3 minutes. Remove from heat. Stir in remaining ingredients, blending until smooth. Spread immediately over hot 9 x 13-inch cake.

Sour Cream Poundcake

350 degrees   10-INCH BUNDT CAKE

1 cup (2 sticks) butter
2¼ cups sugar
6 eggs
3 cups sifted flour
½ teaspoon salt
¼ teaspoon soda
1 cup dairy sour cream
½ teaspoon vanilla
½ teaspoon lemon extract
½ teaspoon orange extract

Cream butter until soft. Add sugar gradually, beating until light and fluffy. Add eggs, one at a time, beating thoroughly after each. Sift together sifted flour, salt and soda; add to batter alternately with sour cream, beating until smooth. Add flavorings. Prepare fluted cake pan by coating generously with vegetable oil spray, then sprinkling with granulated sugar; or grease pan heavily. Pour batter into prepared pan. Bake for 1 hour or until done. Cool cake for 10 minutes; remove from pan.

Walnut Honey Cake

350 degrees   14 TO 16 SERVINGS

   1 cup (2 sticks) butter or margarine
1½ cups sugar
   6 eggs
   1 teaspoon vanilla
   2 cups flour, scooped and leveled
   1 teaspoon baking soda
   1 teaspoon ground cloves
1½ teaspoons ground cinnamon
   1 cup plain yogurt
   2 cups walnuts, finely chopped
   Honey Syrup (below)

In large bowl cream butter; add sugar gradually. Add eggs, one at a time, and beat well after each until blended. Add vanilla. Add sifted dry ingredients alternately with yogurt; blend well. Stir in nuts. Bake in large (12 cup) bundt pan that's been generously greased and floured. Bake for 40 minutes or until done. (Cake will pull away from sides of pan.) Cool 10 minutes, then carefully turn cake onto wire rack to cool. When thoroughly cool, return cake to pan. Carefully pour hot honey syrup over cake and allow to cool. Turn out of pan onto rack to allow any excess syrup to drip out. Cut thin slices and serve plain or with whipped cream.

HONEY SYRUP: Combine in medium saucepan 2 cups water, 1½ cups sugar, ½ cup honey and ½ teaspoon lemon juice. Boil together 15 minutes. Remove from heat; add 1½ teaspoons vanilla. Pour hot over cooled walnut cake.

NOTE: Cake may be baked in a 10½ x 14½ x 2-inch baking pan, generously greased and lightly floured. Bake as above, cool in pan and pour hot syrup over. Allow to stand until thoroughly cooled.

Brown Sugar Frosting

FROSTS 1 LAYER CAKE

½ cup butter
1 cup brown sugar, packed
¼ cup milk
3 cups confectioners' sugar
½ teaspoon vanilla

In saucepan melt butter. Add brown sugar; cook over low heat for 2 minutes, stirring. Add milk; continue to cook until mixture comes to a boil. Remove from heat. Gradually add confectioners' sugar. Add vanilla; mix well. Thin, if necessary, with few drops of evaporated milk.

Strawberry Angel Cake

10 TO 12 SERVINGS

1 10-inch angel food cake
1 package (10 oz.) frozen strawberries, thawed
1 envelope (1 T.) unflavored gelatin
2 cups heavy cream
¼ cup sugar

Cut angel food cake into two layers. Drain juice from thawed strawberries into small glass dish. Sprinkle gelatin over juice; allow to stand until softened. Set dish into boiling water; stir until gelatin is dissolved. Combine warm gelatin mixture with berries; do not allow to congeal. Whip cream until stiff, sweetening with sugar. Fold liquid strawberry mixture carefully into cream. Spread strawberry cream over bottom layer of angel food cake. Replace top layer and frost entire cake with remaining cream. Refrigerate for several hours.

Cookies and Candies

Let's face it, Mormons love sweets! Of the *Deseret News* recipes returned by readers as their favorites, cookie recipes exceeded them all.

Why should this be, we wondered, and could think of several reasons.

Family nights, 52 of them a year, encourage cookie baking. What's more fun for children to make as their family treat than easy Peanut Butter Mallow Bars? And everyone clamors for mother's big, soft Gingersnaps.

Family reunions (and Mormons have lots of them) call for potluck foods to be carried and shared. Milk chocolate-laden Parfait Cookies are always a hit.

Young Mormon missionaries at the hungry age of 19 are sent all over the world, giving two years to a cause they believe in. Missionaries receive not only financial support from home, but also letters and boxes of goodies. Butterscotch Brownies and Fruit Cocktail Bars ship well when sent uncut in their baking pans.

Christmas for Mormon families is usually a flurry of cookies baking—gingerbread men to hang from the tree, cut out sugar cookies to decorate for gifts and, of course, Jessie's Scotch Shortbread to store in tins.

"The longer shortbread hangs around," Jessie says with her Scotch brogue, "the better it gets." Meltaways are a drop version of the same cookie.

It was difficult to choose which cookie recipes to include in this chapter, since there wasn't nearly room for all. But readers, we hope, will never know what they missed because they'll be so delighted with what they find!

273

Gingersnaps

350 degrees   5 DOZEN

    ¾ cup (1½ sticks) butter, margarine or shortening
    1 cup sugar
    1 egg
    ¼ cup molasses
    2 cups flour, stirred and measured
    2 teaspoons soda
    ½ teaspoon salt
    1¼ teaspoons ground ginger
    ¾ teaspoon cinnamon
    ½ teaspoon cloves

Cream butter; add sugar gradually. Beat until fluffy. Add egg and molasses; blend. Stir or sift together flour, soda, salt and spices; blend into butter mixture. Roll small portions of dough into balls about the size of walnuts; roll in granulated sugar. Place on ungreased baking sheet about 1½ inches apart. Bake for 8 to 10 minutes or until they have melted and puffed. For crisper cookies, bake until they have flattened. Cookies bake down to form perfect rounds with traditional gingersnap cracks on top.

NOTE: ½ cup chopped raisins may be added to dough.

Chocolate Chews

350 degrees   3 DOZEN

    ½ cup shortening
    1⅔ cups sugar
    1 teaspoon vanilla
    2 eggs
    2 squares (1 oz. each) unsweetened chocolate, melted
    2 cups flour, stirred and measured
    2 teaspoons baking powder

½ teaspoon salt
⅓ cup milk
½ cup nuts, chopped
½ cup confectioners' sugar

Cream shortening, sugar and vanilla. Beat in eggs and melted chocolate. Sift dry ingredients; add to batter alternately with milk. Stir in nuts. Chill 2 to 3 hours. Form into 1-inch balls; roll in confectioners' sugar; place on greased baking sheet 2 to 3 inches apart. Bake for 12 minutes.

Gumdrop Cookies

350 degrees   3 DOZEN

½ cup shortening
½ cup granulated sugar
½ cup brown sugar, packed
1 teaspoon vanilla
1 egg, beaten
1 cup flour, stirred and measured
½ teaspoon soda
½ teaspoon baking powder
¼ teaspoon salt
½ cup grated coconut
½ cup small gumdrops or cut-up large ones (licorice flavor omitted)
1 cup quick cooking rolled oats

Cream together shortening and sugars. Add vanilla and egg; beat until light and fluffy. Sift in dry ingredients; mix thoroughly. Fold in coconut, gumdrops and oatmeal. Pinch off small pieces of dough; roll into one-inch balls. Arrange 2 inches apart on greased cookie sheet. Flatten with fork dipped in milk. Bake 10 minutes.

Sand Balls

375 degrees   4 DOZEN

1 cup butter
½ cup confectioners' sugar
2 tablespoons honey
2¼ cups sifted flour
¼ teaspoon salt
1 teaspoon vanilla
¾ cup walnuts, chopped

Cream together butter, confectioners' sugar and honey thoroughly. Add flour, salt, vanilla and nuts. Mix with hands, if necessary, to blend. Form into balls 1-inch in diameter; chill well. Place 2½ inches apart on greased cookie sheet. Bake 14 to 17 minutes or until barely tinged with brown. While still warm, roll in confectioners' sugar. Cool. Roll in confectioners' sugar again.

Gingerbread Cookies

350 degrees   5 DOZEN

1 cup shortening
1 cup sugar
2 eggs
½ cup cold water
2 teaspoons soda
1 cup molasses
1 teaspoon ginger
1 teaspoon cinnamon
1 teaspoon salt
4 cups (or more) flour

Cream shortening; add sugar gradually, then slightly beaten eggs; beat until well blended. Clean beaters. In very large bowl combine water, soda and molasses; beat vigorously (mixture increases in volume as it's beaten).

Add molasses mixture to shortening mixture; blend. Sift dry ingredients with 3 cups flour; stir into dough. Turn dough out onto well floured board; knead remaining flour into dough until the right texture to roll—smooth to the feel and firm, not soft. Chill several hours or overnight. Roll ¼ to ⅛-inch thick. Cut into desired shapes. Arrange on lightly greased baking sheet. Bake 7 minutes or until done.

Pepper Cookies

350 degrees   8 DOZEN

½ cup sugar
½ cup dark corn syrup
½ cup (1 stick) butter
1½ teaspoons vinegar
 1 egg, slightly beaten
2¼ cups flour, stirred and measured
½ teaspoon soda
¼ teaspoon black pepper
½ teaspoon ginger
½ teaspoon cloves
½ teaspoon cinnamon

Combine in small saucepan sugar, corn syrup, butter and vinegar; bring almost to boiling point; then cool to room temperature. Stir in egg. Add sifted dry ingredients, blending well. Cover; refrigerate several hours or overnight. Divide dough into 4 portions, keeping each part chilled until time to roll out. Roll dough very thinly on floured board. Cut into any desired shapes. Bake on greased cookie sheet 7 to 8 minutes. Remove from baking sheet immediately; cool; store in tight tins. Recipe may be doubled.

Cut Out Sugar Cookies

375 degrees   2 DOZEN

⅔ cup shortening
¾ cup sugar
1 egg
½ teaspoon vanilla
½ teaspoon almond extract
1¾ cups flour, stirred and measured
1 teaspoon baking powder
¼ teaspoon salt
4 teaspoons milk

Thoroughly cream shortening and sugar. Add egg; beat until mixture is light and fluffy. Add vanilla and almond; mix in thoroughly. Add sifted dry ingredients together with milk. Chill 1 hour for ease in handling. Roll out dough to ⅛-inch thickness. Cut into desired shapes. Arrange on greased cookie sheet. Bake 6 to 8 minutes or until done. Cool; frost as desired.

Jessie's Scotch Shortbread

325 degrees   6 DOZEN SQUARES

1 lb. butter (no substitute), at room temperature
1 cup confectioners' sugar
4 cups flour, scooped and leveled
⅓ cup cornstarch

In large bowl cream butter with wooden spoon. Gradually add sugar, creaming well. Add flour and cornstarch (which have been sifted together) a little at a time, creaming until dry ingredients have been blended. Gather mixture into ball; knead with warm hands on lightly floured board for 5 to 10 minutes. With rolling pin, roll out about ½ inch-thick. Cut into 1½-inch squares; prick top with fork tines; bake on ungreased cookie sheet for 25 to 30 minutes or until barely showing signs of browning. Tops of cookies do not brown much nor do shapes of cookies change. Remove cookies to rack; allow to cool. Store in foil-lined, tightly covered tin. Shortbread may be eaten at once, but ripens and mellows with age. Keeps indefinitely.

Butterscotch Brownies

350 degrees   40 BARS

¾ cup (1½ sticks) butter or margarine
3 cups brown sugar, packed
3 eggs, beaten
2¼ cups flour, stirred and measured
2 teaspoons baking powder
¾ teaspoon salt
1 teaspoon vanilla
1 cup walnuts, coarsely chopped
1 cup grated or flaked coconut

Grease 9 x 13-inch baking pan. Melt butter or margarine; remove from heat. Blend in brown sugar. Stir in beaten eggs. Blend in sifted dry ingredients, then vanilla, nuts and coconut. Spread in prepared pan. Bake 35 minutes or until just done. Do not overbake. Cut into bars while warm.

Peanut Butter Mallow Bars

3 DOZEN

½ cup smooth peanut butter
¼ cup (½ stick) butter or margarine
½ lb. marshmallows
5 cups unsweetened prepared cereal

Melt together peanut butter, butter and marshmallows over low heat, stirring constantly. Measure cereal into large bowl. Pour syrup over cereal, blending well. Spoon mixture into buttered 9-inch square pan. Cool. Cut into 1½-inch bars.

Lemon Frosted Nut Bars

350 degrees   5 DOZEN

> ½ cup (1 stick) butter or margarine
> 1 cup flour, stirred and measured
> ½ cup brown sugar, packed
> 2 eggs
> 1½ cups brown sugar, packed
> ½ teaspoon vanilla
> 3 tablespoons flour
> ¼ teaspoon baking powder
> ¼ teaspoon salt
> 1½ cups (3½ oz.) coconut
> 1 cup nuts, chopped

Grease 9 x 13 x 2-inch pan. In small bowl cream butter. Add 1 cup flour and ½ cup brown sugar; blend well. Spread in prepared pan. Bake 12 to 15 minutes, until light brown on top. Remove from oven. In medium bowl beat together eggs, 1½ cups brown sugar and vanilla. Add sifted dry ingredients; then coconut and ¾ cup nuts; stir thoroughly. Spoon carefully over baked crust. Lower oven heat to 325 degrees; bake 20 to 25 minutes or until firm. Frost while warm with Lemon Icing (below); sprinkle with remaining chopped nuts.

LEMON ICING: To 1¾ cups confectioners' sugar add enough lemon juice to make thin icing. Spread carefully over warm cake.

NOTE: If using glass baking dish, lower baking temperatures by 25 degrees.

Quick Butterscotch Crunchies

3 DOZEN

> 2 packages (6 oz. each) butterscotch chips
> ½ cup peanut butter
> 6 cups cornflakes

Melt butterscotch chips and peanut butter together over medium heat. Stir in cornflakes. Drop from teaspoon onto waxed paper, shaping cookies with spoon. Allow to set.

Maple Pumpkin Cookies

350 degrees   3 DOZEN

- ¾ cup shortening
- 1 cup sugar
- 1 egg
- 1 cup cooked or canned pumpkin
- ½ teaspoon vanilla
- ½ teaspoon lemon extract
- 2 cups flour, stirred and measured
- 4 teaspoons baking powder
- 1 teaspoon cinnamon
- ½ teaspoon nutmeg
- ¼ teaspoon ginger
- ½ cup shredded coconut
- ½ cup nuts, chopped

In large mixing bowl, cream together shortening and sugar. Add egg, pumpkin, vanilla and lemon extract; beat well. Sift in dry ingredients; mix thoroughly. Fold in coconut and nuts. Drop onto greased cookie sheet by teaspoonfuls. Bake for 15 minutes. When cooled, frost with Maple Frosting (below).

Maple Frosting

½ CUP

- 2 tablespoons butter, softened
- 1 cup confectioners' sugar
- 2 tablespoons milk
- ½ teaspoon maple flavoring

Blend ingredients together until smooth and creamy.

Layered Party Bars

350 degrees   2 DOZEN

  ½ cup (1 stick) butter or margarine
1½ cups graham cracker crumbs (16 single crackers)
  1 can (14 oz.) sweetened condensed milk
  1 package (6 oz.) semi-sweet chocolate chips
1½ cups (3½ oz.) flaked coconut
  1 cup nuts, chopped

In 13 x 9-inch baking pan, melt butter. Sprinkle graham cracker crumbs over butter. Pour sweetened condensed milk evenly over crumbs. Top evenly with remaining ingredients, pressing down gently. Bake 25 to 30 minutes or until lightly browned. Cool thoroughly before cutting. Store, loosely covered, at room temperature.

NOTE: If using glass baking dish, lower temperature to 325 degrees.

Pineapple Bars

325 degrees   2 DOZEN

  ½ cup (1 stick) butter, softened
  ½ cup shortening
  ¾ cup sugar
  1 teaspoon vanilla
  ¼ teaspoon salt
  2 cups flour, stirred and measured
  1 can (1 lb. 4 oz.) crushed pineapple, undrained
  2 tablespoons cornstarch
  ¾ cup sugar
  1 egg yolk
  ½ teaspoon salt
  1 teaspoon lemon juice

Make crumb mixture by combining butter, shortening, sugar, vanilla, salt and flour. Press ⅔ of mixture into bottom of ungreased 8 x 12-inch baking pan. Drain a little juice from pineapple to blend with cornstarch. In medium saucepan combine remaining crushed pineapple and juice, sugar, egg yolk, salt, lemon juice and cornstarch mixture. Cook over medium heat, stirring until mixture thickens and is clear. Spread over crumb mixture in pan; sprinkle remaining crumbs over top. Bake for 50 to 60 minutes. Cut into 1 x 2-inch bars.

Rich Fudge Nut Bars

350 degrees   5 DOZEN

1 package (6 oz.) semi-sweet chocolate chips
3 tablespoons butter
1 can (14 oz.) sweetened condensed milk
2 teaspoons vanilla
¾ cup nuts, coarsely chopped
1 cup (2 sticks) butter or margarine
2 cups brown sugar, packed
2 eggs
2½ cups flour, stirred and measured
1 teaspoon baking powder
¾ teaspoon salt
¾ cup quick cooking rolled oats

Grease 10 x 15 x 1-inch baking or jelly roll pan. Melt chocolate chips, 3 tablespoons butter and sweetened condensed milk together in medium saucepan; add vanilla and nuts; cool. In large bowl cream together 1 cup butter and brown sugar; beat in eggs. Add flour, baking powder and salt that have been mixed together. Stir in rolled oats. Spread three-quarters of dough in prepared pan to make bottom crust. Spread fudge mixture evenly over crust. Dot remaining dough over top. Bake 20 to 25 minutes or until done. Cool; cut into bars.

Brownies

325 degrees   4 DOZEN

      2 cups sugar
      1 cup (2 sticks) butter or margarine
      4 eggs
      4 squares (4 oz.) unsweetened chocolate, melted and slightly
        cooled
   2½ cups sifted flour
      ¼ teaspoon salt
      ¼ teaspoon baking powder
      2 teaspoons vanilla
      1 cup nuts, broken

Grease 9 x 13 x 2-inch pan. In large bowl cream together
sugar and butter until fluffy. Beat in eggs until well
blended. Add melted chocolate; blend. Sift measured
sifted flour with salt and baking powder. Stir into batter.
Stir in vanilla and nuts. Spread into prepared pan. Bake 30
to 35 minutes or until point at which top barely springs
back when touched; do not overbake. Cool. Frost with
Chocolate Cream Cheese Frosting (below).

Chocolate Cream Cheese Frosting

                                                1½ CUPS

      1 package (3 oz.) cream cheese, softened
      1 tablespoon milk
   2½ cups sifted confectioners' sugar
      1 square (1 oz.) unsweetened chocolate, melted and cooled
        slightly
      1 teaspoon vanilla
        Dash salt

Cream together cream cheese and milk. Blend in confectioners' sugar. Stir in chocolate, then vanilla and salt. If
necessary, thin with a little milk for spreadability.

Fruit Cocktail Bars

350 degrees
27 BARS

 1 *can (17 oz.) fruit cocktail (1½ cups drained fruit)*
 2 *eggs*
1⅓ *cups sugar*
2¼ *cups flour, stirred and measured*
 ¾ *teaspoon soda*
 ½ *teaspoon salt*
 1 *teaspoon vanilla*
1¼ *cups (3½ oz.) coconut*
 ¼ *cup walnuts, chopped*
  Glaze (below)

Grease 9 x 13 x 2-inch baking pan. Drain fruit cocktail. Beat eggs and sugar together until fluffy. Add drained fruit cocktail, flour, soda, salt and vanilla. Beat at medium speed until mixture forms a batter, about 1 minute. Spread batter in prepared baking pan. Sprinkle coconut and nuts over top. Bake for 30 to 35 minutes or until cake tests done. (If glass baking dish is used, lower oven temperature to 325 degrees.) While cake is still hot, drizzle glaze over top. Cool and cut into bars.

GLAZE:

 ¾ *cup sugar*
 ½ *cup (1 stick) butter or margarine*
 ¼ *cup evaporated milk*
 ½ *teaspoon vanilla*
 ½ *cup walnuts, chopped*

Combine sugar, butter and evaporated milk in small saucepan. Bring to boil; boil 2 minutes, stirring constantly. Remove from heat. Stir in vanilla and nuts. Pour over warm cake.

Applesauce Brownies

350 degrees   35 SQUARES

  ¾ cup plus 2 tablespoons vegetable oil
  2 cups sugar
  4 eggs
  1 cup applesauce
  2 teaspoons vanilla
  2 cups plus 2 tablespoons sifted whole wheat flour
  1 teaspoon baking powder
  ½ teaspoon salt
  ½ teaspoon soda
  ½ cup cocoa
  1 cup nuts, chopped

Grease 9 x 13 x 2-inch pan. In large bowl blend together oil and sugar. Beat in eggs, applesauce and vanilla. Sift measured sifted whole wheat flour with other dry ingredients; add to batter. Stir in nuts. Pour batter into prepared pan. Bake for 35 to 40 minutes. Cut into squares. Especially good when eaten warm.

Lemon Bars

350 degrees   3 DOZEN

  2 cups flour, stirred and measured
  ½ cup confectioners' sugar
  1 cup (2 sticks) butter or margarine
  4 eggs
  2 cups granulated sugar
  5 tablespoons flour
  1 teaspoon baking powder
    Pinch salt
  ¼ teaspoon nutmeg
  ⅓ cup lemon juice
  2 tablespoons grated lemon rind (2 lemons)
    Confectioners' sugar

In large bowl combine flour and confectioners' sugar; cut in butter until crumbly. Press evenly in 9 x 13-inch pan. Bake 20 minutes. In meantime, in small bowl beat eggs and sugar together until light colored; stir in flour, baking powder, salt, nutmeg, lemon juice and rind. While crust is still hot, spread immediately with lemon mixture; continue to bake for another 25 to 30 minutes or until light golden brown. While warm, sprinkle with additional confectioners' sugar. Cool; cut into bars.

Tea Bars

3 DOZEN

½ cup (1 stick) butter
5 tablespoons cocoa
1 egg, slightly beaten
¼ cup sugar
1 teaspoon vanilla
1 cup coconut
½ cup walnuts, chopped
2 cups (20 single crackers) graham cracker crumbs
3 tablespoons milk
2 cups sifted confectioners' sugar
¼ cup (½ stick) butter, softened
2 tablespoons packaged vanilla pudding and pie filling mix
4 squares (4 oz.) semi-sweet chocolate
1 tablespoon butter

In double boiler melt together ½ cup butter, cocoa, egg, ¼ cup sugar and vanilla; blend until smooth. Add coconut, walnuts and graham cracker crumbs; stir until blended. Pat evenly in 9 x 9-inch pan. Cream together milk, confectioners' sugar, ¼ cup butter and pudding mix; spread over crumb mixture. Melt and blend chocolate and 1 tablespoon butter over low heat; spread over cookie mixture. Refrigerate for at least 1 hour or until ready to serve. Cut into 1½-inch squares.

Easy Filled Cookies

375 degrees   5 DOZEN

    1 cup shortening, softened
    2 cups brown sugar (packed)
    3 eggs
    ½ cup water
    1 teaspoon vanilla
    3½ cups sifted flour
    ½ teaspoon salt
    1 teaspoon soda
    ¼ teaspoon cinnamon
       Date Filling (below)

In large bowl cream together shortening, brown sugar and eggs. Stir in water and vanilla. Sift together dry ingredients; stir into batter. Drop dough by teaspoonfuls at least 2 inches apart onto ungreased baking sheet. Place ½ teaspoon date filling on top of dough, then cover with another ½ teaspoon dough. Bake for 10 to 12 minutes or until lightly browned.

DATE FILLING: In saucepan combine 2 cups chopped dates (½ lb. pitted), ¾ cup sugar and ¾ cup water. Cook slowly, stirring constantly, until thickened. Add ½ cup chopped nuts, if desired.

Lace Cookies

375 degrees   16 TO 18

    ⅔ cup blanched almonds, finely chopped
    ¼ cup sifted flour
    ¼ teaspoon salt
    ½ cup sugar
    ½ cup (1 stick) butter, melted
    2 tablespoons light cream or half-and-half

Combine almonds in saucepan with flour, salt, sugar, butter and cream. Cook until mixture begins to bubble (about 5 minutes). Remove from heat; stir briskly for a few seconds. Drop by teaspoonfuls, about 4 inches apart, on greased, lightly floured baking sheet, doing only 4 to 5 cookies at a time. Bake 5 or 6 minutes. Cool 2 minutes on baking sheet before lifting with spatula. Shape cookies over bottom of juice glass into ruffled basket. Cool. If cookies harden before they can be removed from cookie sheet, return to oven for a few seconds to soften. Fill baskets with vanilla ice cream; top with chocolate sauce or crushed sweetened strawberries, if desired. Or cookies can be rolled around handle of wooden spoon to make rolled cookies.

Pecan Kisses

300 degrees   3 DOZEN

  2 egg whites
⅛ teaspoon salt
  2 cups sifted confectioners' sugar
  1 teaspoon white vinegar
  1 teaspoon vanilla
1½ cups pecans, chopped

Beat egg whites with salt until soft peaks form. Gradually add sugar, vinegar and vanilla, beating until stiff. Stir in nuts. Drop teaspoon of mixture from tip of teaspoon onto greased baking sheet. Bake for 13 to 15 minutes. Cookies hardly change color. Cool completely; then remove carefully from baking sheet.

Zucchini Drop Cookies

350 degrees   3 DOZEN

  ½ cup (1 stick) butter or margarine
  1 cup sugar
  1 egg, beaten
  2 cups flour, stirred and measured
  ½ teaspoon salt
  1 teaspoon soda
  1 teaspoon cinnamon
  ½ teaspoon cloves
  1 cup zucchini, grated
  1 cup raisins
  1 cup nuts, chopped

Cream together butter, sugar and beaten egg on high speed for 5 minutes. Sift together flour, salt, soda and spices; stir into batter. Add zucchini; mix well. Stir in raisins and nuts. Drop by heaping teaspoonfuls onto greased cookie sheet. Bake for 12 to 15 minutes.

Oatmeal Chocolate Chip Cookies

375 degrees   3 DOZEN

  1 cup shortening
  ¾ cup granulated sugar
  ¾ cup brown sugar, packed
  2 eggs
  1 teaspoon vanilla
  1½ cups flour, scooped and leveled
  ½ teaspoon salt
  1 teaspoon soda
  1 tablespoon hot water
  2 cups quick cooking rolled oats
  1 package (6 oz.) chocolate chips
  ½ cup nuts, coarsely chopped

Cream shortening; add sugars and cream until fluffy. Beat in eggs and vanilla. Add flour and salt; then add soda that's been dissolved in hot water; blend. Stir in rolled oats, chocolate chips and nuts. Drop by teaspoonfuls onto ungreased baking sheet about 1½ inches apart. Bake for 10 minutes or until barely brown and still a little puffy. For crisper cookies bake until cookies flatten.

NOTE: Coconut, raisins and/or peanuts may be added to this basic cookie dough. Or 1 cup coarsely grated carrots, cooked in 2 tablespoons boiling water for 5 minutes, may be added.

NOTE: Recipe may be doubled.

Meltaways

350 degrees   2 DOZEN

  ½ *lb. (2 sticks) butter (no substitute)*
  ¾ *cup cornstarch*
  ⅓ *cup confectioners' sugar*
  1 *cup flour, stirred and measured*
     Meltaway Frosting (below)

Cream butter; gradually add cornstarch and sugar. Blend in flour. Drop mixture by teaspoonfuls onto ungreased baking sheet. Bake 10 to 12 minutes until done, but not brown. Cool and frost.

MELTAWAY FROSTING:
  1 *package (3 oz.) cream cheese, softened*
  1 *teaspoon vanilla*
  1 *cup confectioners' sugar*
     Few drops food coloring (yellow, pink or light green)

Cream together all ingredients.

Butterscotch Cookies

350 degrees   5 DOZEN

½ cup (1 stick) butter or margarine
1½ cups brown sugar, packed
2 eggs
1 teaspoon vanilla
2½ cups flour, stirred and measured
1 teaspoon soda
½ teaspoon baking powder
½ teaspoon salt
1 cup dairy sour cream (or 1 cup evaporated milk plus 1
   tablespoon vinegar)
⅔ cup nuts, chopped

In large mixing bowl cream together butter and brown sugar until light and fluffy. Add eggs and vanilla; beat until blended. Add sifted dry ingredients alternately with sour cream, stirring well after each addition. Stir in nuts. Drop by teaspoonfuls onto buttered cookie sheet. Bake 10 minutes. When cool, frost with Browned Butter Icing (below).

Browned Butter Frosting

1½ CUPS

¼ cup (½ stick) butter (no substitute)
2 cups confectioners' sugar
2 to 3 tablespoons boiling water
½ teaspoon vanilla

In small saucepan melt butter; continue cooking over medium heat until butter becomes a nut brown color and stops bubbling. Remove from heat. Blend in confectioners' sugar and enough boiling water to make spreadable. Stir in vanilla. If frosting becomes too stiff, add a few more drops of water.

Parfait Cookies

350 degrees   3 DOZEN

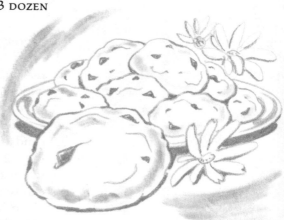

- ¾ cup granulated sugar
- ¾ cup brown sugar, packed
- ¾ cup (1½ sticks) butter or margarine
- 2 eggs
- 2 teaspoons almond extract
- 3 cups (approximately) flour, stirred and measured
- ½ teaspoon salt
- ½ teaspoon soda
- 4 oz. milk chocolate, broken into ½-inch chunks
- ¾ cup nuts, broken

In large bowl cream together sugars and butter. Beat in eggs and flavoring. Blend in 2 cups of the flour mixed with salt and soda. With wooden spoon add additional flour so that dough just barely ceases to be sticky, about 1 more cup. Stir in chocolate and nuts. Drop by heaping teaspoonfuls onto greased baking sheet. Bake for 8 to 9 minutes or until done. Do not overbake. Cookies should have just a tinge of brown but mostly remain white, and soft and high.

Peanut Butter Chews (Uncooked)

30 PIECES

- ½ cup peanut butter
- ½ cup corn syrup
- ⅔ cup confectioners' sugar
- ¾ to 1 cup instant nonfat dry milk

Combine peanut butter and corn syrup. Gradually add sugar; stir until smooth. Add dry milk a little at a time until mixture is stiff enough to handle. Shape into roll 15 inches long by 1 inch in diameter; slice off ½-inch pieces. If desired, wrap individually in plastic wrap, twisting ends.

Candy Cookery

Cooking candy to the correct degree of doneness is critical to success. There are two ways to determine when candy is cooked sufficiently—making the cold water test and checking the temperature with a good candy thermometer. Good candy makers usually make both tests as a double check.

COLD WATER TEST: Remove saucepan of cooking candy from heat when candy thermometer registers at least 2 degrees below temperature specified in recipe or when candy seems to be nearing the "done" stage. (If candy is left on heat while being tested, it may overcook.) Drop ½ teaspoon of hot syrup from tip of spoon into very cold (but not ice) water. Let stand 1 minute. Pick up and test candy between thumb, index and middle fingers and feel the stage to which candy has cooked.

SOFT BALL - Hot syrup makes a soft ball when you pick it up, but it does not hold its shape. For fudge, penuche and fondant.

FIRM BALL - Hot syrup makes a firm ball that holds its shape when picked up. For caramels and caramel corn.

SOFT CRACK - Syrup forms hard, but not brittle, threads rather than a ball. For toffee and butterscotch.

HARD CRACK - Syrup forms brittle threads that break between fingers. For brittles, lollipops and caramel or candy apples.

HIGH ALTITUDE ADJUSTMENTS IN CANDY MAKING: Temperatures in candy recipes are for sea level. If you are using a candy thermometer, you will need to make adjustments for high altitudes. To determine temperature adjustment for your altitude, check the temperature registered on your thermometer when it is set in saucepan of vigorously boiling water for 1 minute. Without removing thermometer, record temperature. If you are at sea level, the thermometer will register 212 degrees. If you are at a high altitude, the temperature on your thermometer will be less than 212 degrees. Subtract the temperature registered on your thermometer from 212 degrees. This will be your adjustment. Subtract that difference from each temperature given in the recipes. For example, if your thermometer registers 203 degrees, you will subtract 9 degrees (212 degrees minus 203 degrees) from candy temperature given in a recipe. It is suggested you write down adjustment on each recipe so it will always be handy.

DURING HUMID WEATHER or on rainy days, cook candy 1 or 2 degrees higher than you would on a normal day.

Old Fashioned Fudge

64 PIECES (1½ LBS.)

3 squares (3 oz.) unsweetened chocolate
1 cup milk
3 cups sugar
2 tablespoons light corn syrup
⅛ teaspoon salt
¼ cup (½ stick) butter or margarine
1 teaspoon vanilla
1 cup nuts, coarsely broken

In heavy 3-quart saucepan combine chocolate and milk. Cook over low heat, stirring constantly until milk is scalded and chocolate is melted. Add sugar, 1 cup at a time, stirring thoroughly to be sure it is dissolved after each addition. Add corn syrup and salt; bring to boil. Cover pan for 3 minutes. Cook without stirring to soft ball stage (235 to 238 degrees). Remove from heat; add butter without stirring. Let stand without disturbing until mixture is cool enough to touch on bottom of pan. Add vanilla. Beat until candy loses its gloss and starts to thicken. Stir in nuts and pour quickly into lightly buttered 8-inch square pan. (Do not scrape pan.) Cool and cut into pieces.

NOTE: Candy temperature is for sea level. For high altitude adjustment, p. 294.

American Style Nougat

162 PIECES (5 LBS.)

PART 1:

1½ cups sugar
1¼ cups light corn syrup
¼ cup water
3 small egg whites

PART 2:

3 cups sugar
3 cups light corn syrup
4 teaspoons vanilla
½ cup melted butter
1 teaspoon salt
3 cups blanched slivered almonds, delicately toasted

PART I: Combine sugar, corn syrup and water in 3-quart heavy saucepan. Cook over medium heat, stirring until sugar dissolves. Continue to cook at low boil to soft ball stage (238 degrees). When syrup reaches 230 degrees, beat egg whites until they stand in peaks. When syrup reaches 238 degrees, add it in a fine stream to egg whites, beating constantly with electric mixer on medium speed, or with wooden spoon, until mixture becomes thick and is lukewarm. It will keep several days if well covered with foil or waxed paper and stored in refrigerator.

PART II: Combine sugar and corn syrup in 4-quart heavy saucepan. Cook over medium heat, stirring constantly, to 275 degrees. Meanwhile, place Part I in lightly buttered large bowl. Pour hot candy (Part II) over it all at one time. Mix with heavy wooden spoon. Slowly add vanilla and butter, continuing to mix with heavy wooden spoon. Add salt and nuts; mix again. Turn into 2 well buttered 9-inch square pans, flattening top of candy with buttered hands. Let stand several hours. Turn onto cutting board; cut each pan of candy into 1-inch squares (81 pieces) and wrap immediately with waxed paper. Keeps well in refrigerator or freezer.

NOTE: Candy temperature is for sea level. For high altitude adjustment, see p. 294.

Spun Peanut Brittle

2¼ LBS.

2 cups sugar
1 cup light corn syrup
1 cup water
2 cups raw peanuts
¼ teaspoon salt
¼ cup (½ stick) butter or margarine
1 teaspoon soda

In heavy saucepan combine sugar, corn syrup and water. Cook over medium heat, stirring constantly until sugar is dissolved. Continue cooking until mixture reaches soft ball stage (236 degrees). Add peanuts and salt. Cook to just beyond soft crack stage (300 degrees). Remove from heat. Add butter and soda, stirring to blend. (Mixture will foam.) Pour onto 2 large buttered baking sheets. Lift candy around edges with spatula and run spatula under candy to cool it partially and to keep it from sticking. As soon as it begins to set, stretch out with forks and fingers to make it as thin as possible. (Since you need to work fast, it is helpful if there are two people working.) When cold, break carefully into pieces. Store in airtight containers or tightly closed plastic bags in freezer or cold place.

NOTE: Candy temperature is for sea level. For high altitude adjustment, see p. 294.

Almond Crunch Toffee

1¼ LBS.

1 cup (2 sticks) butter or margarine
1 cup sugar
2 tablespoons water
1 tablespoon light corn syrup
¼ teaspoon salt
¾ cup slivered blanched almonds
½ teaspoon vanilla
1 milk chocolate bar (8 oz.)
¼ cup walnuts, finely chopped

In 2-quart heavy saucepan melt butter over low heat. Remove from heat and add sugar; stir until sugar is dissolved. Add water, corn syrup and salt; mix well. Stir and cook over medium low heat to soft crack stage (290 degrees). Remove from heat. Add ¾ cup almonds and vanilla; stir quickly. Pour into lightly buttered 13 x 9 x 2-inch pan; quickly spread with spatula. When candy is cool, remove without breaking and place on waxed paper. Spread with chocolate that has been melted over hot water. Sprinkle with finely chopped nuts. When candy is cold, break into pieces. Pack between layers of waxed paper in airtight container. Store in cool place.

NOTE: Candy temperature is for sea level. For high altitude adjustment, see p. 294.

Lollipops

2 DOZEN 2-INCH LOLLIPOPS

2 cups sugar
⅔ cup light corn syrup
1 cup water
½ teaspoon oil of peppermint
5 drops red food coloring

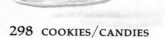

Combine sugar, corn syrup and water in heavy saucepan. Heat until sugar dissolves. Cook, without stirring, to hard-crack stage (300 degrees). Add oil of peppermint and coloring. Cool slightly. Lay 24 skewers 4-inches apart on greased cookie sheet. Drop syrup from tip of teaspoon over skewers to form 2-inch lollipops.

NOTE: Candy temperature is for sea level. For high altitude adjustment, see p. 294.

NOTE: Other flavorings and colors may be used.

Caramels

81 PIECES (3½ LBS.)

  2 cups light corn syrup
  2 cups sugar
  3 cups heavy cream (heavier cream gives greater volume)
  ½ can (14 oz. size) sweetened condensed milk
  1 tablespoon vanilla
  1 cup walnuts, coarsely broken

In heavy saucepan boil together syrup and sugar until mixture changes color and spins a light thread. In mean-time combine heavy cream and sweetened condensed milk in double boiler and scald over boiling water; keep warm. Add warm cream to syrup, ¼ cup at a time, stirring well; allow 45 minutes for total addition. Keep candy boiling lightly over medium heat, stirring frequently. Cook to firm ball stage (242 degrees). Remove from heat; stir in nuts and vanilla. Pour, without scraping pan, into buttered 9 x 9-inch pan. Let stand several hours without moving. Remove candy from pan; cut into 1-inch squares. Wrap in pieces of waxed paper.

NOTE: Candy temperature is for sea level. For high altitude adjustment, see p. 294.

Bavarian Mints

5 DOZEN PIECES (2 LBS.)

1 lb. milk chocolate
1 square (1 oz.) unsweetened chocolate
2 tablespoons butter
1 can (14 oz.) sweetened condensed milk
3 to 6 drops oil of peppermint or 1 teaspoon peppermint extract
¼ teaspoon vanilla

Melt milk chocolate, unsweetened chocolate and butter over hot, not boiling, water. Combine with sweetened condensed milk. Stir in peppermint and vanilla. Pour into buttered 8 x 8 x 2-inch pan. Cool. Cut in 1-inch squares.

Aplets

3 DOZEN PIECES (1½ LBS.)

½ cup cold applesauce
2 envelopes (1 T. each) unflavored gelatin
¾ cup applesauce
2 cups sugar
1 cup walnuts, broken
1 tablespoon vanilla

Soak gelatin in cold applesauce. In meantime, combine ¾ cup applesauce with sugar in medium saucepan; bring to boil; then cook 10 minutes. Add gelatin mixture to hot mixture; cook and stir 15 minutes longer. Remove from heat. Stir in nuts and vanilla. Pour into loaf tin that's been rinsed with cold water. Refrigerate overnight. Loosen edges and, working with fingers, loosen from bottom of pan onto mound of powdered sugar. Cut into 1-inch squares; roll each piece in powdered sugar.

COTLETS: Drain 1 can (29 oz.) or 1 quart apricots. In blender puree apricots. Use in place of applesauce in above recipe.

Vinegar Taffy

1¼ LBS.

2 cups sugar
½ cup vinegar
½ cup water
1 tablespoon butter
¼ teaspoon soda

Combine sugar, vinegar and water in heavy saucepan. Cook, stirring constantly until sugar dissolves. Cook over medium high heat, stirring as little as possible, to the light crack stage (264 degrees). Add butter and soda; stir and remove from heat. Pour onto buttered shallow platter; cool, turning outside edges to inside to speed the cooling. When cool enough to handle, pull with buttered fingers until thick and ropy. Cut into bite-size pieces with buttered scissors. If desired, wrap individual pieces in waxed paper. Place in airtight containers and put into freezer or refrigerator.

NOTE: Candy temperature is for sea level. For high altitude adjustment, see p. 294.

Honey Candy

2 LBS.

2 cups honey
1 cup sugar
1 cup cream

Combine ingredients in heavy saucepan. Stir over low heat until sugar is dissolved. Cook, stirring as little as possible, until mixture reaches hard ball stage (260 degrees). Remove from heat; pour onto buttered shallow pan or buttered platter. Turn edges in with spatula so they will not harden and candy will cool more quickly. When barely cool enough to handle, pull, using only buttered finger tips, until light and fluffy. Twist into ropes of desired thickness. With scissors cut into pieces of desired size.

A Bunch Of Crunch

1 package (any size) cornflakes
1 package (any size) oven-toasted rice cereal
2 cups flaked coconut (sweetened or unsweetened)
1 lb. (4 cups) salted peanuts
2 cups sugar
2 cups white corn syrup
1 cup milk
1 teaspoon vanilla

In large bowl mix together cereals, coconut and peanuts. In medium saucepan combine sugar, corn syrup and milk; cook and stir until mixture reaches soft ball stage, washing down sides of pan. Remove from heat; stir in vanilla. Pour over cereal mixture; stir until entirely coated. Turn out onto counter top; separate into pieces to cool. Store in cool dry place.

Popcorn Balls

18 TO 24 BALLS

2 cups sugar
⅔ cup light corn syrup
⅔ cup water
½ cup (1 stick) butter or margarine
1½ teaspoons salt
1½ teaspoons vanilla
5 quarts popped corn

Combine sugar, corn syrup, water, butter and salt in heavy pan. Cook, stirring until sugar dissolves. Continue cooking without stirring until mixture reaches light crack stage (278 degrees). Add vanilla. Pour syrup slowly over popped corn; mix well. Wet hands slightly and shape into balls 2½ inches in diameter, using only enough pressure to press balls into shape.

NOTE: Candy temperature is for sea level. For high altitude adjustment, see p. 294.

Caramel Apples

15 TO 20 CARAMEL APPLES

15 to 20 small apples (Jonathans best)
4 cups granulated sugar
1 cup (scant) light corn syrup
2⅔ cups evaporated milk

Select small apples free from blemishes; wash and dry thoroughly and stick in wooden skewers. Put sugar, syrup and ⅔ cup evaporated milk in large, heavy kettle; stir to blend well. Heat slowly until sugar is dissolved, stirring constantly. Cook briskly to thick syrup, stirring all the while. Add remainder of milk slowly, keeping mixture boiling briskly. Cook to firm ball stage (242 degrees), stirring constantly to prevent scorching. Remove from heat; let stand until caramel stops bubbling. Working quickly, dip apples, one at a time, in caramel, twisting to get rid of surplus coating and to make smooth. Place on buttered foil. If coating becomes too thick for dipping, add a little evaporated milk and reheat, stirring to keep smooth. The caramel should be kept hot during dipping so coating will not be too heavy.

NOTE: Candy temperature is for sea level. For high altitude adjustment, see p. 294.

Quick Caramel Corn

5 QUARTS

2 cups brown sugar, packed
½ cup (1 stick) butter or margarine
½ cup light corn syrup
5 quarts popped corn

Combine sugar, butter and corn syrup in heavy saucepan. Cook and stir over medium heat until sugar dissolves and mixture boils. Simmer for 5 minutes. Remove from heat. Pour over popped corn, stirring until all corn is coated. Turn out onto clean cool surface; spread out. When thoroughly cooled, break into pieces.

Chocolate Almond Balls

4 DOZEN

3 milk chocolate almond bars (8 oz. each), chopped
1 carton (12 oz.) non-dairy whipped topping
½ package (6 oz.) vanilla wafers, crushed fine

Melt chocolate over hot, not boiling, water. Stir into non-dairy whipped topping; blend well. Chill slightly; with spoons shape into balls about 1½-inch in diameter. Roll in vanilla wafer crumbs. Place on waxed paper; chill in refrigerator until time to serve. May be frozen.

NOTE: 1 teaspoon rum extract may be added for flavor.

Hot Spiced Nuts

3 CUPS

1 cup sugar
1 teaspoon cinnamon
6 tablespoons milk
3 cups unsalted nuts
½ teaspoon vanilla

Combine sugar, cinnamon and milk in saucepan. Cook to soft ball stage (236 degrees). Remove from heat. Add nuts and vanilla; stir until creamy. Turn out at once onto waxed paper; separate. Serve warm or cold.

NOTE: Mixture cooks to soft ball stage quickly, so watch carefully. Cold water test works well with this recipe.

NOTE: Candy temperature is for sea level. For high altitude adjustment, see p. 294.

Chili Nuts

5 CUPS

3 tablespoons butter or margarine
2 cups (8 oz.) unblanched almonds
2 cups (8 oz.) salted blanched peanuts
2 cups (8 oz.) cashews
2 tablespoons sesame seeds, toasted (optional)
1¼ teaspoons chili powder
1 teaspoon ground cumin (cominos)
1 teaspoon paprika
½ teaspoon garlic powder
1½ teaspoons salt

In large skillet melt butter. Add nuts. Cook, stirring constantly, until nuts are golden, 2 to 5 minutes. Remove from heat. Add sesame seeds, spices and salt; mix well. With slotted spoon remove nuts to paper towel to drain. Cool.

NOTE: For Curried Nuts, replace spices in above recipe with 1 teaspoon each curry powder, ground ginger and ground coriander, and ½ teaspoon powdered mustard.

Toasted Salted Nuts

325 degrees

Use any combination desired of shelled nuts. Spread shelled blanched almonds, cashews and/or brazil nuts on baking sheet; bake for 20 minutes; stirring occasionally. Add shelled walnuts and/or pecans; continue baking another 25 minutes, stirring 2 or 3 times more. Put nuts into mixing bowl; add just enough vegetable oil and melted margarine (equal parts combined) to barely coat each nut. Salt to taste.

Preserved Foods

Every spring Utah's fruit crops are in jeopardy. Fragile fruit blossoms and tiny buds are possible prey for the icy fingers of a capricious frost.

That's why Utahns rejoice when their crops survive and go on to mature. With gusto they eat their fruits fresh, then preserve the rest by canning, drying or freezing. They remember the counsel of Brigham Young: "Everything we used to feed the life of man or beast, no grain of it should . . . go to waste."

Recipes for preserving fruits and vegetables are passed from hand to hand and the best ones exchanged again—recipes like the one for Frozen Fruit Cocktail that is used in hundred of homes every fall and the resourceful recipe for freezing peach pie filling without using any pie dishes as freezing containers.

The Slow-Cooked Apple Butter recipe came from a home economist friend. The recipe for Sweet Mustard Pickles was given us by a former Mrs. America who made the pickles every summer with her grandmother in Heber City.

A resident of Davis County shared step-by-step instructions for drying apricots with readers years ago, and many are still following his directions.

Oh, there is reward, not only materially but spiritually, in gathering the fruit of the harvest and preserving it to last beyond its own season.

Apricot Syrup

5 HALF-PINTS

4 cups apricot puree
1 cup water
3 tablespoons lemon juice
4 cups sugar
½ teaspoon butter

Combine all ingredients in a 3-quart saucepan. Bring to boil over medium high heat; boil for 5 minutes, stirring constantly. Remove from heat. Pour into sterilized jars, leaving ¼-inch head space and adjust lids. Process in boiling water bath for 15 minutes. Use as syrup for pancakes or waffles or as sauce for ice cream.

Frozen Peach Pie Filling

425 degrees   FOR 5 PIES

3½ cups sugar
2 teaspoons ascorbic acid powder
4 quarts fresh peaches, sliced
½ cup plus 2 tablespoons quick cooking tapioca
⅓ to ½ cup lemon juice
1 teaspoon salt

Blend together sugar and ascorbic acid powder. Stir in remaining ingredients. Line five 8-inch pie dishes with foil, leaving enough extra foil for each to wrap around frozen filling. Divide fruit mixture evenly among them. Wrap foil loosely around; freeze immediately. When frozen, lift filling out of pie dishes; wrap foil securely around them so they are air-tight. Stack in freezer. To bake, remove frozen pie filling from foil; set into pastry-lined 9-inch pie plate. Dot with 2 tablespoons butter. Arrange top pastry over filling, sealing to lower crust and crimping. Slash top crust to vent. Bake for 1 hour or until done.

Canned Apricot Pie Filling

5 QUARTS

10 lbs. apricots, washed and pitted
2 cups water
4 cups sugar
1 cup plus 2 tablespoons quick cooking tapioca
1½ cups sugar
¾ cup lemon juice

In large heavy kettle combine apricots, water and 4 cups sugar. Cook until mixture is just about ready to boil (190 degrees). Add tapioca, remaining 1½ cups sugar and lemon juice. Barely bring to boiling point again. Pour into sterilized jars. Adjust lids. Process in boiling water bath for 25 minutes. For each pie, pour 1 quart filling into unbaked 9-inch pastry shell. Dot with 2 tablespoons butter. Adjust top pastry over pie. Trim, crimp and cut vent holes. Bake at 400 degrees for 40 minutes or until crust in golden brown.

Frozen Fruit Cocktail

FOUR 1½-PINTS

3 lbs. (12 medium) fresh peaches
2 cups sugar
1 lb. seedless grapes
1 can (15¼ oz.) crushed pineapple, undrained
½ cup lemon juice (2 lemons)
1½ cups orange juice (3 oranges)

Peel peaches; cut into bite-size pieces to make 6 cups. Sprinkle with sugar; set aside while preparing remainder of fruit. Wash grapes; stem. Stir into peaches along with remaining ingredients. Spoon into plastic freezer containers; freeze. To serve while still frosty (which is when it is best), allow to stand at room temperature about 3 hours. Bananas may be added at serving time.

Easy Peach Jam

5 PINTS

5 cups peaches, drained and finely cut
½ cup orange juice (1 orange)
5 cups sugar
1 small bottle maraschino cherries, drained and chopped
1 package (3 oz.) orange flavor gelatin

In large heavy saucepan combine peaches, orange juice and sugar. Boil 15 minutes. Add maraschino cherries; cook for additional 10 minutes. Stir in gelatin. Pour into sterilized jars, leaving ¼-inch head space. Adjust lids. Process for 15 minutes in boiling water bath.

NOTE: When serving jam, stir to distribute fruit evenly.

Slow Cooked Apple Butter

6 HALF-PINTS

10 to 12 large cooking apples (14 cups), chopped
2 cups apple juice or apple cider
3 cups sugar
1½ teaspoons ground cinnamon
½ teaspoon ground cloves

Core and chop unpeeled apples. Combine with apple juice or cider in slow cooker; add sugar. (Pot may be filled to top.) Cover; cook on low setting for 10 hours or on high setting for 4 hours. Put apples into blender; blend on high speed until smooth. Return apples to slow cooker; add spices. Cook on low setting for 1 hour or until mixture reaches desired consistency. For very thick apple butter remove lid while cooking. Ladle into six sterilized half-pint jars, leaving ½-inch headspace. Adjust lids. Process in boiling water bath for 10 minutes. Apple butter will keep several weeks in refrigerator.

Bing Cherry Jam

FIVE HALF-PINTS

4 cups pitted sweet dark cherries
1 package powdered pectin
¼ cup lemon juice (2 lemons)
1 teaspooon almond extract
¼ teaspoon salt
½ teaspoon ground cinnamon
½ teaspoon ground cloves
4½ cups sugar

Place all ingredients but sugar in a 6 quart kettle. Bring mixture to a boil that cannot be stirred down. Immediately add sugar. Bring mixture to a boil; continue boiling for 2 minutes. Skim mixture. Pour hot jam immediately into hot jars, leaving ¼-inch head space. Adjust caps. Process 10 minutes in boiling water bath.

Canned Huckleberries

2 QUARTS

8 quarts stemmed, washed berries
1 teaspoon soda
2 lemons, juiced
5 cups sugar

In large saucepan cover huckleberries with water. Bring to boiling; boil 5 minutes. Add soda; cook another 5 minutes. Drain. Cover berries with fresh water. Bring to boil. Add lemon juice and sugar. Cook for 30 minutes, until juice is slightly heavy. Pour into sterilized quart jars. Adjust lids and seal. Process in boiling water bath for 30 minutes. Two quarts canned huckleberries will make three 8-inch pies.

Dried Apricots

2½ QUARTS

1½ cups sugar
½ cup light corn syrup
1½ teaspoons ascorbic acid powder
2 cups water
1 lug (½ bushel) fresh apricots

Combine all ingredients but apricots. Heat only long enough to dissolve sugar; then cool. Using only small ripe, blemish-free apricots, spray clean with water and allow to dry fully. With knife cut apricots in half. Dip apricots immediately into cooled syrup. Drain thoroughly. Arrange cut side up on drying racks so fruit halves barely touch. Cover with nylon or plastic netting to protect from insects. Allow to dry in direct sun for 2½ to 3 days. When apricots are dry around edges and barely sticky, place in brown paper grocery sack, filling ¼ to ⅓ full. Fold top closed; hang from clothesline with clothespins. Leave for 1 to 3 days, agitating apricots at least once daily. Check fruit each day. When it is rubbery, with no moist spots, and feels like a raisin, it is ready to put into jars. Pack apricots rather tightly into clean fruit jars. (Do not store in plastic bags.) Cover jars with clean lids; screw on bands loosely. Set fruit into preheated 200 degrees oven for 30 minutes. Remove jars from oven, screw bands tightly and cool. Although fruit jars will probably seal as they cool, it is not necessary that they do so.

Apricot Leather

Wash apricots thoroughly, drain well, halve and pit. Measure fruit halves. For every cup of fruit add 1 tablespoon honey and ½ tablespoon lemon juice. Heat slightly in large kettle; then put through food grinder or whir in blender until smooth. Spread fruit puree about ⅛-inch thick on plastic wrap. Lay clean nylon netting over fruit, taking care that it does not touch fruit. Place in direct sunlight. When leather feels firm to touch and is dry in center (may take a couple of days), peel fruit leather in one piece from plastic wrap. Place leather on clean sheet of plastic wrap; roll up, plastic wrap and all, into scroll-like package. Wrap again in plastic wrap; place in airtight container, cover tightly and store in cool place. Several rolls of leather will fit into one fruit jar.

NOTE: Chinese apricots have an especially good flavor for fruit leather.

Poor Man's Strawberry Jam

3½ PINTS

- 2 cups fresh strawberries, mashed
- 2 cups water
- 1 package (0.23 oz.) unsweetened strawberry flavor punch powder
- 1 package (2 oz.) powdered pectin
- 6 cups sugar

In large heavy kettle combine strawberries, water, punch powder and pectin. Bring to boil. Add sugar; stir thoroughly and boil 3 minutes. Remove from heat; let stand 3 minutes. Pour into sterilized jars, adjust lids. Process 15 minutes in boiling water bath. Before serving, stir to distribute strawberries evenly through jam.

NOTE: Other combinations of fruit and punch powder may be used according to availability of fruit and taste.

Watermelon Pickles

5 PINTS

3 quarts watermelon rind (6 lbs. unpared or ½ large melon)
¾ cup salt
3 quarts cold water
2 quarts ice cubes
1 tablespoon whole cloves
3 sticks cinnamon, broken in half
2 pieces ginger root
9 cups sugar
3 cups white vinegar, 4 to 6 percent acidity
3 cups water
1 lemon, thinly sliced

To prepare watermelon rind, trim dark skin and pink flesh from thick watermelon rind. Cut in 1-inch pieces or as wanted. Dissolve salt in 3 quarts cold water; add ice cubes. Pour over rind; let stand 6 hours. Drain; rinse in cold water. Cover with cold water; cook until just tender, about 10 minutes. Drain. Tie spices in cheesecloth bag; combine with remaining ingredients. Simmer 5 minutes; pour over watermelon. Let stand overnight. Heat watermelon in syrup to boiling; cook until watermelon is translucent, about 10 minutes. Pack boiling hot pickles loosely in hot pint jars, adding 1 piece stick cinnamon from spice bag to each jar. Cover with boiling syrup to ½ inch of top. Adjust jar lids. Process 10 minutes in boiling water bath.

Frozen Cream Style Corn

350 degrees

4 QUARTS

4 quarts fresh corn, cut from cobs
1 cup half-and-half cream
⅓ cup sugar
4 teaspoons salt

Combine all ingredients and spread in shallow pan. Bake for approximately 45 minutes or until slightly thickened, stirring frequently. Cool until only slightly warm. Put into freezer containers, allowing ½ cup per serving. Seal and freeze.

NOTE: An electric carving knife works well for cutting fresh corn from cobs.

Sweet Mustard Pickles

12 PINTS

1 quart cucumbers, quartered and sliced
1 quart green tomatoes, quartered and sliced
6 sweet red peppers, cut in ¾-inch chunks
2 bunches celery, thinly sliced
1 head cauliflower, sliced
1 quart pickling onions
3 cups sugar
3 cups white vinegar (4 to 6 percent acidity)
2 cups water
¼ cup pickling salt
¾ cup flour
6 tablespoons dry mustard
1 tablespoon turmeric
1 cup cold water

Clean and cut first five vegetables. Pour boiling water over whole pickling onions; allow to stand 2 or 3 minutes; then slip off skins. In large kettle combine sugar, vinegar, 2 cups water and salt. Add all vegetables but cauliflower. Bring to boil. Blend together flour, mustard, turmeric; stir in cold water to make smooth paste. Stir into vegetables; cook and stir until mixture is thick and smooth. Add cauliflower. Bring to boil; simmer 5 minutes. Pack into hot jars, leaving ¼ inch head space. Adjust caps. Process 10 minutes in boiling water bath.

Hot Dog Relish

8 PINTS

4 cups (7 large) onions
4 cups (1 medium) cabbage
4 cups (10 large) green tomatoes
5 cups (12 large) green peppers
1½ cups (6 large) sweet red peppers
½ cup pickling salt
6 cups sugar
1 tablespoon celery seed
2 tablespoons mustard seed
1½ teaspoons turmeric
4 cups cider vinegar (4 to 6 percent acidity)
2 cups water

Chop or grind vegetables using coarse blade. Sprinkle with ½ cup salt; let stand several hours or overnight. Rinse and drain. Combine remaining ingredients; pour over vegetable mixture. Heat to a boil; simmer 3 minutes. Pour into sterilized jars, leaving ¼-inch head space. Adjust lids. Process in boiling water bath for 10 minutes.

Zucchini Pickles

5 HALF-PINTS

2 lbs. fresh firm zucchini
2 small onions
1 sweet red pepper
1 sweet green pepper
¼ cup salt
2 cups sugar
2 teaspoons mustard seed
1 teaspoon celery salt
1 teaspoon turmeric
3 cups vinegar (4 to 6 percent acidity)

Wash zucchini and cut in thin slices. Peel and cut onions in quarters, then into thin slices. Slice peppers thinly. In large pan combine zucchini, onion, red and green pepper and salt. Cover with ice cubes and let stand 2 hours. Drain thoroughly. Bring remaining ingredients to boiling. Pour over vegetables. Let stand 2 hours. Bring all ingredients to boiling point and heat 5 minutes. Pack, boiling hot, into hot jars, leaving ¼-inch head space. Adjust caps. Process 15 minutes in boiling water bath.

Corn Relish

7 PINTS

2 quarts (16 to 20 medium ears) corn
2 cups (5 medium) sweet red peppers, chopped
2 cups (5 medium) sweet green peppers, chopped
1 quart (1 large bunch) celery, chopped
1 cup (1 medium) onion, chopped
1½ cups sugar
1 quart vinegar (4 to 6 percent acidity)
1½ tablespoons salt
2 teaspoons celery seed
1 tablespoon mustard seed
1 tablespoon dry mustard
1 tablespoon turmeric

To prepare corn, boil 5 minutes, then cut from cob. (An electric knife works well for this.) Combine with remaining ingredients; simmer 20 minutes. Bring to boiling. Pack, boiling hot, into hot pint jars, leaving ¼-inch head space. Adjust caps. Process 15 minutes in boiling water bath.

Pickled Beets

3 quarts cooked small beets, peeled
2 cups sugar
2 sticks cinnamon
1 tablespoon whole allspice
1 tablespoon whole cloves
1½ teaspoons salt
3½ cups vinegar (4 to 6 percent acidity)
1½ cups water

To cook beets: Wash and drain beets. Leave 2 inches of stems and the tap roots. Cover with boiling water; cook until tender. Combine all ingredients except beets; simmer 15 minutes. Pack peeled and trimmed beets into hot jars, leaving ¼-inch head space. Pour liquid over. Adjust caps. Process 30 minutes in boiling water bath.

Dill Pickles Kosher Style

7 PINTS

¾ cup sugar
½ cup granulated salt
1 quart vinegar (4 to 6 percent acidity)
1 quart water
3 tablespoons mixed pickling spices
30 to 40 medium cucumbers, scrubbed and cut in half lengthwise
    Dill plant, fresh or dried (1 head per jar)
    Garlic buds (1 bud per jar)
    Hot red peppers (1 piece per jar)
1 teaspoon mustard seed per jar

Combine sugar, salt, vinegar and water. Tie pickling spices in cheesecloth bag; add to vinegar mixture; simmer 15 minutes. Pack cucumbers into hot jars, leaving ¼-inch head space; put dill, garlic bud, hot red pepper piece and mustard seeds into each jar. Heat brine to boiling. Pour boiling hot vinegar mixture over cucumbers to within ¼-inch of top. Adjust caps. Process 15 minutes in boiling water bath.

NOTE: Leaving dill pickles a full year before opening assures a stronger, better flavor. Some canners plan it so that they are canning dill pickles for use two seasons ahead rather than for the usual winter season just ahead.

Green Tomato Relish

12 PINTS

2 quarts (10 large) green tomatoes
2 quarts (10 large) unpeeled cucumbers
1 quart (2½ lbs.) onions
1 quart (9 large) green peppers
3 red peppers
3 cups vinegar
6 cups sugar
1½ tablespoons mustard seed
2 tablespoons pickling salt
1½ tablespoons turmeric
1½ teaspoons celery seed

Chop or grind all vegetables with coarse blade; combine with remaining ingredients in large heavy kettle. Bring to boil; simmer for 20 minutes. Pour into sterilized jars, leaving ¼-inch head space. Adjust lids. Process in boiling water bath for 10 minutes.

Chili Sauce

8 PINTS

4 quarts (24 large) tomatoes, peeled, cored and chopped
6 cups (6 medium) onions, chopped
1¼ cups (3 medium) green peppers, chopped
2 cups vinegar (4 to 6 percent acidity)
1½ cups sugar
1 tablespoon salt
⅛ teaspoon cayenne pepper
2 teaspoons ground cinnamon
½ teaspoon ground cloves
½ teaspoon ground allspice

Combine all ingredients in large saucepan. Bring to boil; simmer until as thick as desired, about 2 to 3 hours. Stir frequently to prevent sticking. Pour, boiling hot, into hot jars, leaving ¼-inch head space. Pour liquid over. Adjust caps. Process 30 minutes in boiling water bath.

Dilly Pickled Peppers

Green peppers
Dill weed (1 sprig for each bottle)
Garlic buds (1 individual bud for each bottle)
1 cup white vinegar (4 to 6 percent acidity)
3 cups water
3 tablespoons pickling salt

Wash green peppers. Cut off tops, clean out seeds, replace tops and fit two green peppers into each sterilized wide-mouth pint jar. Or cut green peppers into strips; fit lengthwise into sterilized pint jars. Into each jar put one sprig of dill weed, controlling strength of dill flavor by number of dill seeds used. Also into each jar put 1 small garlic bud cut into 3 or 4 slices. Combine vinegar, water and salt in saucepan. Bring to boil; simmer 3 minutes. Pour boiling hot liquid over pickles. Let stand 2 or 3 minutes. Drain off liquid; bring to boil again and pour once again over pickles leaving ¼ inch head space. Adjust lids and seal. Process in boiling water bath for 10 minutes.

Dried Corn

350 degrees   2 QUARTS

  4 quarts fresh corn, cut from cob
  1 cup evaporated milk
  ½ cup sugar
  4 teaspoons salt

Combine all ingredients. Spread evenly in 2 shallow pans; bake for 45 minutes. Drain off any remaining liquid. Arrange on fiberglass or nylon screen (corn is very sticky and almost impossible to scrape off anything else). Dry in dehydrator (400 degrees) for 7 hours or in sun until thoroughly dry. Store in jars. To reconstitute, combine 1 part corn to 2 parts water in saucepan; bring to boil, cover and remove from heat for 10 minutes. To cook, return to heat and continue cooking, uncovered, for about 10 minutes or until done.

NOTE: Dried corn is so delicious eaten out of hand that you may wish to keep supply for snacking.

Index

SUBSTITUTIONS

IF YOU DON'T HAVE: **SUBSTITUTE:**

IF YOU DON'T HAVE:	SUBSTITUTE:
1 ounce chocolate	3 tablespoons cocoa plus 1 tablespoon butter or margarine
1 cup buttermilk or sour milk	1 tablespoon vinegar or lemon juice plus enough sweet milk to make 1 cup; allow to stand 5 minutes
1 cup sour cream (for baking only)	1 tablespoon vinegar or lemon juice plus enough undiluted evaporated milk to make 1 cup; allow to stand 5 minutes
1 tablespoon cornstarch (for thickening)	2 tablespoons flour or 1 tablespoon arrowroot or 2 tablespoons minute tapioca
Buttermilk	1 cup plain yogurt or 1 cup sour milk
1 cup brown sugar	1 cup granulated sugar plus 1 tablespoon molasses, stirred together
1 cup cake flour	1 cup minus 2 tablespoons all purpose flour
1 cup self-rising flour	1 cup all purpose flour plus 1½ teaspoons baking powder plus ½ teaspoon salt
1 clove garlic	⅛ teaspoon garlic powder or 1 teaspoon garlic salt
1 small fresh onion	1 tablespoon instant dried onion
1 cup fresh milk	3 to 5 tablespoons nonfat dry milk powder in 1 cup cold water or ½ cup evaporated milk plus ½ cup water
1 cup honey	1¼ cups sugar plus ¼ cup liquid (whatever liquid is used in recipe)
1 cup sugar	¾ cup honey; decrease liquid in recipe by 2 tablespoons
1 cup butter or margarine	⅞ cup hydrogenated shortening plus ½ teaspoon salt
1 teaspoon baking powder	¼ teaspoon soda plus ⅝ teaspoon cream of tartar
1 egg	1 teaspoon unflavored gelatin plus 3 tablespoons cold water plus 2⅓ tablespoons boiling water; mix well.
1 teaspoon dry mustard	1 tablespoon prepared mustard
1 can (14 oz.) sweetened condensed milk	½ cup hot water plus 1 cup sugar plus 2 tablespoons margarine plus 1 cup instant non-fat dry milk; blend until smooth.

WEIGHTS AND MEASURES

1 tablespoon	=	3 teaspoons
1 fluid ounce	=	2 tablespoons
¼ cup	=	4 tablespoons
⅓ cup	=	5⅓ tablespoons
½ cup	=	8 tablespoons
⅔ cup	=	10⅔ tablespoons
¾ cup	=	12 tablespoons
1 cup	=	16 tablespoons, 8 fluid ounces or ½ pint
1 pint	=	2 cups

1 quart	=	2 pints or 4 cups
1 gallon	=	4 quarts
1 peck	=	8 quarts
1 bushel	=	4 pecks
1 pound	=	16 ounces
¾ pound	=	12 ounces
½ pound	=	8 ounces
¼ pound	=	4 ounces